The Alternative Building
SOURCEBOOK

for
Traditional, Natural and Sustainable Building
Products & Services

Edited by
Steve Chappell

Fox Maple Press, Inc.   Brownfield, Maine

"In designing the house, the first essential, naturally, was that it should be suited exactly to the requirements of the life to be lived in it; the second, that it should harmonize with its environment, and third, that it should be built, so far as possible, from the materials to be had right there on the ground and left as nearly as was practicable in the natural state."

—Gustav Stickley, 1908.

The Alternative Building SOURCEBOOK

Edited by
Steve Chappell

**Research & Development
Copy Editor**
James J. Marks

Design Assistant
Laurie LaMountain

Watercolor Artwork
Benjamin Young

Published by

Fox Maple Press, Inc.
P.O. Box 249
Corn Hill Road
Brownfield, Maine 04010
Phone 207-935-3720
Fax 207-935-4575
email: foxmaple@nxi.com
www.nxi.com//WWW/joinersquarterly

For advertising accounts write to the
above address or call: 207-935-3720

This publication is available in quantities
for newsstand distribution and resale.
For information on setting up a
wholesale account please call:
207-935-3720, or fax query
letter to: 207-935-4575

ISBN 1-889269-01-8

Editor's Notes

Over the last several years our contacts with builders, manufacturers and individuals involved in the alternative building arena have been steadily increasing. These sources cover a wide array of natural and traditional building venues, materials, products, and some extremely exciting design concepts and approaches. Because the majority of these contacts have come to our attention in a random fashion, we've not always been able to put our fingers on the right name for the right product or service when we needed it—primarily because we've never before compiled them in any comprehensive or logistical order. When we finally set about to once-and-for-all organize our myriad hard files and computer databases for our own in-house use, we realized that the list was quite extensive and that it could be an equally valuable resource for JQ readers, workshop students and anyone else attempting to build in an alternative vein. The result is this First Edition of the *Alternative Building SOURCEBOOK*.

Enclosed are over 900 individual listings from more than 400 companies. In an attempt to include all of the potential products and suppliers who are actively engaged in what may be considered avant-garde building, we've tried not to alienate anyone. Most of the products, and or, services, focus on natural, traditional and sustainable building techniques and systems. Where the materials may be synthetic, or petroleum based, we've included them because they offer unique results, energy efficiency and/or exceptional value in relation to labor input.

We have attempted to make this *SOURCEBOOK* comprehensive and easy to use. Many of the companies listed offer more than one product or service which may fall into more than one category. To make it easy to find any and all the sources available for a given product or service, companies have been listed in up to three categories when appropriate. In addition to the category listings, we have also included an alphabetical company directory, along with an additional listing of all companies who have submitted URL's and E-mail addresses.

For the most part, the listings contained within are small, progressive companies and dedicated individuals who have devoted themselves to their own unique style of building, design, or product manufacturing— because they care about quality, and the environment. We encourage you to take advantage of their hard work by using this resource to serve all of your building needs.

—Steve Chappell

Table of Contents

Traditional Building... the Wave of the Future

An alternative undercurrent to the *conventional* building systems of the day has existed throughout the ages, I'm convinced. There was a day, indeed, when timber framing was considered the convention and when thatch or stone were the only viable roofing options. With the natural evolution in technology and an ever changing resource supply, there is a slow, but continual, transformation in the conventions we use to pattern our building models—an endless round from the alternative, to the conventional, to the traditional, to the alternative, etc.

For the most part, change follows in direct line with the availability and cost of materials and labor. The shift from timber framing to stud framing in this country—what we now call 'conventional' or 'balloon framing'—was precipitated by the invention of the circular saw blade in 1840. This single advance in technology, invented by a Shaker woman in New York state, so dramatically increased the speed and efficiency of milling logs that for the first time cutting smaller pieces of lumber and boards became economically viable. Even then, timber framing remained the standard form until after the Civil War, when the demand for housing ushered in new systems that could provide homes quickly and cheaply.

Vernacular styles change also. Frank Lloyd Wright was considered a maverick in the early part of this century when he began developing his prairie style homes. By the end of his career, his design concepts became the pattern for the common house in the post war building boom of the 1950s through the 1960s.

Wright began his career in the 1880s designing the rambling 'shingle style' vacation homes popular with wealthy industrialists on the East Coast. His roots, however, were in the midwest. He felt that a dwelling should reflect the surrounding environment and blend into the landscape. He had wild notions about building with the materials directly from the building site, of doing away with foundations and cellars below frost line by using rubble filled trenches (which he used in all but a handful of his houses), heating systems that radiated directly from the floor—he even pioneered earth bermed houses. For the most part, his designs were practical and affordable. The construction cost for his *Usonian* homes ranged from $5 to $10 per square foot—and he attempted to minimize costs throughout his career.

When we think of Frank Lloyd Wright, we tend to think of modern forms and modern systems. The truth is that his wild notions were nothing more than variations to traditional and indigenous building systems that he had seen and studied in his travels. The rubble trench foundation is as old as the ages. These were what the grand cathedrals in Europe and the New England barn were built upon. The Japanese still used it extensively when Wright visited in 1914. Another tradition in Japan that intrigued him was the mysterious, radiant heated floors. For centuries the Japanese heated their temples and houses by drawing the heat and smoke from outdoor fire pits through flues in their floors. Wright studied these building styles and systems and then adapted them into his own design schemes. Almost overnight these most ancient and traditional building technologies were transformed into the icons of modern architectural engineering.

John Ruskin, the architectural historian, wrote, somewhat mysteriously, that "there is no new architecture." What he meant, I believe, was that while the obtuse functions and architectural forms may appear to change, the essence of a building and our fundamental need for a dwelling or community hall, remains the same throughout all ages. This becomes apparent when we realize that Architectural styles, for the most part, are based on the *revival* of some earlier period. As in the case with Frank Lloyd Wright, perhaps it's through the study of building techniques from the past that our so called *modern forms* will evolve.

While we have called this the Alternative Building Sourcebook, it's really more of a universal/cross platform collection of people and companies who have devoted themselves to developing products and services that currently may appear to be in the *alternative vein*. Fundamentally they are all connected, in that they all, collectively, form a compendium of proven knowledge and wisdom of building crafts both ancient and modern. Our goal in putting this collection together was to provide an easy avenue for people to connect with qualified craftsmen, manufacturers and building suppliers that could help in defining and designing dwellings on a more personal level and with quality paramount. Quality and craftsmanship are two of the most important elements in any building endeavor. Without them, there will be no lasting value, no matter the cost.

—Steve Chappell

"The house of moderate cost is not only a major architectural problem, but the problem most difficult for architects...the chief obstacle to any real solution...is the fact that our people do not really know how to live. They imagine their idiosyncrasies to be their 'tastes,' their prejudices to be their predilections, and their ignorance to be virtue—where any beauty of living is concerned."

—Frank Lloyd Wright

Design & Planning

Design & Planning

The ultimate success, comfort and efficiency of a building project can be linked directly to the thoroughness and attention to details paid during the design and planning process. This is even more important when the style or type of building falls outside the mainstream of the building industry. Finding an architect, designer or designer/builder who has had experience in timber framing is imperative if you want to build a timber frame. Likewise, if your desire is to build a passive solar home, or a dwelling that utilizes natural and nontoxic materials, you'll want to work with someone who is well versed in both the design and construction process.

More and more, especially in the alternative building arena, architects and designers are the builders as well. There can be advantages to this in that the more the designer knows about their client, the better equipped they are at advising during the design phase and directing the building process. While the design and planning stage covers a broad area, there are a few edicts that apply to the process that rise to the top of every client's wish list.

1) The house should be as large as possible, for the least cost per square foot.

2) The construction process should take the least amount of time possible.

3) The project should not go over budget.

As much as these are on the minds of the client, they are the dread of most builders. The fact is, building a dream house is fraught with pitfalls and dilemmas. The more one cares about the structure and the construction process, the more the possibility of cost overruns and delays in the construction schedule. The experienced architect or designer/builder can more than earn their pay by keeping the project on-line, in focus and in check.

The following are some considerations that can be made in the design stage to make the building process a more successful one.

Determining size in relation to budget.

It's very common for non-builders to have a difficult time conceiving of 3-dimensional enclosed space. This phenomenon often leads the homeowner into thinking they need a house larger or smaller than necessary. Size will dictate cost to a large degree, so it's helpful to analyze the actual square footage and volume of a number of spaces that you already use—in your current home, those of friends or at work.

Understanding space, and how you plan to use it, is an important aspect of the design process—one that can save money.

Mechanics & Materials.

The materials and the system you choose to build with have a direct relation to the cost of the project, and perhaps more importantly, to the comfort of living in the house. In conventional residential building the process is one of layering. Several layers are applied to the skeletal frame, with nothing but flat, painted and plastic surfaces exposed in the end. Neither the structure nor the materials that cloth it are acknowledged, but only the decorative elements hung on the walls and placed about the room. Materials can add texture and comfort to an enclosed space. If the materials that make up the structural element are also the finished elements then there is a direct connection with those who enter the environment. Most of the building systems found in this book—log building, timber framing, cob, strawbale, etc.—are whole systems, in that, the structural elements are also the finish elements. In these systems, the environments created stand complete on their own, with little need to embellish or to create illusory decorative touches.

Site planning.

Let the site work for you as opposed to making it conform to your needs. Not all designs are suited for every site, so it is important to choose a site first and design the building to sit comfortably upon it. Up to 30% of the cost of construction can be in site development (driveway, excavation, etc.). Consider all options wisely and get advice from your excavator, surveyor, designer or builder before making the final decision on site planning.

Sweat Equity.

When we think of alternative building, we automatically think of owner-builders as well. Don't be mistaken, the term sweat equity can be taken at face value. Working on your own building project can save money, but it can also cost plenty in commitment and energy output. Most of the people involved in the construction of their own home are motivated by reasons that transcend monetary savings. Because of this, one needs to clearly consider the options available and the practicality in the end result. Consultation with those who have done it, taking classes and workshops, and finding designers who specialize in assisting owner-builders is pretty much a necessity if satisfaction is to be had.

Architects

DC, Washington

Passive Solar Industries Council
1511 K Street, Suite 600
Washington, DC 20005
Tel.(202) 628-7400
Fax (202) 393-5043
PSIC independent nonprofit advancing climate responsive buildings.
E-mail: PSICouncil@aol.com
Web site: http://www.psic.org

Massachusetts

Jack A. Sobon: Architect/Builder
PO Box 201, 613 Shaw Road
Windsor, MA 01270-0201
Tel: (413) 684-3223
Fax: same
Specializing in design and construction of sustainable wooden architecture.

Michigan

Millcreek Classic Homes
1009 Parchment Drive SE
Grand Rapids, MI 49546
Tel: (616) 949-3012
Fax: (616) 949-4477
Design and build Riverbend timber frame custom homes.

Minnesota

Community Eco-Design Network
PO Box 6241, 3151-29th Ave. S, #103
Minneapolis, MN 55406
Tel: (612) 306-2326
Super-insulated construction planbook, design services, northern climate strawbale building system.
E-mail: erichart@mtn.org
Web site: http://www.umn.edu/n/home/m037/kurtdand/cen

Missouri

Timberland Design/Hearthstone
15444 Clayton Road, Ste. 325-6
St. Louis, MO 63011
Tel: (800) 680-8833, (314) 341-8833
Fax: (314) 341-8833
Architect, Hearthstone distributor, specializing in timber frame/log designs & packages.

New Hampshire

Springpoint Design
2210 Pratt Road
Alstead, NH 03602
Tel: (603) 835-2433
Fax: (603) 835-7825
Architectural design/consulting: health, sustainability, efficiency–timber frames, alternative enclosures.

Straw Works
152 West Main St.
Conway, NH 03818
Tel: (603) 447-1701
Fax: (603) 447-6412
Design for those wishing to walk lightly upon the earth.
E-mail: Straw-Works@juno.com

New York

Gallagher Associates
124-01 20th Ave.
College Point, NY 11356
Tel: (718) 539-6576, Fax: (718) 539-6578
Commercial and residential environmentally friendly architecture and landscape design.

Donald J. Berg, AIA
150 Harvard Avenue
Rockville Centre, NY 11570
Tel: (516) 766-5585, Fax: (516) 536-4081
Editor of American Barns and Backbuildings Catalog. Author of American Country Building Design. Historical research. Building plans available.
E-mail:XCBR70A@prodigy.com

Oregon

Sustainable Architecture
PO Box 696, 910 Glendale Ave.
Ashland, OR 97520
Tel: (541) 482-6332, Fax: (541) 488-8299
Architectural services integrating full spectrum of healthy, holistic building.

Pennsylvania

Hugh Lofting Timber Framing, Inc.
339 Lamborntown Road
West Grove, PA 19390
Tel: (610) 444-5382
Fax: (610) 869-3589
Company dedicated to practicing green architecture with sustainable materials.
E-mail: hlofting@aol.com

Washington

Richard Berg, Architect
727 Taylor St.
Port Townsend, WA 98368
Tel: (360) 379-8090, Fax: (360) 379-8324
Architectural practice specializing in comfortable, energy-efficient, quality timber framed homes.
E-mail: rberg@olympus.net

Jean Steinbrecher Architects
PO Box 788
Langley, WA 98260-0788
Tel: (360) 221-0494
Fax: (360) 221-6594
Log & timber design specialists.
E-mail: jsa@whidbey.com

Design Consultants

Arizona

The Canelo Project
HCL Box 324
Elgin, AZ 85611
Tel: (520) 455-5548
Fax: (520) 455-9360
Straw bale building/earthen floors and plasters, workshops, resources, consulting.
E-mail: absteen@dakotacom.net
Web site: http://www.deatech.com/canelo

California

Eos Institute
580 Broadway, Suite 200
Laguna Beach, CA 92651
Tel: (714) 497-1896
Fax: (714) 497-7861
Educational nonprofit for the study of sustainable living. Resources, consulting, and programs on ecological community design. Library, lectures, workshops.
E-mail: eos@igpc.org

Florida

Freedom Builders
1013 Naples Drive
Orlando, FL 32804
Tel: (407) 647-5849
Fax: (407) 645-5652
Internet informational & advertising site–log & t.f design–video productions.
E-mail: freedom@magicnet.net
Web site: www.magicnet.net/freedom

Georgia

Upper Loft Design, Inc.
Rt. 1 Box 2901
Lakemont, GA 30552
Tel: (706) 782-5246
Fax: (706) 782-6840
A timberframe design/build and turn-key housewright company.
Web site: http://www.upperloft@stc.net

Indiana

Timbersmith, Inc.
4040 Farr Road
Bloomington, IN 47408
Tel: (812) 336-7424
Our frames exhibit traditional wooden joinery and can be finely detailed to produce one-of-a-kind creations.

Kansas

Elemental Resources
PO Box 21, 1320 E. 94th St. South
Haysville, KS 67060
Tel: (316) 788-3678
Fax: same
Renewable energy. Specializing in design &
installation of photovoltaic & wind hybrid systems.
E-mail: cvdow@aol.com

Natural Habitat
PO Box 21, 1320 E. 94th St. South
Haysville, KS 67060
Tel: (316) 788-3676
Feng shui/bau-biologie consulting. New and
existing structures.

Kentucky

The Raven River Co., Inc.
125 Twin Creek–Connorsville Road
Sadieville, KY 40370
Tel: (606) 235-0368
Fax: same
Artisans of fine timber frames and other things.
E-mail: ravenriver@kitt.net

Massachusetts

Greenspace Collaborative
PO Box 107, Ashfield, MA 01330
Tel: (413) 369-4905
Buildings of straw bales and other natural
materials detailed for the northeastern
climate.

Maine

Talmage Solar Engineering, Inc.
18 Stone Road
Kennebunkport, ME 04046
Tel: (207) 967-5945, Fax: (207) 967-5754
Design and sale of solar electric components
for off-grid or utility interface.
E-mail: tse@talmagesolar.com
Web site: www.talmagesolar.com

Connolly & Co. Timber Frame Homes & Barns
10 Atlantic Highway
Edgecomb, ME 04556
Tel: (207) 882-4224, Fax: (207) 882-4247
Custom timber frame homes & barns built to
last. Traditional oak-pegged mortise and tenon
joinery. Design services. Project management.
Frames to complete projects. Visit our facility
in Maine and observe our commitment to
excellence.
E-mail: connolly@lincoln.midcoast.com

Fox Maple School of Traditional Building
PO Box 249, Corn Hill Road
Brownfield, ME 04010
Tel: (207) 935-3720, Fax: (207) 935-4575
Workshops in introductory & advanced timber
framing. Design workshops and seminars. Full
design services through the Timber Frame
Apprenticeshop. Natural and traditional
building systems.
E-mail: foxmaple@nxi.com
Web site: http://www.nxi.com/WWW/
joinersquarterly

Minnesota

Carroll, Franck & Associates
1357 Highland Parkway
St. Paul, MN 55116
Tel: (612) 690-9162
Fax: (612) 690-9156
Engineering of architectural structures,
traditional joinery and concealed steel
connections.
E-mail: carrfran@gold.tc.umn.edu

Montana

**Center For Resourceful Building
Technology**
PO Box 100, 516 S. Orange
Missoula, MT 59806
Tel: (406) 549-7678
Fax: (406) 549-4100
Non-profit educating the public on environ-
mentally responsible construction practices.

North Carolina

Goshen Timber Frames, Inc.
104 Wykle Road
Franklin, NC 28734
Tel: (704) 524-8662
Fax: same
Ongoing workshops and apprenticeships in
timber framing and design; design services;
frame sales.
E-mail: goshen@dnet.net
Web site: http://www.timberframemag.com

New Hampshire

Day Pond Woodworking
PO Box 299, Rt. 114
Bradford, NH 03221
Tel: (603) 938-2375
Over 17 years experience designing &
building custom timber frame homes, etc.

Specialty Timberworks
PO Box 261, Brownfield Road
Eaton, NH 03832
Tel: (603) 447-5625
Fax: same
Designers & fabricators of new, and
reconstruction of antique timber frames.
3-D CADD services.

Springpoint Design
2210 Pratt Road
Alstead, NH 03602
Tel: (603) 835-2433
Fax: (603) 835-7825
Architectural design/consulting: health,
sustainability, efficiency–timber frames,
alternative enclosures.

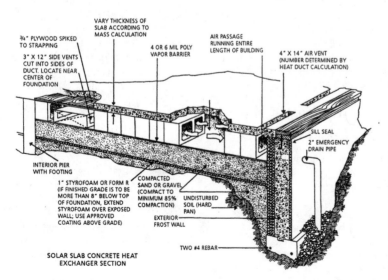

Solar Slab Concrete Heat Exchanger Section

VARY THICKNESS OF SLAB ACCORDING TO MASS CALCULATION

3/4" PLYWOOD SPIKED TO STRAPPING

3" X 12" SIDE VENTS CUT INTO SIDES OF DUCT. LOCATE NEAR CENTER OF FOUNDATION

4 OR 6 MIL POLY VAPOR BARRIER

AIR PASSAGE RUNNING ENTIRE LENGTH OF BUILDING

4" X 14" AIR VENT (NUMBER DETERMINED BY HEAT DUCT CALCULATION)

SILL SEAL

2" EMERGENCY DRAIN PIPE

INTERIOR PIER WITH FOOTING

1" STYROFOAM OR FORM R (IF FINISHED GRADE IS TO BE MORE THAN 8" BELOW TOP OF FOUNDATION, EXTEND STYROFOAM OVER EXPOSED WALL; USE APPROVED COATING ABOVE GRADE)

COMPACTED SAND OR GRAVEL (COMPACT TO MINIMUM 85% COMPACTION)

UNDISTURBED SOIL (HARD PAN)

EXTERIOR FROST WALL

TWO #4 REBAR

SOLAR SLAB CONCRETE HEAT EXCHANGER SECTION

*Solar design offers many advantages and often requires little addition
to the cost of construction. Ingenuity can save in both dollars and
comfort.*

Graphic from 'The Passive Solar House', Chelsea Green Publishing.

New York

Tea House Design, Inc.
PO Box 99, 11 Benedict Road
Waccabuc, NY 10597
Tel: (914) 763-3078
Fax: (914) 763-6165
27 years experience. 100 mile radius NYC.
Innovative and diligent.

Eastfield Village
PO Box 539, 104 Mud Pond Road
Nassau, NY 12062
Tel: (518) 766-2422
Fax: same
School of historic preservation and early
American trades.

Barkeater Design Build Company
35 Wellington Street
Malone, NY 12953
Tel: (518) 483-5282
Fax: same
Designer/builders specializing in stone
slipform construction. Workshops available.
E-mail: barkeatr@slic.com

Ohio

Natural Homesteads
13182 N. Boone Road
Columbia Station, OH 44028
Tel: (440) 236-3344
Natural building design/consultation; slide
presentations; straw-bale and cob workshops.

Oregon

Terry F. Johnson Building Design
1013 NW Taylor Ave.
Corvallis, OR 97330
Tel: (541) 757-8535
Fax: (541) 753-4916
Custom plans for timber framed homes, barns
and outbuildings.
E-mail: sarah@peak.org

Confluence Design & Construction
PO Box 1258, 1013 NW Taylor
Corvallis, OR 97339
Tel: (514) 757-0511
Fax: (541) 753-4916
"Where thinking and doing are still one."
Design, frames, consultation.

Rhode Island

South County Post & Beam
521 Liberty Lane
West Kingston, RI 02892
Tel: (401) 783-4415
Fax: (401) 783-4494
A full service timber frame company, wide pine
distributor.

Texas

**Center For Maximum Potential
Building Systems**
8604 FM 969
Austin, TX 78724
Tel: (512) 928-4786
Fax: (512) 926-4418
E-mail: max_pot@txinfinet.com
Web site: http://www.maxpot.com/maxpot

Vermont

Memphremagog Heat Exchangers, Inc.
PO Box 490
Newport, VT 05855
Tel; (800) 660-5412
Fax: (802) 895-2666
Indoor air quality solutions for tightly built
homes since 1982.
E-mail: info@mhevt.com
Web site: www.mhevt.com

Vermont Sun Structures, Inc.
42 Walker Hill Road
Williston, VT 05495
Tel: (802) 879-6645
Glulam timber framed sunrooms & green-
houses, fully "weeped" & water tight!

Principles of Bau-Biologie

The following list was developed by Prof. Anton Schneider, founder of the Institut fur Baubiologie und Okologie. These principles can be used while planning the construction of a healthy and ecologically friendly home, or while remodeling an existing one. At present, practically every one of these guidelines is being broken or ignored. Isn't it remarkable how far we have strayed from building according to human criteria?

1. Consider geobiology in the process of selecting building sites.

2. Locate habitats at a distance from centers of industry and main traffic routes.

3. Have dwellings well separated from one another in spaciously planned developments, amid green areas.

4. Plan homes and developments individually, taking into consideration the human aspects and the needs of family life.

5. Use building materials of natural origin.

6. Use wall, floor, and ceiling materials that allow air diffusion.

7. Allow for natural regulation of indoor air humidity by the use of hygroscopic building materials.

8. Use interior surface materials that allow air filtration and neutralization of air pollutants (use materials capable of sorption).

9. Consider the balance between indoor heat storage and thermal insulation.

10. Consider the balance between surface temperatures and air temperatures.

11. Use thermal radiation in heating, employing solar energy as much as possible.

12. Promote low humidity and rapid desiccation in new buildings.

13. Ensure that buildings have a neutral or pleasant odor. Toxic fumes should be avoided.

14. Use light, illumination, and color in accordance with nature.

15. Provide adequate protection from noise and infrasonic-sound vibrations or sound conducted through solids.

16. Use building materials that emit little or no radioactivity.

17. Preserve natural electric field conditions and physiologically advantageous ionization.

18. Refrain from altering the natural magnetic fields.

19. Minimize technical electro-magnetic fields.

20. Restrict alteration of important cosmic and terrestrial radiation.

21. Employ physiologically designed furniture and spaces. Apply ergonomic principles.

22. Design shapes and proportions in harmonic order.

23. Be sure that neither the construction nor the production of building materials contributes to environmental problems or high energy costs.

24. Do not allow building and production methods to contribute to the over-exploitation of limited raw materials.

25. Ensure that building activities and production of materials do not promote social damage through harmful side-effects.

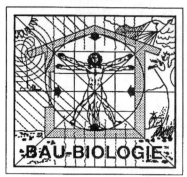

IBE

INTERNATIONAL INSTITUTE for BAU-BIOLOGIE™ & ECOLOGY

The **Institute** provides a holistic viewpoint in this comprehensive education on the subject of

HEALTHY HOMES

Over 1000 students have taken one of our home study courses and/or participated in seminars/workshops.

OUR PROGRAM:
- **Home Study Course** (MCC1) for home dwellers and professionals (ASID & Florida Board of Architects approved for CEU's)
- **Comprehensive Home Study Course** (CC) for the professional (architect, builder, med. practitioner, home inspector)
- **Seminars**
  - •• Introduction to Bau-biologie
  - •• Electrobiology, Indoor Air Quality, Water, Materials
  - •• FengShui & Bau-biologie
  - •• The Natural Building *"the breathing house"* (planning, materials, systems)

Our purpose is to provide information and practical advise to the building professionals and the public which will enable them to build and live/work in healthy buildings. This will prevent illness and destruction of the Earth. To make sure that everyone gets this knowledge **your participation is essential.**

IBE
Box 387, Clearwater, FL 33757
Ph: 813-461-4371 **Fax**: 813-441-4373
Internet:www.bau-biologieusa.com
Email: baubiologie@earthlink.net

Environmental Building News
RR 1, Box 161
Brattleboro, VT 05301
Tel: (802) 257-7300
Fax: (802) 257-7304
The leading publication on environmentally responsible design and construction.
E-mail: ebn@ebuild.com
Web site: http://www.ebuild.com

Washington

Ark II Inc.
HCR 73 Box 67
Twisp, WA 98856
Tel: (509) 997-2418
Fax: (509) 997-4434
Fine quality timber frame & log buildings.

Greenfire Institute
PO Box 1040
Winthrop, WA 98862
Tel: (509) 996-3593
Fax: same
Straw bale construction training, consultation and design.
E-mail: greenfire@igc.org
Web site: www.balewolf.com

Richard Berg, Architect
727 Taylor St.
Port Townsend, WA 98368
Tel: (360) 379-8090
Fax: (360) 379-8324
Architectural practice specializing in comfortable, energy-efficient, quality timber framed homes.
E-mail: rberg@olympus.net

West Virginia

Wind Bell Hollow/C.J. Jammer
HC 40 Box 36
Lewisburg, WV 24901
Tel: (304) 645-6466
Design/drafting of timber framed homes and other natural house designs.

Manitoba

A & K Technical Services
PO Box 22
Anola, MB, Canada R0E 0A0
Tel: (204) 866-3262
Fax: (204) 866-3287
Structural engineering in wood. "Stackwall" house construction design, consulting, manual.
E-mail: krisdick@mb.sympatico.ca

Ontario

Alderaan Stone/Timber Homes
PO Box 313, 6-14845 Yonge Street
Aurora, Ontario, Canada L4G 6H8
Tel: (905) 713-0001
Fax: (905) 713-0134
Traditional materials and craftsmanship.

Comprehensive custom reproductions of early Canadian homes.
Web site: www.craftsman-book.com

Northern Timberhouse, Ltd.
PO Box 71, Hwy. 35 South
Minden, Ontario, Canada K0M 2K0
Tel: (705) 286-3791
Fax: (705) 286-6168
Canadian timber frames and hand-crafted log homes since 1980.
E-mail: nortim@halhinet.on.ca

Bear Timber Frame Homes
PO Box 124
Ajax, Ont, Canada L1S 3C2
Tel: (905) 428-6505
Designers of timber frame and energy-efficient (R2000) homes.

Bau-Biologie & Feng Shui

International Institute for Bau-Biologie
1401 A Cleveland St.
Clearwater, FL 34615
Tel: (813) 461-4371
Holistic education in the creation of homes & offices that are harmonious and healthy to the occupants and have no adverse effect on the environment.
E-mail: baubiologie@earthlink.net
Web site: http://www.bau-biologieusa.com

Natural Habitat
PO Box 21, 1320 E. 94th St. South
Haysville, KS 67060
Tel: (316) 788-3676
Feng Shui/bau-biologie consulting. New and existing structures.

Renaissance Developments
10704 Oviatt Road
Honor, MI 49640
Tel: (616) 326-4009
Sustainable building, healthy creative dreamspaces, bau-biologie, owner-builder involvement welcome.

Home Environmental Options
M. Spark Burmaster, E.E.
RR 1, Box 77A
Chaseburg, WI 54621
Tel/Fax: (608) 483-2604

Structural Engineers

Carroll, Franck & Associates
1357 Highland Parkway
St. Paul, MN 55116
Tel: (612) 690-9162
Fax: (612) 690-9156
Engineering of architectural structures, traditional joinery and concealed steel connections.
E-mail: carrfran@gold.tc.umn.edu

Traditional Building

Chris Barstow, Specialty Timberworks

Traditional Building

The quest to build both quality homes and a better future for the coming generations is no longer the individual musings of a few, but rather a cohesive effort by ever-growing numbers to change the building industry's *modus operandi*. In recent years, some truly different types of homes have begun to filter into the construction industry. Many of these utilize the materials at hand, and integrate modern and ancient technologies to create some of the most efficient and environmentally friendly homes on the planet. Some are built into the ground to make use of the Earth's natural heat—below the frostline in winter, the earth maintains a constant temperature between 50-55 degrees. Some houses are built with walls of straw bales, that not only have insulating values as high as R-50, but make use of a material that would have otherwise been wasted or burned. The attributes of straw and other cellulose fibers from agricultural crops hold a promising future in the building industry. Presently, straw is being used to produce stress skin panels and wafer (OSB) board and its future looks promising.

Timber framing has made an astonishing revival. Thirty years ago, there was little more than a handful of craftsmen with knowledge of joinery and post & beam design. Today, it is a vibrant industry, accessible in all regions of the country. Timber framing was perfected during Medieval times, when the forests of Europe were rapidly disappearing. The large beams, and carefully executed joinery, provided a sturdy and durable frame for homes that would last for many generations.

Even compared to modern construction's "stick frame" technology, a timber frame can provide a structural framework with more design flexibility, while using up to a third less lumber. Providing the structural framework, it opens up a wide variety of alternative enclosure systems to be used. Traditionally, wattle & daub was used as an infill system. The "breathable" walls actually preserved the timbers, and some buildings in Europe are still in use after 600 years. New innovations are evolving using German techniques with light straw/clay and woodchips that can add higher insulation values required in today's building environment. Timber frames are also ideal for panelized systems. Foam core panels have been perfected over the last 20 years and provide superior insulative qualities. Wheat straw panels are coming into the market and can provide a natural option to structural panels.

Innovative new technologies are now being developed that will allow traditional building materials to be more readily available and practical for use in modern applications. Advanced Earthen Construction Technologies, Inc. has come up with a compressed soil block machine that produces an inexpensive, durable, and energy efficient building material from locally available soils. And it can make as many as 960 blocks per hour.

With recent innovations in passive solar design, photovoltaics, renewable energy sources, utilizing materials at hand through traditional building methods, and individual creativity, an infrastructure is beginning to develop that may replace the market-driven economy with a common-sense-driven economy. Families can become less dependent upon industries, utilities, financial institutions and government, and more self-reliant. And isn't that where the true strength of a people lies—in the strength of its individuals?

California

Sierra Timberframers
PO Box 595
Nevada City, CA 95959
Tel: (916) 292-9449
Fax: (916) 292-9460
Timberframed structures. Recycled wood & salvaged trees. Solar & sustainable designs preferred. Classes available.

Pacific Post & Beam
PO Box 13708
San Luis Obispo, CA 93406
Tel: (805) 543-7565
Fax: (805) 543-1287
Full service timber frame and truss design and build.

Colorado

Leopard Creek Timberframe Co.
PO Box 51, 2980 Hwy.62
Placerville, CO 81430
Tel: (970) 728-3590
Fax: same
Hand-crafted timber frame homes, located in southwest Colorado. Call for information.

Connecticut

Post & Beam Homes, Inc.
4 Sexton Hill Road South
East Hampton, CT 06424
Tel: (860) 267-2060, CT (800) 821-8456
Fax: (860) 267-9515
Pine, oak, Doug fir or recycled lumber. Frames hand-crafted in our workshop. Our expert timber framers will construct anywhere.

C&C Home Builders, Inc.
3810 Old Mountain Road
West Suffield, CT 06093
Tel: (860) 668-0382
Building in the New England-New York area using white oak and traditional joinery.

Delaware

Timber Frame Systems, Inc.
PO Box 458, 28 Main St.
Frankford, DE 19945
Tel: (302) 732-9428
Fax: (302) 537-4971
Manufacturer of custom post & beam frame kits.

Florida

R.G. White Construction
PO Box 14734, 5800 Firestone Road
Jacksonville, FL 32238
Tel: (904) 778-8352
Fax: same
Building fine quality cracker style and craftsman style homes.

Georgia

Hearthstone Log & Timberframe Homes
120 Carriage Drive
Macon, GA 31210
Tel: (800) 537-7931
Fax: (912) 477-6535
21 years experience, CADD design, professional erection and dry-in services.
E-mail: hearthstonehomes@mindspring.com
Web site: www.mindspring.com/~hearthstonehomes

Upper Loft Design, Inc.
Rt. 1 Box 2901
Lakemont, GA 30552
Tel: (706) 782-5246
Fax: (706) 782-6840
A timberframe design/build and turn-key housewright company.
Web site: http://www.upperloft@stc.net

Idaho

Jeff Pedersen—Logsmith
PO Box 788, Hwy. 93 North
Challis, ID 83226
Tel: (208) 879-4211
Fax: (208) 879-5574
Traditional broadax-hewn dovetail and round log scribe-fit log homes. Broadax-hewn and round log timber frames.
E-mail: jplogs@cyberhighway.net

Alternative Timber Structures
1054 Rammel Mt. Rd.
Tetonia, ID 83452
Tel: (208) 456-2711
Fax: same
Custom door manufacturer, custom sizes, interior & exterior—Davis Frame rep.

Illinois

Windlass Timber Framing, Inc.
137 N. Center St.
Naperville, IL 60540
Tel: (630) 355-1788
Fax: same
Timber frame barn removal, repair, erection and sales.

The Edge Woodworks
Rt. 1 Box 179
Grafton, IL 62037
Tel: (618) 786-2442
Traditional hand-crafted joinery, portable sawmill, owner-builder friendly.
E-mail: edgewrks@gtec.com

Indiana

Timbersmith, Inc.
4040 Farr Road
Bloomington, IN 47408
Tel: (812) 336-7424
Our frames exhibit traditional wooden joinery and can be finely detailed to produce one-of-a-kind creations.

Kentucky

The Raven River Co., Inc.
125 Twin Creek-Connorsville Road
Sadieville, KY 40370
Tel: (606) 235-0368
Fax: same
Artisans of fine timber frames and other things.
E-mail: ravenriver@kitt.net

Timber framing is based on an ancient tradition that was developed simultaneously in all parts of the world during the first half of the second millennia A.D.
Then, as now, the master carpenters took pride in the quality of their craftsmanship and tended to extend their talents through finer and finer work. The great cathedrals of the world could not have been completed without such dedicated craftsmen. Their legacy is what has inspired many to enter the field today.

Massachusetts

New England Preservation Services
95 West Squantum Street, Suite 705
Quincy,MA 02171
Tel: (617) 472-8934, Fax: (617) 770-8934
Restoration of 18th & 19th century homes &
barns.
E-mail: 74131.1254@Compuserve.com

The Heartwood School
Johnson Hill Road
Washington, MA 01235
Tel: (413) 623-6677
Fax: (413) 623-0277
Workshops in homebuilding, timber framing,
woodworking, and more.
E-mail: info@heartwoodschool.com
Web site: www.heartwoodschool.com

Colonial Restorations
26 Main St.
Brookfield, MA 01506
Tel: (508) 867-4400
Structural restoration/repair of post & beam
homes or barns.

Jack A Sobon: Architect/Builder
PO Box 201, 613 Shaw Road
Windsor, MA 01270-0201
Tel: (413) 684-3223
Fax: same
Specializing in design and construction of
sustainable wooden architecture.

Ellison Timberframes
20 Six Penny Lane
Harwichport, MA 02646
Tel: (508) 430-0407
Award-winning design/build company. No
steel connections used.

Maryland

Craftwright-Timber Frame Company
100 Railroad Ave., #105
Westminster, MD 21157
Tel: (410) 876-0999
Custom hand-crafted timber frames, antique
frames and timbers available.

Maine

New Dimension Homes, Inc.
PO Box 95, RR1
Clinton, ME 04927
Tel: (207) 426-7450
Fax: (207) 426-8837
Affordable panelized western red cedar post
& beam homes & sunrooms.

Wentworth Timberframes
PO Box 1116, 45 Mason Street
Bethel, ME 04217
Tel: (207) 824-4237
25 years experience. Hewn, rough-sawn, or
hand-planed timbers. Mortise and tenon
joinery. Owner friendly

Connolly & Co.
Timber Frame Homes & Barns
10 Atlantic Highway
Edgecomb, ME 04556
Tel: (207) 882-4224
Fax: (207) 882-4247
Custom timber frame homes & barns built to
last. Traditional oak pegged mortise and tenon
joinery. Design services. Project management.
Frames to complete projects. Visit our facility
in Maine and observe our commitment to
excellence.
E-mail: connolly@lincoln.midcoast.com

Authentic Timberframes
Route 302, RR 2 Box 698
Bridgton, ME 04009
Tel: (207) 647-5720
Timber frame homes, barns, cottages, camps
and signs. Traditional joinery, hand-crafted
frames.
E-mail: tenon@maine.com
Web site: http://timberframe.maine.com

Barnstormers
RR 1 Box 566, North Rochester Road
East Lebanon, ME 04027-9730
Tel: (207) 658-9000
The barn recycling specialists. Antique barns
resourced, restored, shipped & reassembled
nationwide. Authentic timber framing. Vintage
lumber.

Timber Frame Apprenticeshop
PO Box 249, Corn Hill Road
Brownfield, ME 04010
Tel: (207) 935-3720
Fax: (207) 935-4575
An extension of Fox Maple School of
Traditional Building, the TF Apprenticeshop
offers students real world working opportuni-
ties from design through construction, while
offering substantial savings to clients. TFA
encourages owner participation.
E-mail: foxmaple@nxi.com
Web site: http://www.nxi.com/WWW/
joinersquarterly

Michigan

Millcreek Classic Homes
1009 Parchment Drive SE
Grand Rapids, MI 49546
Tel: (616) 949-3012
Fax: (616) 949-4477
Design and build Riverbend timber frame
custom homes.

Minnesota

Sandro's Woodshed
20018 486th Ave.
Hendricks, MN 56136
Tel: (605) 479-3875
Custom timber frames. Cabinetry and
furniture built with all natural materials—no
plywood or particle board—non-toxic finishes
available.

Great Northern Woodworks, Inc.
30694 Polk St. NE
Cambridge, MN 55008
Tel: (612) 444-6394
Fax: (612) 444-9552
Timber frame structures, including design,
cutting, raising and panel enclosure.

Missouri

Timberland Design / Hearthstone
15444 Clayton Road, Ste. 325-6
St. Louis, MO 63011
Tel: (800) 680-8833, (314) 341-8833
Fax: (314) 341-8833
Architect, Hearthstone distributor, specializing in timber frame/log designs & packages.

North Carolina

Mountain Construction Enterprises
PO Box 1177, 353 Devonwood Drive
Boone, NC 28607
Tel: (704) 264-1231
Fax: (704) 264-4863
Custom traditionally mortised oak timber frames with stress skin panels.
E-mail: Mtnconst@skybest.com
Web site: http://blowingrock.com/nc/timberframe

Timberfab, Inc.
PO Box 399, 200 W. Hope Lodge St.
Tarboro, NC 27886
Tel: (800) 968-8322
Fax: (919) 641-4142
Log and timber frame structures, components and supplies
E-mail: tfab@coastalnet.com
Web site: http://www4.coastalnet.com/timberfab

Goshen Timber Frames, Inc.
104 Wykle Road
Franklin, NC 28734

Tel: (704) 524-8662
Fax: same
Ongoing workshops and apprenticeships in timber framing and design; design services; frame sales.
E-mail: goshen@dnet.net
Web site: http://www.timberframemag.com

New Hampshire

Timberpeg
PO Box 5474
W. Lebanon, NH 03784
Tel: (603) 298-8820
Fax: (603) 298-5425
Custom designed timber frame homes and commercial structures since 1974.
E-mail: info@timberpeg.com
Web site: www.timberpeg.com

Great Northern Barns
PO Box 912E, RFD2
Canaan, NH 03741
Tel: (603) 523-7134
Fax: (603) 523-7134 *51
Great Northern Barns dismantles and erects antique barn frames.
E-mail: ejl@endor.com
Web site: www.greatnorthernbarns.com

Day Pond Woodworking
PO Box 299, Rt. 114
Bradford, NH 03221
Tel: (603) 938-2375
Over 17 years experience building custom timber frame homes, etc.

Specialty Timberworks
PO Box 261, Brownfield Road
Eaton, NH 03832
Tel: (603) 447-5625, Fax: same
Designers & fabricators of new, and reconstruction of antique timber frames. 3-D CADD services.

A.W. Corriveau Timber Frames
PO Box 421
Gilmanton, NH 03237
Tel: (603) 267-8427
Quality hand cut and erected timber frames in oak, hemlock or pine. Competitive prices due to low overhead. Satisfaction guaranteed.

New Mexico

Natural House Building Center
2300 West Alameda, A5
Santa Fe, NM 87501
Tel: (505) 471-5314
Fax: (505) 471-3714
Hands-on workshops: timber framing, straw-clay construction, earth floors & plastering.

New York

Tea House Design, Inc.
PO Box 99, 11 Benedict Road
Waccabuc, NY 10597
Tel: (914) 763-3078
Fax: (914) 763-6165
27 years experience. 100 mile radius NYC. Innovative and diligent.

The raising

New Energy Works Of Rochester, Inc.
1755 Pioneer Road
Shortsville, NY 14548
Tel: (716) 289-3220
Fax: (716) 289-3221
Timber frame production, reclaimed wood
milling; interior woodworks and design.
E-mail: jononewt@aol.com

Timberbuilt
10821 Schaffstall Dr.
N. Collins, NY 14111
Tel: (716) 337-0012
Fax: (716) 337-0013
We design, cut, erect and enclose fine timber
frame structures.

Alternate Energy Systems
PO Box 344
Peru, NY 12972
Tel: (518) 643-0805
Fax: (518) 643-2012
Masonry heaters-timber frame and log homes-
a natural blend-call.

Pine Grove Post & Beam Builders
4 Bates Road
Johnson City, NY 13790
Tel: (607) 754-0821
Fax: (607) 748-5946
Custom designed timber framed homes,
barns, buildings, and additions.

Cepco Tool Co.
PO Box 153, 295 Van Etten Road
Spencer, NY 14883
Tel: (607) 589-4313
Fax: same
Board straightening/joining tools, Bowrench
deck tool, Quick-Jack construction jack.

Legacy Timber Frames, Inc.
691 County Rd. 70
Stillwater, NY 12170
Tel: (518) 279-9108
Fax: (518) 581-9219
Custom designed, traditional timber frame
construction.

Rondout Woodworking, Inc.
29 Terra Road
Saugerties, NY 12477
Tel: (914) 246-5879, Fax: (914) 246-5845
Restoration specialist. Agricultural-industrial,
waterwheels, windmills, barns, timber
frames.

Ohio

Heartwood Timber Frames
6660 Heartwood Place
Swanton, OH 43558
Tel: (419) 875-5500
Fax: same
Crafting beautiful timber frames, panel homes,
and masonry heaters.

Hearthstone Log & Timberframe Homes
4974 Wortman Road
Zanesville, OH 43701
Tel: (614) 453-6542
Fax: same
Oak or pine timber frames, and square, hand-
hewn log homes.

Pennsylvania

Hessel Valley Timber Framing
2061 Jackson Run Road
Warren, PA 16365
Tel: (814) 489-3018
Unique combinations of Medieval European
and early American timberframe carpentry.

Hugh Lofting Timber Framing, Inc.
339 Lamborntown Road
West Grove, PA 19390
Tel: (610) 444-5382
Fax: (610) 869-3589
Company dedicated to practicing green
architecture with sustainable materials.
E-mail: hlofting@aolcom

Pocono Mt. Timber Frames
PO Box 644, Rt. 115
Brodheadsville, PA 18322
Tel: (717) 992-7515
Fax: (717) 992-9064
Design, fabrication, and erection of timber
frame barns and houses.
E-mail: etreible@ptd.net
Web site: www.pmtf.com

Bruce Cowie Timber Frames
Rt. 34 Box 354
York, PA 17406
Tel: (717) 755-6678
Custom hand-crafted traditional timber framing.
E-mail: bruce220@juno.com

Oregon

Confluence Design & Construction
PO Box 1258, 1013 NW Taylor
Corvallis, OR 97339
Tel: (514) 757-0511
Fax: (541) 753-4916
"Where thinking and doing are still one."
Design, frames, consultation

Rhode Island

South County Post & Beam
521 Liberty Lane
West Kingston, RI 02892
Tel: (401) 783-4415
Fax: (401) 783-4494
A full service timber frame company, wide pine
flooring supplier.

South Carolina

Southern Breeze Timberworks
PO Box 635
Travelers Rest, SC 29690
Tel: (864) 834-3706
Quality hand-wrought joinery.

South Dakota

Northern Lights Woodworks
24144 Pine Grove Road
Rapid City, SD 57701
Tel: (605) 399-9909
Design and construction of timber frame
homes and other timbered projects.

Tennessee

Hearthstone, Inc.
1630 E. Hwy. 25-70
Dandridge, TN 37725
Tel: (800) 247-4442
Fax: (423) 397-9262
Traditionally joined timber frames and finely
crafted dovetailed log homes.
E-mail: sales@hearthstonehomes.com
Web site: www.hearthstonehomes.com

Virginia

Blue Ridge Timberwrights
2030 Redwood Drive
Christiansburg, VA 24073
Tel: (540) 382-1102
Fax: (540) 382-8039
Designers and manufacturers of hand-crafted
timber frame structures.

Dreaming Creek Timber Frame Homes, Inc.
2487 Judes Ferry Road
Powhatan, VA 23139
Tel: (804) 598-4328
Fax: (804) 598-3748
Oak, southern yellow pine. Lengths to 45 ft.
Custom planing to 8" x 20". Fax tally for
prices. Ship nationwide.

Vermont

Liberty Head Post & Beam
PO Box 68, Main Road
Huntington, VT 05462
Tel: (802) 434-2120
Fax: (802) 434-4929
Custom designed timber frames—authenti-
cally joined in the Vermont tradition.

North Woods Joinery
PO Box 1166
Burlington, VT 05402-1166
Tel: (802) 644-5667
Fax: (802) 644-2509
Traditional post and beam construction:
homes, barns, steeples, bridges, towers.

Kondor Post & Beam
RR 2 Box 2794
Cambridge, VT 05444
Tel: (802) 644-5598
Fax: (802) 644-8735
Post & beam frames for residential & lite
commercial buildings.
E-mail: kondor@sover.net
Web site: kondorinc.com

Vermont Frames
PO Box 100, Rte. 116 Varney Hill Road
Hinesburg, VT 05461
Tel: (802) 453-3727
Fax: (802) 453-2339
Traditional affordable timber frame homes.
Building nationwide.
E-mail: foamlam@sover.net
Web site: http://www.sover.net/~foamlam

Washington

Timber Framers Guild of North America
PO Box 1075
Bellingham, WA 98227-1075
Tel: (360) 733-4001
Fax: (360) 733-4002

Ark II Inc.
HCR 73 Box 67
Twisp, WA 98856
Tel: (509) 997-2418
Fax: (509) 997-4434
Fine quality timber frame & log buildings.

The G.R. Plume Company
1373 West Smith Road, Suite A-1
Ferndale, WA 98248
Tel: (360) 384-2800
Fax: (360) 384-0335
Architectural timber millwork fabricated from
reclaimed Douglas fir.

Richard Berg, Architect
727 Taylor St.
Port Townsend, WA 98368
Tel: (360) 379-8090, Fax: (360) 379-8324
Architectural practice specializing in
comfortable, energy-efficient, quality timber
framed homes.
E-mail: rberg@olympus.net

Timbercraft Homes, Inc.
85 Martin Road
Port Townsend, WA 98368
Tel: (360) 385-3051, Fax: (360) 385-7745
Since 1979, high quality timber frame
structures, components, and architectural
engineering.
E-mail: info@timbercraft.com
Web site: http://www.timbercraft.com

Old World Timber Frames
22130 SE Green Valley Road
Auburn, WA 98092
Tel: (253) 833-1760
Heirloom quality timber frame homes and
buildings. Contact Ben Beers.

British Columbia

Gateway Timberframe Construction
8576 Ebor Terrace
Sidney, BC, Canada V8L 1L5
Tel: (250) 655-3476
Fax: (250) 656-7455
Full construction services. Quality timbers &
workmanship. Panels.

The Timber Frame Company
RR #3, Zillinsky Road
Powell River, BC, Canada V8A 5C1
Tel: (604) 487-4396
Fax: same
Home frames of Douglas Fir, Custom design
services. e-mail: tfco@pren.org

Manitoba

Pride Builders Ltd.
Box 12, GRP. 4
Dufresne, Manitoba, Canada R0A 0Y0
Tel: (204) 878-3926
Fax: (204) 878-3927
Design services, frame cutting & raising, with
either your general contractor or ours.

Nova Scotia

Acorn Timber Frames, Ltd.
RR 1, Hantsport, Kings County, NS,
Canada B0P 1P0
Tel: (902) 684-9708, Fax: same
Traditional joinery: homes, churches, farm/
garden/tourism/vacation structures, great
rooms, restorations. Serving Canada and
alluring locations with your requirements since
1978.

Ontario

Alderaan Stone/Timber Homes
PO Box 313, 6-14845 Yonge Street
Aurora, Ontario, Canada L4G 6H8
Tel: (905) 713-0001
Fax: (905) 713-0134
Traditional materials and craftsmanship.
Comprehensive custom reproductions of early
Canadian homes.
Web site: www.craftsman-book.com

**The Timbersmith Log
Construction, Limited**
General Delivery
Hillsdale, Ontario, Canada L0L 1V0
Tel: (705) 725-2585
Fax: (705) 725-2590
Log and timber frame custom hand-crafted
homes.

Northern Timberhouse, Ltd.
PO Box 71, Hwy. 35 South
Minden, Ontario, Canada K0M 2K0
Tel: (705) 286-3791
Fax: (705) 286-6168
Canadian timber frames and hand-crafted log
homes since 1980.
E-mail: nortim@halhinet.on.ca

Bear Timber Frame Homes
PO Box 124
Ajax, Ont, Canada L1S 3C2
Tel: (905) 428-6505
Designers of timber frame and energy-efficient
(R2000) homes.

Designing a Timber Frame

The aesthetic beauty of a timber frame structure is recognized as one of its most dominant features. But a well designed frame offers much more than just beauty, it can provide an efficient and comfortable living environment adaptable to both future changes to accommodate your families needs, and an economical core structural element that can allow a wide variety of natural and progressive enclosure systems to be used.

Maximizing efficiency, while enhancing the aesthetic beauty, requires a little understanding of the structural system, combined with a little artistic talent. By understanding a few of the following general guidelines for designing a timber frame, you will be more equipped to discuss your plans with your designer or

Bent Framing

builder, and you may save some money along the way.

Cost Analysis

About 75% of the cost of the timber frame is in the labor of handling, laying out and cutting the joinery. A quick way to gain comparative costs between frame

designs is by counting the number of timbers in the frame. The labor in a frame can range anywhere from 3 to 10 man hours per timber. This spread is based to large degree on the complexity of the design, but has less to do with the overall size of the frame.

Bents & Bays

Traditional timber frames are built on the bent and bay system. The *bent* is the primary structural framework, and the *bay* is the space between the bents. Four bent, three bay house frames are traditionally most common both in Europe and in the U.S. Most people are familiar with the classic Capes, Saltboxes and Colonials that were built along the east coast from the mid 17th to the late 19th centuries. The bays in these traditional frames provide the living areas, therefore, the greater

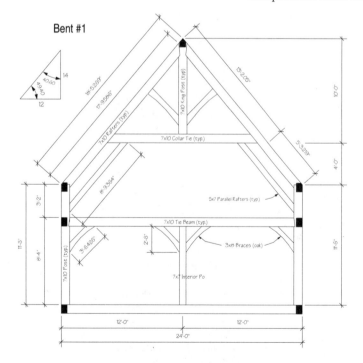

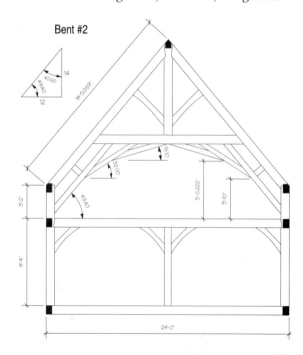

This high-posted frame requires a clear-span second floor. In example #1, the parallel rafters provide an efficient way to transfer loads to make the span possible. In example #2, the same forces are being addressed, however, additional struts are included to add an artistic design element.

the bay spacing, the greater the unobstructed and usable living area. Bays in colonial house frames were commonly spaced from 12 feet to 16 feet. The center bay, known as the *chimney bay*, was the mechanical and transitional area—chimney, stairway, hall/passageway, etc. This bay was usually narrower than the outer bays (8 to 10 feet in most frames), or just enough to fit the essential mechanical and transitional elements. The two outer bays created the primary living areas on the first floor. The kitchen and dining areas were usually on the eastern side, with the parlor and study on the western side. The bedrooms would be on the second floor.

The bent framing and post placement can add to the environment by creating distinct, visual living areas. Often, interior partitions (a costly part of construction) are not necessary to create the sense of separation and privacy.

The greatest amount of labor in cutting the frame lies in the bent framing, therefore, one can easily recognize that the fewer the bents and the greater the bay spacing, the more economical the frame may be.

Design Parameters

The practical limit for a timber to span is 16 feet, therefore, designing the frame in modules of 16 feet is the most economical. By comparing a 4 bent cape frame consisting of three 16 foot bays, and 32 foot bents (32'x 48'), with that of a cape frame of three 12 foot bays and 24 foot bents (24'x 36'), you'll find that the smaller frame will use only 8 to 12 fewer essential timbers, however the larger frame contains over 75% more living area and may cost only 15 to 20% more to produce.

Timber Frame Bent/Bay Plan

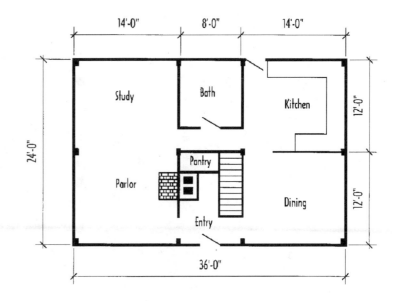

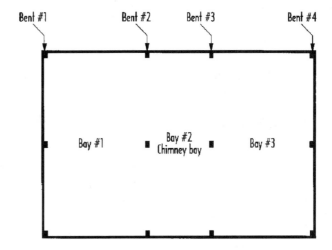

The floor plan for a traditional four bent/three bay cape frame follows a very basic concept—increase living area, and reduce wasted space. In the drawings above, the bent spacing is such that maximum living areas are created on the east and west ends of the house. These become the cooking/dining areas and the main living areas. The central bay, or chimney bay, is where all of the utilities, hallways, and mechanical systems are located. All rooms, upstairs and down, are accessed from a central location with the minimum amount of hall space. Plumbing, heating systems, and all mechanical systems generate and are accessed from the center of the structure. This reduces travel and mechanical runs, and therefore, can reduce construction costs and increase general efficiency of the dwelling.

The overall cost of the house, however, cannot be judged strictly by the frame design alone. Increasing the footprint will proportionally increase all of the surface areas and will have direct and proportionate increases in cost. To determine the final cost, or better, to determine an overall building budget, one has to determine the enclosure system to be used, the finish materials, both interior and exterior, the necessary mechanical systems, and the convenience items.

By understanding the variety of enclosure options available, how the structural elements of the frame can best be used to naturally achieve finish details, and how to allow the frame plan to blend seamlessly with the floor plan, substantial savings can be made. But, as importantly, a more comfortable home can be built.

All decisions in the design and planning stage of the home should not, however, be based strictly on cost. If this were the case, we'd all be living in mobile homes. If the budget limits the size of the home, you'll need to look at ways to increase the feeling of size, and/or design with future additions in mind. Timber framing allows a great amount of flexibility so far as creating a sense of open space, and accommodates future expansion and additions due to the few structural supports in the wall systems.

This four bent cape frame is one of the most economical timber frame designs. A frame of this style uses approximately 70% of the lumber required to build a conventionally framed house and is adaptable to future expansion. Enclosure options range from panels (foam core or compressed wheatstraw structural panels), straw bales, to a variety of traditional clay infill systems.

Does timber framing uses less material than conventional framing?

Back in 1992 we published a short article which compared the use of lumber in both a conventional stick framed house and a timber frame (Stick Frame or Timber Frame, JQ22, Summer 1992). Because of Tracy Kidder's meticulous accounting of every stick of lumber and nail which went into the Souweines' house in his book House , we used this as a model. For comparison, we used a traditional high-posted cape timber frame. To create a comparative formula that could be applied accurately to a broad range of house designs and sizes with reasonable accuracy, we determined the ratio of board feet of lumber by square footage of living area. The Souweine's house used 24,270 board feet of framing lumber. This equated to roughly 8.1 board feet of framing lumber per square foot of framed floor space. The timber frame model used a total of 10,614 board feet of timbers and interior partition framing. This came to roughly 5.5 board feet per square foot of living area. In further examples we found that as the square footage increases in a timber frame, the ratio of timber to living area decreases, while the ratio for a stick frame remains relatively constant.

If we view timber framing as a structural system similar in design and engineering to post and lintel steel structures, and not merely as an aesthetic feature, it becomes evident that it is an extremely practical and flexible method to enclose space. The fact that they're aesthetically pleasing…well, that's just a bonus.   —*Steve Chappell*

Log Home Building

Alaska

Top Notch Log Builders
Box 401, Talkeetna, Alaska 99676
Tel: (907) 733-2427
Scribe fit log joinery, custom designs and
details for the most discerning customers.

Florida

Freedom Builders
1013 Naples Drive
Orlando, FL 32804
Tel: (407) 647-5849, Fax: (407) 645-5652
Internet informational & advertising site–log &
t.f. design–video productions.
E-mail: freedom@magicnet.net
Web site: www.magicnet.net/freedom

Georgia

Hearthstone Log & Timberframe Homes
120 Carriage Drive
Macon, GA 31210
Tel: (800) 537-7931, Fax: (912) 477-6535
21 years experience, CADD design,
professional erection and dry-in services.
E-mail: hearthstonehomes@mindspring.com
Web site: www.mindspring.com/
~hearthstonehomes

Idaho

Woodhouse
PO Box 801
Ashton, ID 83420
Tel: (208) 652-3608, Fax: (208) 652-3628
Supplying all specialized tools and materials
for log-timber construction. Providing owner
and/or professional with largest selection of
quality products available.

Jeff Pedersen–Logsmith
PO Box 788, Hwy. 93 North
Challis, ID 83226
Tel: (208) 879-4211, Fax: (208) 879-5574
Traditional broadaxe-hewn dovetail and
round log scribe-fit log homes. Broadaxe-
hewn and round log timber frames.
E-mail: jplogs@cyberhighway.net

Maine

Timberstone Builders
RR 1 Box 3125
Freedom, ME 04941
Tel: (207) 589-4675, Fax: same
We specialize in chink-style log buildings and
Rumford fireplaces.

Michigan

Northern Land & Lumber Co.
7000 P Rd.
Gladstone, MI 49837
Tel: (906) 786-2994, Fax: (906) 786-2926
Primary manufacturer of log home kits &
components.
E-mail: nlandl@up.net
Web site: www.deltami.org/nlandl

Missouri

Timberland Design/Hearthstone
15444 Clayton Road, Ste. 325-6
St. Louis, MO 63011
Tel: (800) 680-8833, (314) 341-8833
Fax: (314) 341-8833
Architect, Hearthstone distributor, specializing
in timber frame/log designs & packages.

North Carolina

Mountain Construction Enterprises
PO Box 1177, 353 Devonwood Drive
Boone, NC 28607
Tel: (704) 264-1231, Fax: (704) 264-4863
Custom traditionally mortised oak timber
frames with stress skin panels.
E-mail: Mtnconst@skybest.com
Web site: http://blowingrock.com/nc/
timberframe

*No other building art
requires such crafts-
manship and skill as that
of a craftsman built log
structure. This scribe-fit log
corner detail, built by Chris
Mannix and Mark Stasik,
of Top Notch Builders,
Talkeetna, Alaska, is
testament to the patience,
experience and dedication
that fine joinery can
wrangle out of a body.*

Enertia Building Systems, Inc.
13312 Garffe Sherron Road
Wake Forest, NC 27587
Tel: (919) 556-0177
Fax: (919) 556-1135
Design/prefabrication of solid wood solar/
geothermal environmental homes.

Timberfab, Inc.
PO Box 399, 200 W. Hope Lodge St.
Tarboro, NC 27886
Tel: (800) 968-8322
Fax: (919) 641-4142
Log and timber frame structures, components
and supplies.
E-mail: tfab@coastalnet.com
Web site: http://www4.coastalnet.com/
timberfab

New Hampshire

Dan Dustin–Custom Hand-Hewing
1107 Penacook Road
Contoocook, NH 03229
Tel: (603) 746-5683
Expert adze and broadaxe work–your
material–my yard.

New York

Alternate Energy Systems
PO Box 344
Peru, NY 12972
Tel: (518) 643-0805
Fax: (518) 643-2012
Masonry heaters–timber frame and log
homes–a natural blend–call.

Lok-N-Logs, Inc.
PO Box 677, Route 12
Sherburne, NY 13460
Tel: (800) 343-8928, (607) 674-4447
Fax: (607) 674-6433
Producer of top quality, pre-cut log home packages–lifetime limited warranty!
E-mail: lnlinfo@loknlogs.com
Web site: http://www.loknlogs.com
Catalog: $12.95

Ohio

Hochstetler Milling
552 St. Rt. 95
Loudonville, OH 44842
Tel: (419) 281-3553, (419) 368-0004
Oak timber 4-sided planing. Pine log home logs 10 profiles.

Hearthstone Log & Timberframe Homes
4974 Wortman Road
Zanesville, OH 43701
Tel: (614) 453-6542
Fax: same
Oak or pine timber frames, and square, hand-hewn log homes.

Tennessee

Hearthstone, Inc.
1630 E. Hwy. 25-70
Dandridge, TN 37725
Tel: (800) 247-4442
Fax: (423) 397-9262
Traditionally joined timber frames and finely crafted dovetailed log homes.
E-mail: sales@hearthstonehomes.com
Web site: www.hearthstonehomes.com

Vermont

Real Log Homes
PO Box 202, National Information Center
Hartland, VT 05048
Tel: (800) 732-5564
Fax: (802) 436-2150
Pre-cut log home packages over 19,000 worldwide since 1963. Catalog $10.
Web site: http://www.realloghomes.com

Washington

Ark II Inc.
HCR 73 Box 67
Twisp, WA 98856
Tel: (509) 997-2418, Fax: (509) 997-4434
Fine quality timber frame & log buildings.

Timbercraft Homes, Inc.
85 Martin Road
Port Townsend, WA 98368
Tel: (360) 385-3051, Fax: (360) 385-7745
Since 1979, high quality timber frame structures, components, and architectural engineering.
E-mail: info@timbercraft.com
Web site: http://www.timbercraft.com

Wisconsin

Standard Tar Products Co., Inc.
2456 West Cornell St.
Milwaukee, WI 53209-6294
Tel: (800) 825-7650
Fax: (414) 873-7737
"Organiclear" protective wood coatings & finishes for log homes & restoration.

Canada

Goldec International Equipment, Inc.
6760   65 Ave.
Red Deer, Alberta, Canada T4R 1G5
Tel: (403) 343-6607
Fax: (403) 340-0640
De-bark logs with our chainsaw attachment. The amazing Log Wizard!
E-mail: goldec@telusplanet.net
Web site: goldec.com

The Timbersmith Log Construction, Ltd.
General Delivery
Hillsdale, Ontario, Canada L0L 1V0
Tel: (705) 725-2585
Fax: (705) 725-2590
Log and timber frame custom hand-crafted homes.

Northern Timberhouse, Ltd.
PO Box 71, Hwy. 35 South
Minden, Ontario, Canada K0M 2K0
Tel: (705) 286-3791
Fax: (705) 286-6168
Canadian timber frames and hand-crafted log homes since 1980.
E-mail: nortim@halhinet.on.ca

Canadian Log Home Supply
RR 2
Eganville, Ontario, Canada K0J 1T0
Tel: (800) 746-7773, (613) 628-2372
Fax: same
Sealants, finishes, preservatives, cleaners and restoration products. Retail and wholesale. Authorized Perma-Chink distributor.

Wooden Boatbuilding

Wooden Boat School
PO Box 78
Brooklin, ME 04616
Tel: (207) 359-4651
Fax: (207) 359-8920

The Atlantic Challenge Foundation
Apprenticeshop of Rockland
Box B
Rockland, ME 04841

International Yacht Restoration School
449 Thames Street
Newport, RI 02840
Tel: (401) 848-5777
Fax: (401) 842-0669

The Center for Wooden Boats
1010 Valley Street
Seattle, WA 98109
Tel: (206) 382-2628
Fax: (206) 382-2699
Traditional wooden boatbuilding workshops offered. To do is to learn.
E-mial: cwboats@eskimo.com/-cwboats

Wooden boatbuilding offers unique challenges to the craftsman and a viable dwelling in an ever changing world.

Natural Building

Natural Building

Cob Cottage Company

The concern that people are having over the materials that we use to build our homes is increasing on almost a daily basis. The increase in chemical sensitivity is escalating at an alarming rate. If for no other reason than health, we all should be considering more closely the materials that we are using in the construction of the spaces we inhabit. As important as the health reasons are, there are also many other compelling reasons for taking a closer look at the way in which we build.

While general health plays a large role in most of the decisions that we make as a people, there is also our socioeconomic health to consider. What are we building? And how are we doing it? In the last three decades we have systematically separated ourselves from the production oriented economic base. Most of the employment in the nation is in the governmental and intellectual arena. Farming is now the process of multinational giants. Aside from the automobile manufacturers, and the people who are out there building houses for a living, our nation is basically producing paper and electronic transactions.

The odds are good that in the next millennium people will need to take a more active role in the construction of their own houses. The environmental concerns that are beginning to face us now may be the impetus that makes everyone take a closer look at what we are building. The Natural Building Movement, if it can be so dubbed, is opening the eyes of many to more practical ways to build and the benefits of natural materials.

Natural materials, when used as the structural element of a building, are usually less expensive than their synthetic counterparts. Using materials in a more natural state, however, usually requires increased labor on the site. This is a great exchange as long as the builder and client understand it from the outset. Natural materials for the interior and exterior finish applications (slate tiles for counter tops and flooring as opposed to laminates and linoleum, as an example) are also less expensive, and they most often have a longer life cycle as well.

Wood, stone, earth and straw have been the universal building materials since the beginning of civilization. With the appropriate design and planning, coupled with creative and progressive approaches to working with these materials, they will most likely remain for a long time to come.

Straw bales used as enclosure for a timber frame home in Alaska.

Strawbale Construction

Arizona

The Canelo Project
HCL Box 324
Elgin, AZ 85611
Tel: (520) 455-5548
Fax: (520) 455-9360
Straw bale building/earthen floors and plasters, workshops, resources, consulting.
E-mail: absteen@dakotacom.net
Web site: http://www.deatech.com/canelo

The Last Straw
PO Box 42000
Tucson, AZ 85733
Tel: (520) 882-3848
The Last Straw: the quarterly journal of straw-bale construction.
E-mail: thelaststraw@igc.apc.org
Web site: http://www.netchaos.com/+ls

Out On Bale, "un" Ltd.
1037 E. Linden St.
Tucson, AZ 85719
Tel: (520) 624-1673, Fax: (520) 299-9099
Strawbale workshops, presentations, wall raising, planning and supervision, consulting and publishing.
E-mail: binb@juno.com

Sustainable Systems Support
PO Box 318
Bisbee, AZ 85603
Tel: (520) 432-4292
Offers books and videos on plastered straw bale construction, including an excellent 90 min. "how-to" video with a 62 page manual. Wall raising workshops and consultations.

Colorado

Solar Energy International
PO Box 715
Carbondale, CO 81623
Tel: (970) 963-8855
Fax: (970) 963-8866
Hands-on workshops on renewable energy and environmental building technologies.
E-mail: sei@solarenergy.org
Web site: http://www.solarenergy.org

Massachusetts

Greenspace Collaborative
PO Box 107, Ashfield, MA 01330
Tel: (413) 369-4905
Buildings of straw bales and other natural materials detailed for the northeastern climate.

Maine

Wentworth Timberframes
PO Box 1116, 45 Mason Street
Bethel, ME 04217
Tel: (207) 824-4237
25 years experience. Hewn, rough-sawn, or hand-planed timbers. Mortise and tenon joinery. Owner friendly

Proclay
c/o Fox Maple
PO Box 249
Brownfield, ME 04010
Tel: (207) 935-3720
Fax: (207) 935-4575
Light-clay infill techniques, clay & lime plasters, clay building materials, workshops and consulting.
E-mail: foxmaple@nxi.com

Fox Maple School of Traditional Building
PO Box 249, Corn Hill Road
Brownfield, ME 04010
Tel: (207) 935-3720
Fax: (207) 935-4575
Timber framing and natural building workshops. Other workshops available in the areas of thatch, straw clay and strawbale enclosures and alternative building systems. Fox Maple strives for quality craftsmanship, with a view towards a sustainable future.
E-mail: foxmaple@nxi.com
Web site: http://www.nxi.com/WWW/joinersquarterly

Minnesota

Community Eco-Design Network
PO Box 6241, 3151-29th Ave. S, #103
Minneapolis, MN 55406
Tel: (612) 306-2326
Super-insulated construction planbook, design services, northern climate strawbale building system.
E-mail: erichart@mtn.org
Web site: http://www.umn.edu/n/home/m037/kurtdand/cen

New Hampshire

Straw Works
152 West Main St.
Conway, NH 03818
Tel: (603) 447-1701
Fax: (603) 447-6412
Design for those wishing to walk lightly upon the earth.
E-mail: Straw-Works@juno.com

Ohio

Natural Homesteads
13182 N. Boone Road
Columbia Station, OH 44028
Tel: (440) 236-3344
Natural building design / consultation; slide presentations; straw-bale and cob workshops.

Oregon

Sustainable Architecture
PO Box 696, 910 Glendale Ave.
Ashland, OR 97520
Tel: (541) 482-6332
Fax: (541) 488-8299
Architectural services integrating full spectrum of healthy, holistic building.

Aprovecho Research Center
80574 Hazelton Road
Cottage Grove, OR 97424
Tel: (541) 942-8198
Fax: (541) 942-0302
Demonstration research and education center for sustainable living.
E-mail: apro@efn.org/~apro
Web site: http://www.efn.org/~apro

Gringo Grip
4951 Netarts Hwy. W. #2041
Tillamook, OR 97141
Tel: (800) 734-8091
Fax: (800) 734-8071
A simple thru-the-bale anchor for fastening cabinets, interior wall sections, electrical boxes, fixtures, and pipe to straw-bale walls.

Vermont

Yestermorrow Design/Build School
RR 1 Box 97-5
Warren, VT 05674
Tel: (802) 496-5545
Fax: (802) 496-5540
Offers hands-on courses in residential design and "green" construction.
E-mail: ymschool@aol.com
Web site: www.yestermorrow.org

Organic Oat Straw
RR#1 Box 520
Orleans, VT 05860
Tel: (802) 754-2028
Straw bales for building.

Washington

Greenfire Institute
PO Box 1040
Winthrop, WA 98862
Tel: (509) 996-3593
Fax: same
Straw bale construction training, consultation and design.
E-mail: greenfire@igc.org
Web site: www.balewolf.com

Sustainable Building

Arizona

The Last Straw
PO Box 42000
Tucson, AZ 85733
Tel: (520) 882-3848
The Last Straw: the quarterly journal of straw-bale construction.
E-mail: thelaststraw@igc.apc.org
Web site: http://www.netchaos.com/+ls

California

Sierra Timberframers
PO Box 595
Nevada City, CA 95959
Tel: (916) 292-9449
Fax: (916) 292-9460
Timberframed structures. Recycled wood & salvaged trees. Solar & sustainable designs preferred. Classes available.

Eos Institute
580 Broadway, Suite 200
Laguna Beach, CA 92651
Tel: (714) 497-1896
Fax: (714) 497-7861
Educational nonprofit for the study of sustainable living. Resources, consulting, and programs on ecological community design. Library, lectures, workshops.

Colorado

Solar Energy International
PO Box 715
Carbondale, CO 81623
Tel: (970) 963-8855
Fax: (970) 963-8866
Hands-on workshops on renewable energy and environmental building technologies.
E-mail: sei@solarenergy.org
Web site: http://www.solarenergy.org

DC, Washington

Passive Solar Industries Council
1511 K Street, Suite 600
Washington, DC 20005
Tel: (202) 628-7400, Fax: (202) 393-5043
PSIC independent nonprofit advancing climate responsive buildings.
E-mail: PSICouncil@aol.com
Web site: http://www.psic.org

Sandra Leibowitz
Eco-Building Schools
3220 N Street NW #218
Washington, DC 20007
$7 ($6 + $1 postage) for Eco-Building Schools: A directory of alternative educational resources in environmentally sensitive design. Detailed info on 35 eco-building schools across the U.S.
Web site: http://www.ecodesign.org/edi/eden

Illinois

Davis Caves Construction, Inc.
PO Box 69
Armington, IL 61721
Tel: (309) 392-2574, Fax: (309) 392-2578
We will design and build to your specific floorplan, or choose from our 80 page planbook.
E-mail: earthome@daviscaves.com
Web site: www.daviscaves.com/builder.htm

Iowa

Lite-Form International
PO Box 774, 1210 Steuben St.
Sioux City, IA 51102
Tel: (712) 252-3704, Fax: (712) 252-3259
Insulating forms for cast in place foundations & walls.
E-mail: liteform@pionet.net
Web site: http://www.pionet.net/~liteform/index.html

Wheat Straw Panels offer a unique alternative to urethane and EPS construction panels commonly used to enclose timber frames.
The future of wheat straw and other grain and agricultural by-products manufactured into panelized and familiar construction products looks promising as more research and development takes place, and as the demand increases.

Agriboard Industries
PO Box 645
Fairfield, IA 52556
Tel: (515) 472-0363
Complete, OSB laminated, compressed
wheat straw panel building systems.
E-mail: agriboard@lisco.com

Massachusetts

The Heartwood School
Johnson Hill Road
Washington, MA 01235
Tel: (413) 623-6677
Fax: (413) 623-0277
Workshops in homebuilding, timber framing,
woodworking, and more.
E-mail: info@heartwoodschool.com
Web site: www.heartwoodschool.com

Greenspace Collaborative
PO Box 107
Ashfield, MA 01330
Tel: (413) 369-4905
Buildings of straw bales and other natural
materials detailed for the northeastern
climate.

Jack A. Sobon: Architect/Builder
PO Box 201, 613 Shaw Road
Windsor, MA 01270-0201
Tel: (413) 684-3223
Fax: same
Specializing in design and construction of
sustainable wooden architecture.

Maine

Talmage Solar Engineering, Inc.
18 Stone Road
Kennebunkport, ME 04046
Tel: (207) 967-5945, Fax: (207) 967-5754
Design and sale of solar electric compo-
nents for off-grid or utility interface.
E-mail: tse@talmagesolar.com
Web site: www.talmagesolar.com

Wentworth Timberframes
PO Box 1116, 45 Mason Street
Bethel, ME 04217
Tel: (207) 824-4237
25 years experience. Hewn, rough-sawn, or
hand-planed timbers. Mortise and tenon
joinery. Owner friendly.

Proclay
c/o Fox Maple
PO Box 249
Brownfield, ME 04010
Tel: (207) 935-3720
Fax: (207) 935-4575
Light-clay infill techniques, clay & lime
plasters, clay building materials, workshops
and consulting.
E-mail: foxmaple@nxi.com

Wood Chip/Clay Infill

Wood chips are an abundant by-product of the forest industry in the U.S. German clay builders began experimenting with woodchips in place of straw in the early 80s. It has proven satisfactory on all accounts. The woodchip system has several advantages over straw because; 1) it takes less time to prepare, 2) it's easier to place into the wall, and 3) no shrinkage. The house above in Alfred, Maine, was infilled with a 12" thick wood chip/ clay enclosure using wooden lathing to 'cage' the mixture.

Michigan

Renaissance Developments
10704 Oviatt Road
Honor, MI 49640
Tel: (616) 326-4009
Sustainable building, healthy creative
dreamspaces, bau-biologie, owner-builder
involvement welcome.

Missouri

Industrial AG Innovations
2725 N. Westwood Blvd, Suite 7
Poplar Bluff, MO 63901
Tel: (573) 785-3355, Fax: (573) 785-3059
Hemp fiberboard products. 100% hemp
particles and a typical UF resin.

Cob was a traditional construction method in Great Britian. Today, Cob Cottage, a design construction group in Oregon, is adapting it to our modern needs.

Montana

Center For Resourceful Building Technology
PO Box 100, 516 S. Orange
Missoula, MT 59806
Tel: (406) 549-7678
Fax: (406) 549-4100
Non-profit educating the public on environmentally responsible construction practices.

North Carolina

Enertia Building Systems, Inc.
13312 Garffe Sherron Road
Wake Forest, NC 27587
Tel: (919) 556-0177
Fax: (919) 556-1135
Design/prefabrication of solid wood solar/geothermal environmental homes.

New Mexico

Natural House Building Center
2300 West Alameda, A5
Santa Fe, NM 87501
Tel: (505) 471-5314
Fax: (505) 471-3714
Hands-on workshop: timber framing, straw-clay construction, earth floors & plastering.

Pumice-Crete Building Systems
PO Box 539
El Prado, NM 87529
Tel: (505) 776-5879
Fax: (505) 758-6954
E-mail: machardy@newmex.com
Web site: www.taosnet.com/pumice-crete/index.html

New Hampshire

Springpoint Design
2210 Pratt Road
Alstead, NH 03602
Tel: (603) 835-2433
Fax: (603) 835-7825
Architectural design / consulting: health, sustainability, efficiency—timber frames, alternative enclosures.

New York

Rector Cork Insulation
9 West Prospect Ave.
Mount Vernon, NY 10550
Tel: (914) 699-5755,6,7
Fax: (914) 699-5759
Architects and engineers specify cork because of its superior insulation values, long life, structural strength & decorative values.

Oregon

Cob Cottage Co.
PO Box 123
Cottage Grove, OR 97424
Tel: (541) 942-2005
Fax: (541) 942-3021
Information and workshops on building with cob (sand, clay, straw).
Web site: http://www.deatech.com/cobcottage

Sustainable Architecture
PO Box 696, 910 Glendale Ave.
Ashland, OR 97520
Tel: (541) 482-6332
Fax: (541) 488-8299
Architectural services integrating full spectrum of healthy, holistic building.

Terry F. Johnson Building Design
1013 NW Taylor Ave.
Corvallis, OR 97330
Tel: (541) 757-8535, Fax: (541) 753-4916
Custom plans for timber framed homes, barns and outbuildings.
E-mail: sarah@peak.org

Aprovecho Research Center
80574 Hazelton Road
Cottage Grove, OR 97424
Tel: (541) 942-8198, Fax: (541) 942-0302
Demonstration research and education center for sustainable living.
E-mail: apro@efn.org/~apro
Web site: http://www.efn.org/~apro

Groundworks
PO Box 381
Murphy, OR 97533
Tel: (541) 471-3470
Workshops and handbook available on cob (hand-sculpted earth) construction.
Web site: http://www.cpros.com/~sequoia

Pennsylvania

Hugh Lofting Timber Framing, Inc.
339 Lamborntown Road
West Grove, PA 19390
Tel: (610) 444-5382, Fax: (610) 869-3589
Company dedicated to practicing green architecture with sustainable materials.
E-mail: hlofting@aolcom

Tennessee

ORNL Buildings Technology Center
PO Box 2008, 1 Bethel Valley Road
Oak Ridge, TN 37831
Tel: (423) 574-4345, Fax: (423) 574-9338
Whole wall & roof R-value measurements.
E-mail: jef@ornl.gov
web site: www.ornl.gov/roofs+walls

Texas

Advanced Earthen Construction Technologies, Inc.
7334 Blanco Road, Suite 109
San Antonio, TX 78216-4978
Tel: (210) 349-6960
Fax: (210) 349-2561, or 492-0222
Compressed Soil Block machine produces an inexpensive, durable, attractive , and energy efficient building material from locally available soils. Produces 960 blocks per hour.
E-mail: vwehman@connecti.com

Virginia

Masonry Heater Association of N.A.
11490 Commerce Pk. Dr., Suite 300
Reston, VA 20191
Tel: (703) 620-3171, Fax: (703) 620-3928
Association of builders, designers & researchers of masonry heaters.
Web site: http://mha-net.org/

Vermont

Yestermorrow Design/Build School
RR 1 Box 97-5
Warren, VT 05674
Tel: (802) 496-5545
Fax: (802) 496-5540
Offers hands-on courses in residential design and "green" construction.
E-mail: ymschool@aol.com
Web site: www.yestermorrow.org

Environmental Building News
RR 1, Box 161
Brattleboro, VT 05301
Tel: (802) 257-7300
Fax: (802) 257-7304
The leading publication on environmentally responsible design and construction.
E-mail: ebn@ebuild.com
Web site: http://www.ebuild.com

Washington

Bear Creek Lumber
PO Box 669, 495 Eastside County Road
Winthrop, WA 98862
Tel: (800) 571-7191
Fax: (509) 997-2040
Western cedar, fir, redwood. Traditional patterns, decking, timbers and beams. Delivery available nationwide.

West Virginia

Wind Bell Hollow/C.J. Jammer
HC 40 Box 36
Lewisburg, WV 24901
Tel: (304) 645-6466
Design/drafting of timber framed homes and other natural house designs.

Canada

Bear Timber Frame Homes
PO Box 124
Ajax, Ont, Canada L1S 3C2
Tel: (905) 428-6505
Designers of timber frame and energy-efficient (R2000) homes.

A & K Technical Services
PO Box 22
Anola, MB, Canada R0E 0A0
Tel: (204) 866-3262
Fax: (204) 866-3287
Structural engineering in wood. "Stackwall" house construction design, consulting, manual.
E-mail: krisdick@mb.sympatico.ca

What is Cob?

The word *cob* comes from an Old English root meaning "a lump or rounded mass". It's a traditional building technique using hand-formed lumps of earth mixed with sand and straw. Cob is easy to learn and inexpensive to build. It dries to a hardness similar to lean concrete and is used like adobe to create self-supporting, load-bearing walls. Cob has been used for centuries throughout Western Europe, even in rainy and windy climates, as far north as the latitude of Alaska. This ancient technology doesn't contribute to deforestation, pollution or mining, nor depend on manufactured materials or power tools. Cob is non-toxic and completely recyclable, which is important in this era of environmental degradation, dwindling natural resources and chemical contaminants.

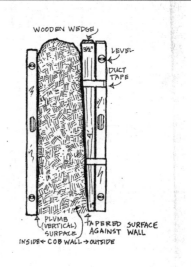

Reprinted from *The Cobber's Companion*, by Michael Smith, A Cob Cottage Publication

Straw: a versatile building material

As pure cellulose fiber, straw lends itself to many useful forms and building systems. In its natural state, straw can be mixed directly with mud and clay to form bricks and blocks. Baled, it can be stacked to make structural wall systems. Chopped straw can be used as a binder for natural clay plasters. Modern manufacturing technology can form and compress straw into structural construction panels. One company in South Dakota is making a 100% wheat straw OSB (oriented strand board). Under heat and pressure, straw exudes its own resin, which acts as a natural binder in the production of straw panels. The qualities, characteristics and abundance of straw make it one of the most promising *new* building materials for the future as issues of health and sustainability play a more significant role in the selection of building materials.

The following is a brief outline of just a few of the ways that straw can be utilized—right now—as an appropriate building material:

Types of straw

Most straw produced in the U.S. is a waste product, which must be disposed of at a considerable cost to farmers. What little market exists for straw has been primarily as bedding for farm animals. Straw should not be confused with hay, which is a mixture of legumes and grasses, including the seed heads. As it is a feedstuff, hay is much more valuable. Wheat, rye, rice, oats and barley are few of the grains produced commercially in the U.S. All types produce suitable straw for construction purposes.

Straw bales

Straw bales are attractive for insulating value (R 45-50) and the apparent ease, speed and low-tech installation requirements. The Greenfire Institute, which pro-

duced western Washington's first code-approved straw bale building in a 1994 workshop, gives straw a rating of "100% Wolf Proof: despite the story of the three little pigs, straw walls stand up to lateral load tests simulating 100 mph winds, passing with flying colors." When plastered or stuccoed, straw walls have been proven to be more fire-resistant than stud-wall construction.

Straw is resistant to moisture and rot as long as there is sufficient air circulation. Bales, due to their density, cannot get wet, so extreme care must be taken to protect them from rain during the building process.

Straw panels

Straw panels may well be the building panel of the future, but are hard to come by at present. Stramit USA has ceased production, but Agriboard Industries, another Texas based company, started production of a similar structural compressed straw panel

Bill Steen demonstrates the art of bale leaning.

in the spring of 1997. Stramit's Enviropanels were attractive at about a third of the cost of foam-core panels, but carried no reliable information on R-value. An experimental straw paneled structure in Maine proved quick and efficient to build, and insulates better than the manufacturer's stated R-value. Reports in JQ30's News & Information citing an incidence of scraps left out in a light rain exploding to five times their size may have exaggerated the panels' vulnerability to moisture. Full panels, completely soaked by rain during the construction process were unaffected. While straw may give the impression of being lightweight and fragile, 2 1/2" 4' by 8' Enviropanels weigh 130-140 lbs. and proved surprisingly strong. If, and when, consistent sources of straw panels become available, they may prove to be the most cost efficient method to enclose a timber frame using natural materials.

Light straw clay

Light straw clay is made by mixing a clay slip (100% clay mixed with water to the consis-

Window opening cut into straw panel wall after panel installation.

tency of thick paint) with straw. While the clay slip can be mixed in a mortar mixer, the straw must be mixed into it by hand and pitchfork, therefore it is rather labor intensive. On the other hand, the materials are extremely inexpensive. Light straw clay has been proven to resist water and moisture both during construction and over the life of the building. Many examples of light straw clay walls date back to the 16th century.

Once mixed, the straw clay is packed into slip forms to create a wall of anywhere from 6" to 18" thick. Colder climates would require a minimum of 12". One drawback is that it must be completed during warm weather, as it cannot freeze prior to drying. This can take anywhere from 6 to 12 weeks, depending on wall thickness and climate. A similar wall system can be made using wood chips instead of straw.

Straw clay bricks

Bricks are formed in the same way, with the advantage of being manufactured off-site under controlled conditions and installed in any season.

Straw clay plaster

Clay plaster can be applied to any surface that masonry or gypsum plaster can be adhered to. The advantages are that it is breathable and most of the materials can come from the building site. The mix will vary in accordance with the quality of the clay and sand or aggregate used, however, the basic recipe is two parts sand, one part clay and one part finely chopped straw for the base coat. Finish coats can range from one part each of fine sand, clay and very finely chopped straw, to 100% clay. Straw can be chopped using garden shredders. Rough coat straw can be chopped with one to two passes through a shredder, and finish coat three to four passes.

Structural Hybrid Straw-Bale Construction

"Structural" hybrids are those in which both compressive straw-bale walls and non-compressive walls/frameworks, made with other materials, carry roof weight. Combining both of these wall types in a design can release you from some of the constraints, or disadvantages, of each. In a single story building this could mean, for example, a central adobe wall carrying half of the roof load, with the other half shared by two exterior load bearing straw-bale walls. Or it could mean a shed-roofed building with lots of windows in a "post-and-beam" framework on the south side, and a load bearing bale wall on the north side.

Designs of this type must take into consideration the fact that the bale walls will compress, lowering the RBA and changing the pitch of the roof. In a building involving a heavy roof system, long rafter spans and spongy bales, the problem could be significant.

In a full, two-story structure, this could mean an engineered, "post-and-beam" framework (wrapped or infilled with bales) topped with a deck. Upon this deck, for a second story, could sit full-height, load bearing straw-bale walls capped with a roof. Or, it could mean a full, designed-to-be-lived-in basement, with a load bearing bale building on top of it.

Our Model as a "Structural" Hybrid

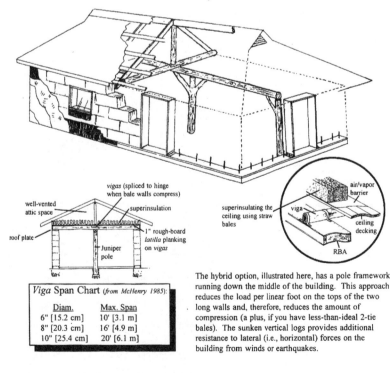

Viga Span Chart (*from McHenry 1985*):

Diam.	Max. Span
6" [15.2 cm]	10' [3.1 m]
8" [20.3 cm]	16' [4.9 m]
10" [25.4 cm]	20' [6.1 m]

The hybrid option, illustrated here, has a pole framework running down the middle of the building. This approach reduces the load per linear foot on the tops of the two long walls and, therefore, reduces the amount of compression (a plus, if you have less-than-ideal 2-tie bales). The sunken vertical logs provides additional resistance to lateral (i.e., horizontal) forces on the building from winds or earthquakes.

Reprinted from *Build it with Bales*, published by Out on Bale,"un" Ltd.

Notes & Numbers

Wood

Wood

Trees to lumber...for centuries the premier building material. But with a burgeoning world population, our forests' limits as a natural resource are stretched more and more each day. Europe and Asia both know the value of good timberland...they've squandered their supplies before–in fact, centuries ago. New England was once bared of 90% of its forests. But back then, there was always a new frontier. The United States, once thought to have an unlimited supply of timber, now has less than 10 percent of its original virgin forest.

Environmentalists have done their part...putting grassroots organizations together to enact protective legislation...creating scientifically sustainable certification commissions to guarrantee the viability of both resources and the environment. And all the while being denigrated as "treehuggers" intent upon destroying the economy, when in fact, though they do love trees, the results of

their actions upon the economy have proven to be just the opposite.

Now, new breeds of lumber suppliers are coming into play that will have an equally beneficial effect. Recycled lumber is fast becoming a mainstay in the building economy. In fact, there are now more than 600 wood recycling facilities in the US, alone. Old mills, bridges, fire towers and tenement tracts are proving to be treasure troves of serviceable, and in many cases, preferred, sources of lumber. Even sunken logs, decades old, and driftwood have found their way into the market.

Woodlot owners have taken great strides in learning to maintain the integrity of their forests, and ironically, it has also made them more profitable. Not only are they producing higher quality timber, and more of it, but they're working with nature instead of against it. Many corporate entities, though, are still focused on the short term, concerned more with quarterly profit margins and

liquidity, than in long term, common sense goals.

With the growing contingent of portable sawmill operators, homeowners are now opting to procure their lumber directly from the building site. Many areas of the country offer wooded lots which need to be cleared for the home and yard. Rather than wasting this wood, it can all be transformed into timbers and lumber with the help of a portable sawmill that can be towed behind a pickup truck. This not only cuts the lumber bill, but eliminates the cost of transportation and the polluting effects of diesel fuel. In some instances, even the slash from these trees can be run through a chipper and used with a clay infill system.

The wood suppliers in this section provide the best quality lumber, with the least amount of damage to the environment. The infrastructure is there–as consumers, all we have to do is build on it.

Timbers

Arizona

Sirocco Trading Company
110 East Wing Drive
Sedona, AZ 86336
Tel: (520) 204-2516
Fax: (520) 282-3716
Recycled wood products, solid timbers,
boards; Douglas fir, redwood, more.
E-mail: eeh3@sedona.net

California

Granberg International
PO Box 70425, 200 South Garraro Blvd.
Richmond, CA 94807-0425
Tel: (510) 237-2099
Fax: (510) 237-1667
Manufacturer of the Alaskan sawmill.
Attachments and accessories for sharpening
chainsaws.
E-mail: granberg@aol.com
Web site: www.granberg.com

Pacific Post & Beam
PO Box 13708
San Luis Obispo, CA 93406
Tel: (805) 543-7565
Fax: (805) 543-1287
Full service timber frame and truss design and
build.

Maxwell Pacific
PO Box 4127
Malibu, CA 90264
Tel: (310) 457-4533
Douglas fir, redwood, pine, cedar, barnwood,
used and new.

Michael Evenson Natural Resources
PO Box 157
Petrolia, CA 95558
Tel: (707) 629-3679
Fax: same
Recycled old growth redwood, Douglas-fir,
custom remilling.
E-mail: evenson@igc.apc.org

Recycled Lumberworks
596 Park Blvd.
Ukiah, CA 95482
Tel: (707) 462-2567, Fax: (707) 462-8607
Quality recycled old growth timber, clear
heart redwood lumber from 100 year old vat
staves and Douglas fir flooring is our
specialty.

Colorado

Greenleaf Forest Products, Inc.
102 Greenleaf Lane
Westcliffe, CO 81252
Tel: (719) 783-2487
Fax: (719) 783-0212
Logs, poles and rough-sawn from sustainably-
managed private forests.

*Richard Babcock, the master of ancient barns, proves that any timber can
become fodder for a frame.*

Connecticut

Hull Forest Products
101 Hampton Road
Pomfret Center, CT 06259
Tel: (860) 974-2083
Fax: (860) 974-2963
Producers of quality oak timbers, band sawn,
up to 26'6" long.
Web site: http://www.HullForest.com

Post & Beam Homes, Inc.
4 Sexton Hill Road South
East Hampton, CT 06424
Tel: (860) 267-2060, CT (800) 821-8456
Fax: (860) 267-9515
Pine, oak, Doug fir or recycled lumber.
Frames hand-crafted in our workshop. Our
expert timber framers will construct
anywhere.

Delaware

Timber Frame Systems, Inc.
PO Box 458, 28 Main St.
Frankford, DE 19945
Tel: (302) 732-9428
Fax: (302) 537-4971
Manufacturer of custom post & beam frame kits.

Florida

Tropical American Tree Farms
C/O AAA Express Mail, 1641 NW 79th Ave.
Miami, FL 33126
Tel: (800) 788-4918, 011 (506) 787-0020
Fax: 011 (506) 787-0051
Growing precious tropical hardwoods on tree
farms in Costa Rica.
E-mail: tatfsa.sol.racsa.co.cr

R.G. White Construction
PO Box 14734, 5800 Firestone Road
Jacksonville, FL 32238
Tel: (904) 778-8352
Fax: same
Building fine quality cracker style and
craftsman style homes.

Idaho

Stein & Collett
PO Box 4065, 201 South Mission Street
McCall, ID 83638
Tel: (208) 634-5374
Fax: (208) 634-8228
Beams, flooring, doors, stair systems. Both
new and recycled woods custom architec-
tural millwork. Unique and unusual species
are our specialty.

Massachusetts

W.D. Cowls, Inc.
PO Box 9677, 134 Montague Road
North Amherst, MA 01059-9677
Tel: (413) 549-1403
Fax: (413) 549-0000
Timbers to 26', NELMA certified to grade
boards, structural lumber and timbers.

Maryland

Vintage Lumber Co., Inc.
PO Box 104, 1 Council
Woodsboro, MD 21798
Tel: (800) 499-7859, Fax: (301) 845-6475
Reclaimed, remilled and remarkable tongue
and groove antique wood flooring.
E-mail: woodfloors@vintagelumber.com
Web site: www.vintagelumber.com

Maine

Natural Knees
281 Hartland Road
St. Albans, ME 04971
Tel: (207) 938-2380
Natural grown knees for timber frame
construction and boat building.
E-mail: kneeman@somtel.com

Churchill Hill Woodworks
Churchill Hill Road
Parsonfield, ME
Tel: (207) 625-7302
Custom sawing. Quality work.

Michigan

Northern Land & Lumber Co.
7000 P Rd.
Gladstone, MI 49837
Tel: (906) 786-2994
Fax: (906) 786-2926
Primary manufacturer of log home kits &
components.
E-mail: nlandl@up.net
web site: www.deltami.org/nlandl

Minnesota

Duluth Timber Company
PO Box 16717, Duluth, MN 55816
Tel: (218) 727-2145
Recycled timbers and planks from U.S. &
Canada. Doug fir, redwood and pine.
Resawn beams, flooring; "as is" wholesale
timbers.

North Carolina

Harmony Exchange
Route 2, Box 843-A
Boone, NC 28607
Tel: (800) 968-9663
Antique, reclaimed & new growth. Flooring,
timber trusses, decking, exposed beam
systems, siding & more. Catalog.

New Hampshire

Great Northern Barns
PO Box 912E, RFD2
Canaan, NH 03741
Tel: (603) 523-7134
Fax: (603) 523-7134 *51
Great Northern Barns dismantles and erects
antique barn frames.
E-mail: ejl@endor.com
Web site: www.greatnorthernbarns.com

New York

M. Fine Lumber Co., Inc.
175 Varick Ave.
Brooklyn, NY 11231
Tel: (718) 381-5200
Fax: (718) 366-8907
Buyer & seller of reusable lumber, timber &
flooring available.
E-mail: MerritF@Fine-Lumber.com
Web site: www.Fine-Lumber.com/Lumber.html

Pioneer Millworks
1755 Pioneer Road
Shortsville, NY 14548
Tel: (716) 289-3220
Fax: (716) 289-3221
Reclaimed timbers from turn-of-the-century
buildings, S4S or rough sawn. Hand-hewn
barn timbers. Antique pine and fir flooring.
Custom millwork.

Ohio

Hochstetler Milling
552 St. Rt. 95
Loudonville, OH 44842
Tel: (419) 281-3553, (419) 368-0004
Oak timber 4-sided planing. Pine log home
logs 10 profiles.

Pennsylvania

Conklin's Authentic Barnwood
RR 1, Box 70, Butterfield Road
Susquehanna, PA 18847
Tel: (717) 465-3832
Fax: same
Supplier antique barnwood, hand-hewn
beams, flooring and rustic materials.
E-mail: conklins@epix.net
Web site: conklins barnwood.com

Pocono Mt. Timber Frames
PO Box 644, Rt. 115
Brodheadsville, PA 18322
Tel: (717) 992-7515
Fax: (717) 992-9064
Design, fabrication, and erection of timber
frame barns and houses.
E-mail: etreible@ptd.net
web site: www.pmtf.com

Rhode Island

Liberty Cedar
535 Liberty Lane
W. Kingston, RI 02892
Tel: (800) 882-3327, (401) 789-6626
Fax: (401) 789-0320
Naturally decay-resistant exterior wood
products specializing in wood roofing.

Tennessee

Hearthstone, Inc.
1630 E. Hwy. 25-70
Dandridge, TN 37725
Tel: (800) 247-4442
Fax: (423) 397-9262
Traditionally joined timber frames and finely
crafted dovetailed log homes.
E-mail: sales@hearthstonehomes.com
web site: www.hearthstonehomes.com

Texas

What Its Worth, Inc.
PO Box 162135
Austin, TX 78716
Tel: (512) 328-8837, Fax: same
Recycled heart pine. Timbers, planks,
custom flooring, cabinet, door and moulding
stock. Sold by piece or truck load. Virgin
tidewater cypress mined from south
Louisiana waterway, cut wet to spec. or sold
in log form.

Precision Woodworks
507 E. Jackson St.
Burnet, TX 78611
Tel: (512) 756-6950
Fax: same
New products from antique longleaf pine and
other used timbers.

Utah

**Trestlewood (A Division Of Cannon
Structures, Inc.)**
PO Box 1728, 241 W 500 N, Suite A
Provo, UT 84603-1728
Tel: (801) 375-2779
Fax: (801) 375-2757
Wholesaler of recycled Douglas fir, redwood,
SYD, etc. Timbers & products.
E-mail: bradnate@burgoyne.com

Virginia

Blue Ridge Timberwrights
2030 Redwood Drive
Christiansburg, VA 24073
Tel: (540) 382-1102
Fax: (540) 382-8039
Designers and manufacturers of hand-crafted
timber frame structures.

Dreaming Creek Timber Frame Homes, Inc.
2487 Judes Ferry Road
Powhatan, VA 23139
Tel: (804) 598-4328
Fax: (804) 598-3748
Oak, southern yellow pine. Lengths to 45 ft.
Custom planing to 8" x 20". Fax tally for
prices. Ship nationwide.

Vermont

Second Harvest Salvage & Demo
PO Box 194-E, RR1
Jeffersonville, VT 05464
Tel: (802) 644-8169
Specializing in hand hewn frames and antique
flooring and lumbers.

North Woods Joinery
PO Box 1166
Burlington, VT 05402-1166
Tel: (802) 644-5667
Fax: (802) 644-2509
Traditional post and beam construction:
homes, barns, steeples, bridges, towers.

Washington

Bear Creek Lumber
PO Box 669, 495 Eastside County Road
Winthrop, WA 98862
Tel: (800) 571-7191
Fax: (509) 997-2040
Western cedar, fir, redwood. Traditional
patterns, decking, timbers and beams.
Delivery available nationwide.

R.W. Rhine, Inc.
1124 112th St. E
Tacoma, WA 98445
Tel: (253) 531-7223
Fax: (253) 531-9548
Salvage timbers, piling and wood products.

Resource Woodworks
627 E. 60th Street
Tacoma, WA 98404
Tel: (206) 474-3757
Fax: (206) 474-1139
Custom milling & planing of reclaimed
Douglas fir timbers, also flooring & trim
package available. We ship anywhere.

British Columbia

Evergreen Specialties
1619 Evelyn
North Vancouver, BC, Canada V7K 1T9
Tel: (604) 988-8574
Fax: (604) 988-8576
Dry fir, cedar. Architectural beams, poles,
lumber, decking, masts & planking.

Steward Management Ltd.
11110-284th Street
Maple Ridge, BC, Canada V2W 1T9
Tel: (604) 462-7712
Fax: (604) 462-8311
Recyclers of old growth timbers--will cut &
plane to size.

Pegs

Scott Northcott Woodturning
RR#1 Box 624
Walpole, NH 03608
Tel: (603) 756-4204
Hardwood pegs for timber framing

Recycled Lumber

Arizona

Sirocco Trading Company
110 East Wing Drive
Sedona, AZ 86336
Tel: (520) 204-2516
Fax: (520) 282-3716
Recycled wood products, solid timbers,
boards; Douglas fir, redwood, more.
E-mail: eeh3@sedona.net

California

Crossroads Recycled Lumber
PO Box 184
O'Neals, CA 93645
Tel: (209) 868-3646
Fax: same
Demolition salvage, portable sawmills, dead &
dying trees, timbers, flooring. Natural
buildings.

Maxwell Pacific
PO Box 4127
Malibu, CA 90264
Tel: (310) 457-4533
Douglas fir, redwood, pine, cedar, barnwood,
used and new.

Michael Evenson Natural Resources
PO Box 157
Petrolia, CA 95558
Tel: (707) 629-3679
Fax: same
Recycled old growth redwood, Douglas-fir,
custom remilling.
E-mail: evenson@igc.apc.org

Urban Ore, Inc.
1333 Sixth St.
Berkeley, CA 94710
Tel: (510) 559-4460
Fax: (510) 528-1540
Buy, sell, trade good used lumber, doors,
windows, fixtures, hardware.

Jefferson Recycled Woodworks
PO Box 696, 1104 Firenze Ave.
McCloud, CA 96057
Tel: (916) 964-2740
Fax: (916) 964-2745
Reclaimed timbers, lumber and millwork.
Milled to your specifications.
E-mail: goodwood@telis.org
Web site: http://www.ecowood.com

Recycled Lumberworks
596 Park Blvd.
Ukiah, CA 95482
Tel: (707) 462-2567
Fax: (707) 462-8607
Quality recycled old growth timber, clear heart
redwood lumber from 100 year old vat staves
and Douglas fir flooring is our specialty.

Old growth Douglas fir logs salvaged from industrial logging 'waste' in Washington state, 1987. Can you believe that they'd leave this behind?

Connecticut

Chestnut Specialists, Inc.
PO Box 217, 365 Harwinton Ave.
Plymouth, CT 06782
Tel: (860) 283-4209
Fax: same
Remanufactured flooring from reclaimed antique lumber. Dimensional antique lumber.

Post & Beam Homes, Inc.
4 Sexton Hill Road South
East Hampton, CT 06424
Tel: (860) 267-2060, (800) 821-8456 (CT only)
Fax: (860) 267-9515
Pine, oak, Doug fir or recycled lumber. Frames hand-crafted in our workshop. Our expert timber framers will construct anywhere.

Idaho

Alternative Timber Structures
1054 Rammel Mt. Rd.
Tetonia, ID 83452
Tel: (208) 456-2711, Fax: same
Custom door manufacturer, custom sizes, interior & exterior—Davis Frame rep—

Stein & Collett
PO Box 4065, 201 South Mission Street
McCall, ID 83638
Tel: (208) 634-5374
Fax: (208) 634-8228
Beams, flooring, doors, stair systems. Both new and recycled woods custom architectural millwork. Unique and unusual species are our specialty.

Illinois

Windlass Timber Framing, Inc.
137 N. Center St.
Naperville, IL 60540
Tel: (630) 355-1788
Fax: same
Timber frame barn removal, repair, erection and sales.

Massachusetts

Cataumet Sawmill
494 Thomas Landers Road
E. Falmouth, MA 02536
Tel: (508) 457-9239
Fax: (508) 540-3626
Antique heart pine flooring "for a home of distinction".

Maryland

Vintage Lumber Co., Inc.
PO Box 104, 1 Council
Woodsboro, MD 21798
Tel: (800) 499-7859
Fax: (301) 845-6475
Reclaimed, remilled and remarkable tongue and groove antique wood flooring.
E-mail: woodfloors@vintagelumber.com
Web site: www.vintagelumber.com

Craftwright-Timber Frame Company
100 Railroad Ave., #105
Westminster, MD 21157
Tel: (410) 876-0999
Custom hand-crafted timber frames, antique frames and timbers available.

Maine

Barnstormers
RR 1 Box 566, North Rochester Road
East Lebanon, ME 04027-9730
Tel: (207) 658-9000
The barn recycling specialists. Antique barns resourced, restored, shipped & reassembled nationwide. Authentic timber framing. Vintage lumber.

Michigan

Renaissance Developments
10704 Oviatt Road
Honor, MI 49640
Tel: (616) 326-4009
Sustainable building, healthy creative dreamspaces, bau-biologie, owner-builder involvement welcome.

Minnesota

Duluth Timber Company
PO Box 16717
Duluth, MN 55816
Tel: (218) 727-2145
Recycled timbers and planks from U.S. and Canada. Doug fir, redwood and pine. Resawn beams, flooring; "as is" wholesale timbers.

North Carolina

Woodhouse, Inc.
PO Box 7336, 105 Creek Street
Rocky Mount, NC 27804
Tel: (919) 977-7336
Fax: (919) 641-4477
French oak, chestnut, antique heart pine solid or laminate flooring.

The Joinery Co.
PO Box 518, 1600 Western Blvd.
Tarboro, NC 27886
Tel: (919) 823-3306
Fax: (919) 823-0818
Antique heart pine, engineered solid wood flooring, stair parts, mouldings, beams.

Harmony Exchange
Route 2, Box 843-A
Boone, NC 28607
Tel: (800) 968-9663
Antique, reclaimed & new growth. Flooring, timber trusses, decking, exposed beam systems, siding & more. Catalog.

New Hampshire

Carlisle Restoration Lumber
HCR 32 Box 556C
Stoddard, NH 03464
Tel: (800) 595-9663
Fax: (603) 446-3540
Traditional wide plank flooring custom milled up to 20" wide.
Web site: www.wideplankflooring.com

New Mexico

Plaza Hardwood, Inc.
5 Enebro Court
Santa Fe, NM 87505
Tel: (800) 662-6306
Fax: (505) 466-0456
Distributor of wood flooring and lumber from
certified sustainable forest resources.

New York

New Energy Works Of Rochester, Inc.
1755 Pioneer Road
Shortsville, NY 14548
Tel: (716) 289-3220
Fax: (716) 289-3221
Timber frame production, reclaimed wood
milling; interior woodworks and design.
E-mail: jononewt@aol.com

M. Fine Lumber Co., Inc.
175 Varick Ave.
Brooklyn, NY 11231
Tel: (718) 381-5200
Fax: (718) 366-8907
Buyer & seller of reusable lumber, timber &
flooring available.
E-mail: MerritF@Fine-Lumber.com
Web site: www.Fine-Lumber.com/Lumber.html

Pioneer Millworks
1755 Pioneer Road
Shortsville, NY 14548
Tel: (716) 289-3220
Fax: (716) 289-3221
Reclaimed timbers from turn-of-the-century
buildings, S4S or rough sawn. Hand-hewn
barn timbers. Antique pine and fir flooring.
Custom millwork.

Pennsylvania

Conklin's Authentic Barnwood
RR 1, Box 70, Butterfield Road
Susquehanna, PA 18847
Tel: (717) 465-3832
Fax: same
Supplier antique barnwood, hand-hewn
beams, flooring and rustic materials.
E-mail: conklins@epix.net
Web site: conklins barnwood.com

Texas

What Its Worth, Inc.
PO Box 162135
Austin, TX 78716
Tel: (512) 328-8837
Fax: same
Recycled heart pine. Timbers, planks, custom
flooring, cabinet, door and moulding stock.
Sold by piece or truck load. Virgin tidewater
cypress mined from south Louisiana
waterway, cut wet to spec. Or sold in log form.

Precision Woodworks
507 E. Jackson St.
Burnet, TX 78611
Tel: (512) 756-6950
Fax: same
New products from antique longleaf pine and
other used timbers.

Utah

**Trestlewood (A Division Of Cannon
Structures, Inc.)**
PO Box 1728, 241 W 500 N, Suite A
Provo, UT 84603-1728
Tel: (801) 375-2779
Fax: (801) 375-2757
Wholesaler of recycled Douglas fir, redwood,
SYD, etc. Timbers & products.
E-mail: bradnate@burgoyne.com

Virginia

Blue Ridge Timberwrights
2030 Redwood Drive
Christiansburg, VA 24073
Tel: (540) 382-1102
Fax: (540) 382-8039
Designers and manufacturers of hand-crafted
timber frame structures.

Vintage Pine Co.
PO Box 85
Prospect, VA 23960
Tel: (804) 574-6531
Fax: (804) 574-2401
Antique heart pine flooring and stair parts.

Mountain Lumber Co.
PO Box 289, 6812 Spring Hill Road
Ruckersville, VA 22968
Tel: (804) 985-3646
Fax: (804) 985-4105
Flooring, moldings, and stair parts milled from
reclaimed wood.
E-mail: sales@mountainlumber.com
Web site: http://www.mountainlumber.com

Washington

R.W. Rhine, Inc.
1124 112th St. E
Tacoma WA 98445
Tel: (253) 531-7223
Fax: (253) 531-9548
Salvage timbers, piling and wood products.

The G.R. Plume Company
1373 West Smith Road, Suite A-1
Ferndale, WA 98248
Tel: (360) 384-2800
Fax: (360) 384-0335
Architectural timber millwork fabricated from
reclaimed Douglas fir.

Resource Woodworks
627 E. 60th Street
Tacoma, WA 98404
Tel: (206) 474-3757
Fax: (206) 474-1139
Custom milling & planing of reclaimed
Douglas fir timbers, also flooring & trim
package available. We ship anywhere.

British Columbia

Evergreen Specialties
1619 Evelyn
North Vancouver, BC, Canada V7K 1T9
Tel: (604) 988-8574
Fax: (604) 988-8576
Dry fir, cedar. Architectural beams, poles,
lumber, decking, masts & planking.

Steward Management Ltd.
11110-284th Street
Maple Ridge, BC, Canada V2W 1T9
Tel: (604) 462-7712
Fax: (604) 462-8311
Recyclers of old growth timbers–will cut &
plane to size

Certified & Sustainably Harvested Wood Suppliers

California

Crossroads Recycled Lumber
PO Box 184
O'Neals, CA 93645
Tel: (209) 868- 3646, Fax: same
Demolition salvage, portable sawmills, dead &
dying trees, timbers, flooring. Natural
buildings.

Michael Evenson Natural Resources
PO Box 157
Petrolia, CA 95558
Tel: (707) 629-3679, Fax: same
Recycled old growth redwood, Douglas-fir,
custom remilling.
E-mail: evenson@igc.apc.org

Jefferson Recycled Woodworks
PO Box 696, 1104 Firenze Ave.
McCloud, CA 96057
Tel: (916) 964-2740, Fax: (916) 964-2745
Reclaimed timbers, lumber and millwork.
Milled to your specifications.
E-mail: goodwood@telis.org
Web site: http://www.ecowood.com

Colorado

Greenleaf Forest Products, Inc.
102 Greenleaf Lane
Westcliffe, CO 81252
Tel: (719) 783-2487, Fax: (719) 783-0212
Logs, poles and rough-sawn from sustainably-
managed private forests.

Florida

Tropical American Tree Farms
C/O AAA Express Mail, 1641 NW 79th Avenue
Miami, FL 33126
Tel: (800) 788-4918, 011 (506) 787-0020
Fax: 011 (506) 787-0051
Growing precious tropical hardwoods on tree farms in Costa Rica.
E-mail: tatfsa.sol.racsa.co.cr

Massachusetts

Karp Woodworks
136 Fountain Street
Ashland, MA 01721
Tel: (508) 881-7000
Fax: (508) 881-7084
Sustainably harvested certified tropical & domestic woods. "Furnature", an organic, sustainable and chemical-free line of upholstered furniture. "Certified Serenity", a line of comfortable and colorful sunroom/patio furniture from certified sustainable sources.

Green River Lumber, Inc.
PO Box 329
Gt. Barrington, MA 01230
Tel: (413) 528-9000
Fax: (413) 528-2379
Manufacturer of certified and non-certified plank hardwood flooring.

Bamboo Fencer
31 Germania St.
Jamaica Plain, MA 02130-2314
Tel: (617) 524-6137, Fax: (617) 524-6100
Manufactures and imports fences, gates, and other products.
E-mail: Dave@bamboofencer.com
Web site: http://www.bamboofencer.com

Maryland

Craftwright-Timber Frame Company
100 Railroad Ave., #105
Westminster, MD 21157
Tel: (410) 876-0999
Custom hand-crafted timber frames, antique frames and timbers available.

Maine

Natural Knees
281 Hartland Road
St. Albans, ME 04971
Tel: (207) 938-2380
Natural grown knees for timber frame construction and boat building.
E-mail: kneeman@somtel.com

Michigan

Northern Land & Lumber Co.
7000 P Rd.
Gladstone, MI 49837
Tel: (906) 786-2994, Fax: (906) 786-2926
Primary manufacturer of log home kits & components.
E-mail: nlandl@up.net
Web site: www.deltami.org/nlandl

Minnesota

The Woodworkers' Store
4365 Willow Dr.
Medina, MN 55340
Tel: (800) 279-4441, Fax: (612) 478-8395
Woodworking hardware, wood, tools and know-how.
E-mail: rocklerl@pclink.com
web site: www.woodworkerstore.com

Midwest Hardwood Corp.
9540 83rd Ave. N
Maple Grove, MN 55369
Tel: (612) 425-8700, Fax: (612) 391-6740
Northern hardwood lumber manufacturer.
E-mail: MWHWD@ix.netcom.com

New Mexico

Plaza Hardwood, Inc.
5 Enebro Court
Santa Fe, NM 87505
Tel: (800) 662-6306, Fax: (505) 466-0456
Distributor of wood flooring and lumber from certified sustainable forest resources.

Ohio

Hochstetler Milling
552 St. Rt. 95
Loudonville, OH 44842
(419) 281-3553, (419) 368-0004
Oak timber 4-sided planing. Pine log home logs 10 profiles.

Pennsylvania

Conklin's Authentic Barnwood
RR 1, Box 70, Butterfield Road
Susquehanna, PA 18847
Tel: (717) 465-3832, Fax: same
Supplier antique barnwood, hand-hewn beams, flooring and rustic materials.
E-mail: conklins@epix.net
Web site: conklinsbarnwood.com

Vermont

Tree Talk
PO Box 426, 431 Pine Street
Burlington, VT 05402
Tel: (802) 865-1111, Fax: (802) 863-4344
Multimedia CD-ROM on wood. 900 species. Database. Video. Pictures. Maps.
E-mail: wow@together.net
Web site: www.woodweb.com/~treetalk/home.html

Belgian Woodworks
1068 Ireland Road
Starksboro, VT 05487
Tel: (802) 453-4787
Custom mouldings, banisters and newels in sustainably harvested northern hardwoods.

Washington

Environmental Home Center
1724 4th Ave. South
Seattle, WA 98134
Tel: (800) 281-8275, (206) 682-8275
Retail / wholesale—environmentally responsible building materials and decorating supplies.
E-mail: info@enviresource.com
Web site: www.enviresource.com

British Columbia

Evergreen Specialties
1619 Evelyn
North Vancouver, BC, Canada V7K 1T9
Tel: (604) 988-8574
Fax: (604) 988-8576
Dry fir, cedar. Architectural beams, poles, lumber, decking, masts & planking.

Wood Siding

Johnson Clapboard Mill
134 Wendell Road
Shutesbury, MA 01072
Tel: (413) 259-1271, Fax: same
Manufacturer of restoration quality clapboard siding.

Using our Timber Resources Wisely

Stepping outside of the commodities building materials market, there are many sources for high grade saw logs that are often reduced to mere fiber.

The issue of how best to use our timber resources is often the debate over a morning cup of coffee or in conference gatherings between builders, architects and engineers. There are those who believe that conventional framing lumber or glulam beams in some way use younger, smaller, less valuable trees than those milled into timber. While there may be a bit of truth to this, it does not, however, prove to be the case on the broader scale. When the issues of sustainability come to the forefront in these dialogs, an even closer look needs to be taken concerning the total energy draw required to produce not only the wood portion of the product, but also the chemical adhesives. Assuming the adhesives are of the natural sort, and that the structural attributes of the manufactured end product are superior, the manufacture of engineered timber products can still be likened to that of raising beef—the grain required to raise a beef critter to slaughter consumes ten times more energy, and could provide 10 times more net calories, if it were fed directly to people.

Being round in section, it's clear that a log large enough to produce a 2 by 10 joist can also produce a 10 by 10 timber. Beyond the fact that structural framing lumber is graded in part due to the density of the growth rings, the logging industry customarily produces structural lumber—two by fours to two by twelve's—from logs in excess of 50 years old. These being a

minimum of 12 inches to over 24 inches in diameter (It takes a 16 inch dia. log to produce a 2 by 12. At an annual growth rate of 3/16" per year, this would take a minimum of 42 years.). There are a few mills in northern New England and in the southeast that produce nothing but two by four studs from small trees harvested during the thinning process, but studs do not fall into the same category as structural framing lumber over two by six.

If we take a broader definition of sustainability, we must also consider the total consumption of energy to produce the finished product, the ratio of waste to net finished product, and waste disposal in all steps of the process. Milling two 6 by 12's from a 16" dia. log produces approximately 18% more usable lumber than if it were sawn into 2 x 6's (you'd only get ten of them due to the loss to the saw kerf). Planing reduces the net quantity of usable lumber by another 16%, resulting in a net reduction of usable timber due to waste to nearly 35%.

As for the use of large timbers, surprisingly, the average timber frame actually uses fewer large timbers than one might think. There is a certain amount of

illusion to be taken into consideration. One of our recent design projects can be used to illustrate this point. The frame is for a 2,200 square foot house and uses a total of 7,410 bd. ft. of timbers (3.36 bd. ft. per square foot of living area). The largest timbers are 7 x 10's, of which there is 2,700 bd. ft. (36%). The balance consist of 3x8, 6x8 and 7x8 in about equal board footage. No log need be larger than 14 inches in dia., or much over 37 years old, and the majority (3,627 bd. ft.) can be milled from logs less than 10 inches in diameter (trees less than 27 years old).

It's my bet that the average glulam beam uses a higher grade lumber, milled from older trees than most timbers used in timber framing, and this is not to mention the additional manufacturing process required to produce the finished product (a sustainability issue). More importantly, glulam's cannot, by code, be notched or mortised without losing their structural integrity, and therefore, are restricted to the use of bolt and plate connections. Paralam's, while they are produced from lower grade wood fiber, are likewise governed by the same code restrictions as glulam's.

—*Steve Chappell*

Notes & Numbers

Tools & Equipment

Tools & Equipment

Tools

California

Abbey Tools
1132 N. Magnolia
Anaheim, CA 92801
Tel: (800) 225-6321

Bailey's
PO Box 550, 44650 Hwy. 101
Laytonville, CA 95454
Tel: (800) 322-4539
Fax: (707) 984-8115
Free catalog: world's largest mail order
woodsman supplies company.
E-mail: baileys@bbaileyscom
Web site: http://www.bbaileys.com

Granberg International
PO Box 70425, 200 South Garraro Blvd.
Richmond, CA 94807-0425
Tel: (510) 237-2099
Fax: (510) 237-1667
Manufacturer of the Alaskan sawmill.
Attachments and accessories for sharpening
chainsaws.
E-mail: granberg@aol.com
Web site: www.granberg.com

Makita U.S.A., Inc.
14930 Northam St.
La Mirada, CA 90638
Tel: (714) 522-8088
Fax: (714) 522-8194
Corded and cordless portable electric power
tools.

Connecticut

Constitution Saw Co.
310 Nutmeg Road South
South Windsor, CT 06074
(203) 289-7696

Florida

International Tool Corporation
2590 Davie Road
Davie, FL 33317
Tel: (800) 338-3384, Fax: (954) 792-3560
Woodworking & construction power tools at
the guaranteed lowest prices.
Web site: http://www.internationaltool.com

Idaho

Woodhouse
PO Box 801
Ashton, ID 83420
Tel: (208) 652-3608, Fax: (208) 652-3628
Supplying all specialized tools and materials
for log-timber construction. Providing owner
and/or professional with largest selection of
quality products available.

Barr Specialty Tools
PO Box 4335
McCall, ID 83638
Tel: (800) 235-4452, Fax: (208) 634-3541
Quality hand-forged framing chisels, slicks,
adzes, draw knives, and gouges for the
serious woodworker. Simply the best.

Illinois

Estwing Mfg. Co.
2647 8th St.
Rockford, IL 61109-1190
Tel: (815) 397-9558, Fax: (815) 397-8665
Manufacturer of world's first & finest all steel
hammers.
E-mail: estwing@estwing.com
Web site: www.estwing.com

Frog Tool Co., Ltd.
2169 IL Rt. 26
Dixon, IL 61021
Tel: (800) 648-1270
Fax: (815) 288-3919
Timber framing and handling tools, hand
woodworking tools, books. Catalog $5.

S. B. Power Tool Co.
4300 W. Peterson Ave.
Chicago, IL 60646
Tel: (800) 301-8255
Fax: (773) 794-6615
Skil and Bosch portable power tools and
accessories.

Indiana

Wood-Mizer Products, Inc.
8180 W. 10th Street
Indianapolis, IN 46214
Tel: (317) 271-1542
Fax: (317) 273-1011
Transportable sawmills and accessories:
lowers lumber costs and improves quality.
E-mail: adindy@woodmizer.com
Web site: http://www.woodmizer.com

Trusty-Cook, Inc.
10530 E. 59th St.
Indianapolis, IN 46236
Tel: (317) 823-6821
Fax: (317) 823-6822
Deadblow urethane hammers and sledges for
maximum power, sustained impact.

Massachusetts

U.S. Cutting Chain Mfg. Co.
PO Box 437, 95 Spark Street
Brockton, MA 02403
Tel: (508) 588-0322
Fax: (508) 583-7808
Heavy duty chain mortisers, mortise chains,
guide bars and sprockets.

Maine

Lie-Nielsen Toolworks, Inc.
PO Box 9
Warren, ME 04864
Tel: (800) 327-2520
Fax: (207) 273-2657
Makers of heirloom quality hand tools for
woodworkers.
E-mail: toolwrks@lie-nielsen.com
Web site: http://ww.lie-nielsen.com

Barn Masters, Inc.
PO Box 258
Freeport, ME 04032
Tel: (207) 865-4169
Fax: (207) 865-6169
Makita tools for timber framing: chain
mortisers, stationary routers, chisel
mortisers, groove cutters, circular saws, 6" x
12" planers, tenon cutters. Free brochure.

Minnesota

Tools On Sale Div. Of
Seven Corners Hdwr., Inc.
216 West 7th Street
St. Paul, MN 55102
Tel: (800) 328-0457
Fax: (612) 224-8263
496 page catalog of power tools and related
accessories featuring the most respected
brands in the business.

The Woodworkers' Store
4365 Willow Dr.
Medina, MN 55340
Tel: (800) 279-4441
Fax: (612) 478-8395
Woodworking hardware, wood, tools and
know-how.
E-mail: rocklerl@pclink.com
Web site: www.woodworkerstore.com

Missouri

Woodmaster Tools
1431 N. Topping Ave.
Kansas City, MO 64120
Tel: (816) 483-7203
Make mirror-smooth custom molding with the
Woodmaster planer/molder.

North Carolina

Country Workshops
90 Mill Creek Road
Marshall, NC 28753
Tel: (704) 656-2280
Tools, books and instruction in traditional
woodworking with hand tools
E-mail: langsner@countryworkshops.org
Web site: countryworkshops.org

Klingspor's Sanding Catalogue
PO Box 3737
Hickory, NC 28603-3737

North Dakota

Tool Crib Of The North
PO Box 14040, 1603 12th Ave. N
Grand Forks, ND 58206-4040
Tel: (701) 780-2882
Fax: (701) 746-2869
96 color pages of woodworking tools and
accessories, free!
E-mail: kcolman@corpcomm.net
Web site: www.toolcribofthenorth.com

New York

Cepco Tool Co.
PO Box 153, 295 Van Etten Road
Spencer, NY 14883
Tel: (607) 589-4313
Fax: same
Board straightening/joining tools, Bowrench
deck tool, Quick-Jack construction jack.

Lee Valley Tools Ltd.
PO Box 178012 East River St.
Ogdensburg, NY 13669-0490
Tel: (800) 871-8158, Fax: (800) 513-7885
Our 236-page full-color catalog has the widest
selection of woodworking hand tools on the
market. Web site: http://www.leevalley.com

Crosscut Saw Company
PO Box 7871
Seneca Falls, NY 13148
(315) 568-5755

Martin J. Donnelly Antique Tools
PO Box 281
Bath, NY 14810-0281
Tel: (607) 776-9322
Fax: (607) 776-6064
Antique tools.
E-mail: MJDtools@servtech.com

Mafell North America, Inc.
80 Earhart Drive, Unit 9
Williamsville, NY 14221
Tel: (716-626-9303
Specialized tools for working big timbers.
Mortising machines, band saws, planers, etc.

Ohio

Miller's Sharpening Service
11301 N. Webb
Alliance, OH 44601
Tel: (330) 821-6240

Pennsylvania

Wilke Machinery Co.
3230 Susquehanna Trail
York, PA 17402
Tel: (717) 764-5000, Fax: (717) 764-3778
Distributors of quality woodworking
machinery and home of Bridgewood Brand
machinery.
Web site: www.wilkemach.com

Virginia

Quick Gauge, Inc.
5237 Clifton Street
Alexandria, VA 22312
Tel: (800) 916-9646
Fax: (703) 941-7415
Quick Clamp installs on any square for fast &
accurate layout of stair stringers & rafters.
Long-lasting aluminum. Dealers welcome.

Vermont

Trow & Holden Co.
45 So. Main St.
Barre, VT 05641
Tel: (800) 451-4349
Tel: (802) 476-7025
Stone carving and splitting tools, mortar-
removal tools.
E-mail: trowco@aol.com

Tools Of The Trade
PO Box 2001, West Main St.
Richmond, VT 05477
Tel: (800) 375-5981, Fax: (802) 434-4467
The only magazine devoted exclusively to
tools for construction professionals.
Web site: www.bginet.com

Bethel Mills, Inc.
PO Box 61, 1 North Main
Bethel, VT 05032
Tel: (800) 234-9951, Fax: (802) 234-5631
Retail lumber, building materials, and tools for
the serious contractor.
E-mail: bml@sover.net
Web site: bethelmills.com

Washington

Systimatic
12530   135th Ave. NE
Kirkland, WA 98034
Tel: (800) 426-0035, Fax: (425) 821-0801
Manufacturer of carbide tipped circular saw
blades.

West Virginia

Woodcraft Supply
PO Box 1686, 210 Wood County Industrial Pk
Parkersburg, WV 26102
Tel: (800) 225-1153, Fax: (304) 428-8271
Quality woodworking tools, books, hardware,
hardwoods; plus tool sharpening service.
E-mail: custserv@woodcraft.com
Web site: www.woodcraft.com

Portable Sawmills

Alabama

Sawmill Exchange
PO Box 131267
Birmingham, AL 35213
Tel: (205) 969-3963
Fax: (205) 967-4620
Buy/sell service for used portable sawmills.
E-mail: nml@mindspring.com
(Note: letter preceding @ is an "L")
Web site: http://www.sawmill-exchange.com/

California

Crossroads Recycled Lumber
PO Box 184
O'Neals, CA 93645
Tel: (209) 868- 3646
Fax: same
Demolition salvage, portable sawmills, dead &
dying trees, timbers, flooring. Natural
buildings.

Granberg International
PO Box 70425, 200 South Garraro Blvd.
Richmond, CA 94807-0425
Tel: (510) 237-2099
Fax: (510) 237-1667
Manufacturer of the Alaskan sawmill.
Attachments and accessories for sharpening
chainsaws.
E-mail: granberg@aol.com
Web site: www.granberg.com

Illinois

The Edge Woodworks
Rt. 1 Box 179
Grafton, IL 62037
Tel: (618) 786-2442
Traditional hand-crafted joinery, portable
sawmill, owner-builder friendly.
E-mail: edgewrks@gtec.com

Indiana

Wood-Mizer Products, Inc.
8180 W. 10th Street
Indianapolis, IN 46214
Tel: (317) 271-1542
Fax: (317) 273-1011
Transportable sawmills and accessories:
lowers lumber costs and improves quality.
E-mail: adindy@woodmizer.com
Web site: http://www.woodmizer.com

Missouri

TimberKing
1431 N. Topping Ave.
Kansas City, MO 64120
Tel: (800) 942-4400
Fax: (816) 483-7203
Cut 45 foot beams with TimberKing's
bandmill.

**Woodland Manufacturing; Vertical Band
Sawmills**
PO Box 1540, 1409 Black River Ind. Road
Poplar Bluff, MO 63902-7720
Tel: (573) 785-3810
Fax: (573) 785-0962
Advanced design, high production one-man
sawmills, built-in edger.

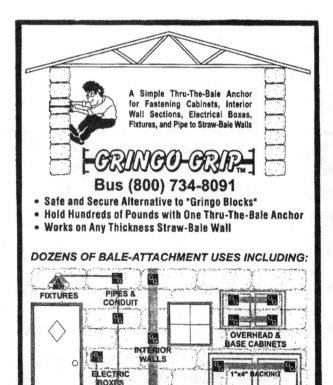

*Portable sawmills can handle big jobs if the operator
sets up the mill site efficiently.*

New York

Norwood Industries Inc.
90 Curtwright Dr., Unit 3
Amherst, NY 14221
Tel: (800) 567-0404
Portable sawmills.
E-mail: norwood@norwoodindustries.com
Web site: www.norwoodindustries.com

Pennsylvania

Pocono Mt. Timber Frames
PO Box 644, Rt. 115
Brodheadsville, PA 18322
Tel: (717) 992-7515
Fax: (717) 992-9064
Design, fabrication, and erection of timber
frame barns and houses.
E-mail: etreible@ptd.net
Web site: www.pmtf.com

Allen Woodworking And Cupolas
2242 Bethel Road
Lansdale, PA 19446
Tel: (215) 699-8100
Fax: same
Custom redwood, cedar, poplar cupolas;
portable sawmill with backhoe services.

Alberta

Goldec International Equipment, Inc.
6760   65 Ave.
Red Deer, Alberta, Canada T4R 1G5
Tel: (403) 343-6607
Fax: (403) 340-0640
De-bark logs with our chainsaw attachment.
The amazing Log Wizard!
E-mail: goldec@TelusPlanet.net
Web site: goldec.com

HEAVY DUTY CHAIN MORTISERS

MODEL FPM-8 & FPM-12

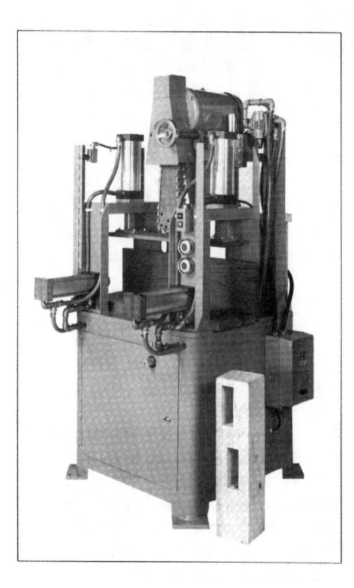

SPECIFICATIONS AND STANDARD EQUIPMENT

Motor - Ten HP, Three Phase

Stock Capacity –
Model FPM-8	8" x 8"
Model FPM-12	12" x 12"

Machine Height –
Model FPM-8	72"
Model FPM-12	80"

Machine Weight –
Model FPM-8	700 lbs.
Model FPM-12	1,200 lbs.

Space Required – 6 ft. x 6 ft.

Chain Sizes Available –
3/4 x 3-1/4 to 2-3/4 x 6-3/4

Magnetic motor starter.

Carbide tipped Chains.

Chain Lubricator.

Chain Guards and Dust Hood.

U.S. MORTISE CHAINS
and Woodworking Machinery
Phone (508) 588-0322

U.S. CUTTING CHAIN MFG. CO.
P.O. BOX 437 ★ BROCKTON, MA 02403

Portable Sawmills
The Economic and Environmental Benefits

Portable sawmills offer many advantages to small woodlot owners over traditional milling options, from both an economic and environmental standpoint.

Environmental Benefits

• *Reduce fuel consumption*–Approximately 15% to 25% of the weight and volume of a saw log is waste wood–slabs and sawdust. By delivering the sawmill to the site, transportation costs and energy consumption is reduced because the whole log does not have to be transported. In addition, the smaller engines on portable mills are more fuel efficient than stationary mills.

• *Less waste, more lumber*–On average, the narrower kerf of portable sawmill blades produce nearly 30% more usable lumber from a log than stationary circular saw mills.

• *Sawdust and waste remain in ecosystem*–Sawdust and slab wood remain in the same ecosystem in which they grew. This is returned to the soil as nourishment, and does not need to be transported or handled further. Slab wood can be used for firewood, fencing, or in many creative and useful ways.

• *Sustainable forest management*–Portable sawmills make it practical to saw less desirable or low grade species of timber, and lower quality logs which are selectively thinned from small woodlots, into usable lumber. Selective thinning increases yield and quality of remaining timber. This can be a win-win situation.

Economic Benefits

• *Direct cost savings*–If you own a small woodlot or building lot with standing timber, out-of-pocket saving of up to 50% can be realized over purchasing sawn timber from traditional sources. Milling costs range from $100 to $200 per 1,000 board feet (comparable to a commercial sawmill custom milling prices). Felling and yarding the trees will cost another $40 to $50 per 1,000. With incidental expenses, the total cost of milling the timber on-site will run between $250 to $300 per 1,000 bd. ft. Based on species and grade, this same timber would cost anywhere from $400 to $1,000 per 1,000 bd. ft., at the mill (trucking is extra).

• *Less waste, more lumber*–As mentioned above, less waste translates directly into money saved.

• *Quality control*–Portable sawmills tend to mill squarer and more uniform timber than the average stationary circular sawmill. In many cases (if used for a timber frame), planing may be unnecessary. This produces additional direct savings, however, planed timbers will save time in layout and cutting.

Comparison of board foot yield–Bandsaw/Circular saw	
Portable Bandsaw Yield	**Circular Sawmill Yield**
61-1x4's	54 -1x4's
4 -1x6's	0 -1x6's
6 -1x7's	3 -1x7's
2 -1x9's	0 -1x9's
2 -1x10's	0 -1x10's
289 board feet	192 board feet

The above comparison is based on milling a 24" diameter by 10 foot long log.
Provided by Wood-Mizer Manufacturing.

Notes & Numbers

Enclosure Systems

Enclosure Systems

Jason Morley, English Master Thatcher, on the roof.

The walls, roofs and foundation systems of any house can make a big difference in functionality, practicability, energy savings, and health. Using the materials at hand can often result in a natural, breatheable, durable and energy-efficient home. They save the costs and pollution of transportation, utilize materials from clearing the land that might otherwise be wasted...or go up in smoke. They create bonds and a sense of community. And often, they come from renewable sources. In the case of thatch, for instance, an introduced reed is taking over many of the wetlands throughout the eastern part of the country. They are a threat to wetland environments, but at the same time, a viable roofing material. Though at the current time little use is being made of them, and they continue to invade swamps and saltwater marshes, perhaps we can begin to harvest them in an efficient manner and use them as a renewable source for roofing material...kill two birds with one stone, so to speak.

Clay, strawbale and cob can be used individually or in various combinations to provide comfortable shelter from resources that shift away the burdens from our heavily abused forests–provide a balance in the relation between civilization and the natural world. Wheat straw panels are now available with beneficial R-values, and they also come from renewable sources. Slipforms can be used in conjunction with rammed earth, clay & woodchips, and even mortar and stone to create walls from readily available materials.

Stresskin panels can save time and labor, while drastically reducing the costs of heating and cooling. The right foundation can utilize the earth's natural heat, or provide healthy alternatives to preferences of the building industry at large. All in all, each of these systems can contribute to healthier homes, relief to the environment, less dependence on fossil fuels, or all three.

Clay

Maine

Proclay
c/o Fox Maple
PO Box 249
Brownfield, ME 04010
Tel: (207) 935-3720
Fax: (207) 935-4575
Light-clay infill techniques, clay & lime
plasters, clay building materials, workshops
and consulting.
E-mail: foxmaple@nxi.com

Timber Frame Apprenticeshop
PO Box 249, Corn Hill Road
Brownfield, ME 04010
Tel: (207) 935-3720
Fax: (207) 935-4575
Traditional timber frame structures using
traditional straw/clay infill systems.
Apprentice built structures from design to
completion. Extending the talents of people
to create a better built environment.
E-mail: foxmaple@nxi.com
Web site: http://www.nxi.com/WWW/
joinersquarterly

Ohio

Superior Clay Corporation
PO Box 352, 6566 Superior Road SE
Uhrichsville, OH 44683
Tel: (614) 922-4122
Fax: (614) 922-6626
Clay flue lining, Rumford fireplace compo-
nents, clay chimney pots, ground fired clay.
E-mail: mcclave@tusconet.com
Web site: rumford.com

Natural Homesteads
13182 N. Boone Road
Columbia Station, OH 44028
Tel: (440) 236-3344
Natural building design/consultation; slide
presentations; straw-bale and cob workshops.

Quikspray, Inc.
PO Box 327
Port Clinton, OH 43452-9485
Tel: (419) 732-2611, (419) 732-2601
Fax: (419) 734-2628
Spray guns for clay & plaster.

Oregon

Cob Cottage Co.
PO Box 123
Cottage Grove, OR 97424
Tel: (541) 942-2005
Fax: (541) 942-3021
Information and workshops on building with
cob (sand, clay, straw).
Web site: http://www.deatech.com/cobcottage

Germany

Uelzener Maschinenfabrik
Friedrich Maurer Gmbh
D-65843 Sulzbach/Ts.
Wiesenstrasse 18
Germany
Tel: 06196-05840
Fax: 06196-71273
Professional German-made clay construction
equipment.

Arizona

The Canelo Project
HCL Box 324
Elgin, AZ 85611
Tel: (520) 455-5548, Fax: (520) 455-9360
Straw bale building/earthen floors and
plasters, workshops, resources, consulting.
E-mail: absteen@dakotacom.net
Web site: http://www.deatech.com/canelo

The Last Straw
PO Box 42000
Tucson, AZ 85733
Tel: (520) 882-3848
The Last Straw: the quarterly journal of straw-
bale construction.
E-mail: thelaststraw@igc.apc.org
Web site: http://www.netchaos.com/+ls

Out On Bale, "un" Ltd.
1037 E. Linden St.
Tucson, AZ 85719
Tel: (520) 624-1673, Fax: (520) 299-9099
Strawbale workshops, presentations, wall
raising, planning and supervision, consulting
and publishing.
E-mail: binb@juno.com

Sustainable Systems Support
PO Box 318
Bisbee, AZ 85603
Tel: (520) 432-4292
Offers books and videos on plastered straw
bale construction, including an excellent 90
min. "how-to" video with a 62 page manual.
Wall raising workshops and consultations.

Wrapping a timber frame with straw bales can be a viable option to panels and conventional 'stick-framed' infill. There are a few design considerations that can make the process faster and easier.
The two primary considerations are the eave/gable transitions, and the foundation/deck detail.
High gable walls require a lot of custom bales, staging and strong arms. Hip roofs with a level eave require less cutting and less labor in general.

Colorado

Solar Energy International
PO Box 715
Carbondale, CO 81623
Tel: (970) 963-8855
Fax: (970) 963-8866
Hands-on workshops on renewable energy
and environmental building technologies.
E-mail: sei@solarenergy.org
Web site: http://www.solarenergy.org

Massachusetts

Greenspace Collaborative
PO Box 107
Ashfield, MA 01330
Tel: (413) 369-4905
Buildings of straw bales and other natural
materials detailed for the northeastern climate.

Maine

Wentworth Timberframes
PO Box 1116, 45 Mason Street
Bethel, ME 04217
Tel: (207) 824-4237
25 years experience. Hewn, rough-sawn, or
hand-planed timbers. Mortise and tenon
joinery. Owner friendly

Proclay
c/o Fox Maple
PO Box 249
Brownfield, ME 04010
Tel: (207) 935-3720
Fax: (207) 935-4575
Light-clay infill techniques, clay & lime
plasters, clay building materials, workshops
and consulting.
E-mail: foxmaple@nxi.com

Fox Maple School of Traditional Building
PO Box 249, Corn Hill Road
Brownfield, ME 04010
Tel: (207) 935-3720, Fax: (207) 935-4575
Workshops for introductory & advanced timber
framing, natural & traditional enclosure
systems, thatch, clay and alternative building
systems. Quality craftsmanship is paramount,
with a view towards a sustainable future.
E-mail: foxmaple@nxi.com
Web site:
http://www.nxi.com/WWW/joinersquarterly

Minnesota

Community Eco-Design Network
PO Box 6241, 3151-29th Ave. S, #103
Minneapolis, MN 55406
Tel: (612) 306-2326
Super-insulated construction planbook, design
services, northern climate strawbale building
system.
E-mail: erichart@mtn.org
Web site: http://www.umn.edu/n/home/m037/
kurtdand/cen

New Hampshire

Straw Works
152 West Main St.
Conway, NH 03818
Tel: (603) 447-1701
Fax: (603) 447-6412
Design for those wishing to walk lightly upon
the earth.
E-mail: Straw-Works@juno.com

Ohio

Natural Homesteads
13182 N. Boone Road
Columbia Station, OH 44028
Tel: (440) 236-3344
Natural building design / consultation; slide
presentations; straw-bale and cob workshops.

Oregon

Sustainable Architecture
PO Box 696, 910 Glendale Ave.
Ashland, OR 97520
Tel: (541) 482-6332
Fax: (541) 488-8299
Architectural services integrating full spectrum
of healthy, holistic building.

Aprovecho Research Center
80574 Hazelton Road
Cottage Grove, OR 97424
Tel: (541) 942-8198
Fax: (541) 942-0302
Demonstration research and education center
for sustainable living.
E-mail: apro@efn.org/~apro
Web site: http://www.efn.org/~apro

Gringo Grip
4951 Netarts Hwy. W. #2041
Tillamook, OR 97141
Tel: (800) 734-8091
Fax: (800) 734-8071
A simple thru-the-bale anchor for fastening
cabinets, interior wall sections, electrical
boxes, fixtures, and pipe to straw-bale walls.

*Thatch is one of the earliest known roof coverings. The early settlers of
Massachusetts Bay found a ready supply of cattails and reeds in the bogs
and lowlands, and used it extensively in the early years of settlement. Today,
some fine examples can be seen at Plimouth Plantation. Plymouth, MA.*

Vermont

Yestermorrow Design/Build School
RR 1 Box 97-5
Warren, VT 05674
Tel: (802) 496-5545, Fax: (802) 496-5540
Offers hands-on courses in residential design
and "green" construction.
E-mail: ymschool@aol.com
Web site: www.yestermorrow.org

Organic Oat Straw
RR#1 Box 520
Orleans, VT 05860
Tel: (802) 754-2028
Straw bales for building.

Washington

Greenfire Institute
PO Box 1040
Winthrop, WA 98862
Tel: (509) 996-3593, Fax: same
Straw bale construction training, consultation
and design.
E-mail: greenfire@igc.org
Web site: www.balewolf.com

Thatch & Wood Roofing

Custom Roof Thatching & Supplies
PO Box 62054
Cincinnati, OH 45262
Tel: (513) 772-4979, Fax: (513) 772-6313
Has thatched in U.S. since 1986. A guide to
roof thatching in the U.S. $6.00
web site: http://www.roofthatch.com

Fox Maple School of Traditional Building
PO Box 249, Corn Hill Road
Brownfield, ME 04010
Tel: (207) 935-3720, Fax: (207) 935-4575
Workshops in thatching, stray clay and
alternative building systems. Supplies and
materials for native reed thatch, clay and
straw projects.
E-mail: foxmaple@nxi.com
Web site:
http://www.nxi.com/WWW/joinersquarterly

Thatching Advisory Services, Ltd.
Faircross Offices
Stratfield Saye,
Reading, Berks
United Kingdom RG7 2BT
Tel: 01256 880828, Fax: 01256 880866
Complete thatching services: design,
thatching crews worldwide, materials, tools,
supplies, books and publications.

Liberty Cedar
535 Liberty Lane
W. Kingston, RI 02892
Tel: (800) 882-3327, (401) 789-6626
Fax: (401) 789-0320
Naturally decay-resistant exterior wood
products specializing in wood roofing.

Wheat straw panel installation.

Wheat Straw Panels

Agriboard Industries
PO Box 645, Fairfield, IA 52556
Tel: (515) 472-0363
Complete, OSB laminated, compressed wheat
straw panel building systems.
E-mail: agriboard@lisco.com

Structural Insulated Panels

Indiana

Angela's Unique Homes–Panel Pros
7096 NCR 490 W., Bainbridge, IN 46105
Tel: (765) 739-1268
Specializing in panel installs for "Thermocore
Panel" systems. General contracting–
construction managers.

Maine

Maine Panel
PO Box 277, Rockland, ME 04841
Tel: (207) 236-2369, Fax: (207) 236-8568
Manufacturer of stress-skin panels for timber
frame homes. Available with urethane or EPS.
Priced to be competitive. Installation available.

Minnesota

AFM Corporation
PO Box 246, 24000 W. Hwy. 7, Ste. 201
Excelsior, MN 55331
Tel: (612) 474-0809, Fax: (612) 474-2074
Mfg. of insulated structural building panels.
E-mail: afmcorp@worldnet.att.net
Web site: www.afmcorp-spsfoam.com

Vermont

Vermont Stresskin Panels
RR 2 Box 2794
Cambridge, VT 05444
Tel: (802) 644-8885, Fax: (802) 644-8797
Stresskin panel enclosure systems for timber
frame structures.

Foard Panel, Inc.
8 Marlboro Avenue
Brattleboro, VT 05301
Tel: (802) 254-3972
Fax: same
Manufacturers and professional installers of
high-quality urethane and EPS panels.
E-mail: shippees@sover.net

Kentucky

Fischer Sips
1843 Northwestern Pkwy.
Louisville. KY 40203
Tel: (800) 792-7477
Structural insulated panels.

Insulating Concrete Forms

Lite-Form International
PO Box 774, 1210 Steuben St.
Sioux City, IA 51102
Tel: (712) 252-3704
Fax: (712) 252-3259
Insulating forms for cast in place foundations
& walls.
E-mail: liteform@pionet.net
Web site: http://www.pionet.net/~liteform/
index.html

Notes & Numbers

Mechanical
Systems

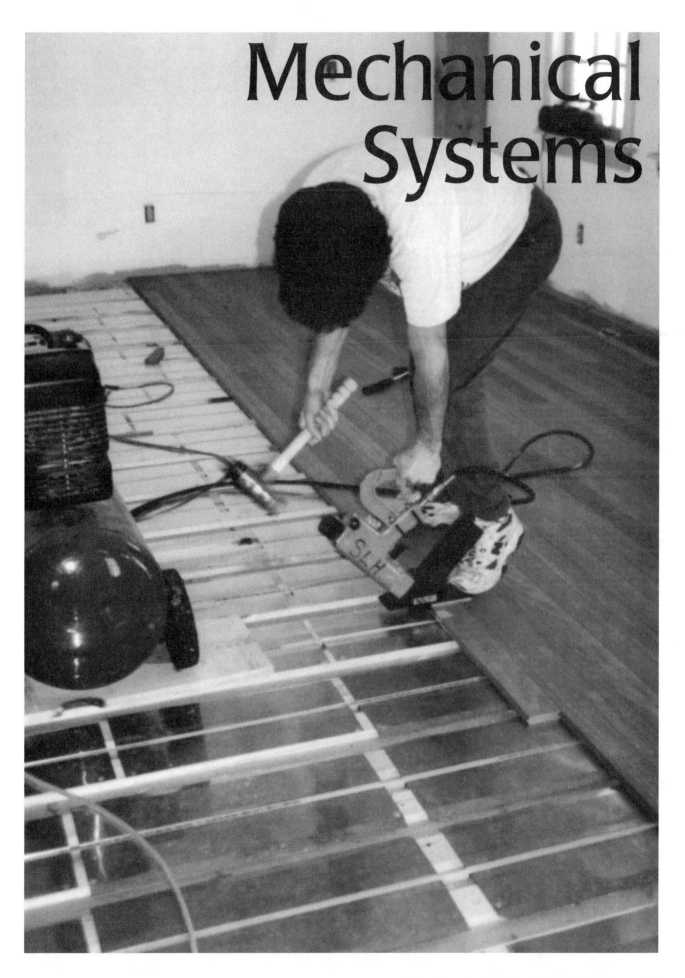

Mechanical Systems

Different homes require the integration of certain mechanical systems in order to provide optimum levels of health, comfort and efficiency. Super-insulated homes using stresskin enclosure systems also require air exchangers or ventilation to insure healthy levels of Indoor Air Quality (IAQ). The air in a home should be completely exchanged every two hours to maintain optimum IAQ, which will solve problems of off-gassing, mildew, fogging and dry-rot. Some of the systems available today not only provide solutions for poor IAQ, but can recover up to 95% of cooling and heating energy that would normally be lost. These systems work great with older, drafty homes, inground homes, and "airtight" homes.

Radiant heat, while comfortable and energy-efficient, can be improved even further when integrated with a solar hot water system. Over the years, architects, engineers, builders and homeowners have combined their experiences to insure affordable, lasting, and environmentally compatible housing. These systems have proven themselves time and again, and truly help bring about the practical use of our resources.

Air Exchange Systems

Allermed Corp.
31 Steel Road
Wylie, TX 75098
Tel: (214) 442-4898
Air exchangers.

American Aldes Ventilation Corporation
Northgate Center Business Park
Sarasota, FL 34234-4864
Tel: (800) 255-7749
Exhausts from several rooms at low economical airflow rates and assures a healthy environment within the home.

Memphremagog Heat Exchangers, Inc.
PO Box 490
Newport, VT 05855
Tel: (800) 660-5412
Fax: (802) 895-2666
Indoor air quality solutions for tightly built homes since 1982.
E-mail: info@mhevt.com
Web site: www.mhevt.com

The Non-Toxic Hotline
830 Meadow Road
Aptos, CA 95003
Tel: (408) 684-0199
Austin Air, Allermed, Aireox, Foust, Pure Air Systems, Nilfisk Allergy Vaccums, Rainbow Ozone Generators, Ionizers at discount prices.

Ozark Air & Water Service
114 Spring St.
Sulphur Springs, AR 72768
Tel: (800) 835-8908
Fax: (501) 298-3421
Testing, sales, installations and service of air & water equipment.

Passive Solar Industries Council
1511 K Street, Suite 600
Washington, DC 20005
Tel: (202) 628-7400
Fax: (202) 393-5043
PSIC independent nonprofit advancing climate responsive buildings.
E-mail: PSICouncil@aol.com
Web site: http://www.psic.org

Sanologistics Inc., Environmental Alternatives
7200 West Camino Real, Ste. 102
Boca Raton, FL 33433
Tel: (407) 394-0203
Fax: (407) 394-9421
Water-Air purification systems for POE and POU. Most advanced, utilizing Ozone, UV, & patented exotic multi-media filtering.

Venmar Ces
2525 Wentz Avenue
Saskatoon, SK, Canada S7K 2K9
Tel: (306) 242-3663
Fax: (306) 242-3484
Commercial HRV's (heat recovery ventilators) and ERV's (energy recovery ventilators).

Worldwide Technology, Inc.
PO Box 272302
Tampa, FL 33688
Tel: (813) 855-2443
Fax: (813) 855-2655
Manufacturer of air & water purification systems for residential, commercial and industrial environments.

Radiant Heat Suppliers

Connecticut

New England Hearth And Soapstone
127 North Street
Goshen, CT 06756
Tel: (860) 491-3091, Fax: same
Hand-crafted masonry heaters, fireplaces, countertops and more in soapstone and other materials, also parts.
E-mail: nehearth@bigfoot.com
Web site: http://mha-net.org/users/nehs

Indiana

Easy Heat, Inc.
31977 US 20 E.
New Carlisle, IN 46552
Tel: (219) 654-3144
Fax: (219) 654-7739
Electrical radiant heating cable solutions.
E-mail: mgb~1@msn.com
Web site: www.easyheat.com

Massachusetts

Runtal North America, Inc.
187 Neck Road
Ward Hill, MA 01835
Tel: (508) 373-1666
Fax: (508) 372-7140
Decorative panel radiators, towel radiator.

Maine

Earthstar Energy Systems
PO Box 626
Waldoboro, ME 04572
Tel: (800) 323-6749, (800) 660-6749 (in ME)
Complete energy system design & product sales.

Minnesota

Maxxon Corporation
PO Box 253, 920 Hamel Road
Hamel, MN 55340
Tel: (612) 478-9600
Fax: (612) 478-2431
Radiant floor heating systems—hot water or electric.
E-mail: debi@maxxon.com
Web site: http://www.maxxon.com

Montana

Cornerstone Masonry Distributing, Inc.
PO Box 83
Pray, MT 59065
Tel: (406) 333-4383
Fax: same
Specializing in Tulikivi soapstone masonry heaters, bakeovens, and cookstoves.
E-mail: radiant@alpinet.com
Web site: http://www.tulikivi.com

New York

Radiant Technology
11A Farber Drive
Bellport, NY 11713
Tel: (800) 784-0234
Fax: (516) 286-0947
E-mail: radtech2@usa.pipeline.com
Web site: http://www.radiant-tech.com

Ohio

Top Hat Chimney Sweeps D.B.A. TNT Masonry Heaters
12380 Tinker's Creek Road
Cleveland, OH 44125
Tel: (216) 524-5431
Wood-fired masonry heaters, bake ovens, and cookstoves.
Web site: http://mha-net.org/users/tnt/index.htm

Pennsylvania

Mid-Atlantic Masonry Heat, Inc.
PO Box 277
Emigsville, PA 17318-0277
Tel: (800) 213-0903
Fax: (717) 854-1373
Mid-Atlantic and southeastern regional distributor Tulikivi natural soapstone fireplaces, bake ovens, cookstoves, heater benches, floor and wall tile.

Virginia

Masonry Heater Association of North America
11490 Commerce Pk. Dr., Suite 300
Reston, VA 20191
Tel: (703) 620-3171
Fax: (703) 620-3928
Association of builders, designers & researchers of masonry heaters.
Web site: http://mha-net.org/

Tulikivi U.S.
PO Box 7825
Charlottesville, VA 22906-7825
Tel: (804) 977-5500
Fax: (804) 977-5164
Tulikivi (two-lee-kee-vee) soapstone fireplaces, bake ovens, cookstoves—efficient radiant heat.

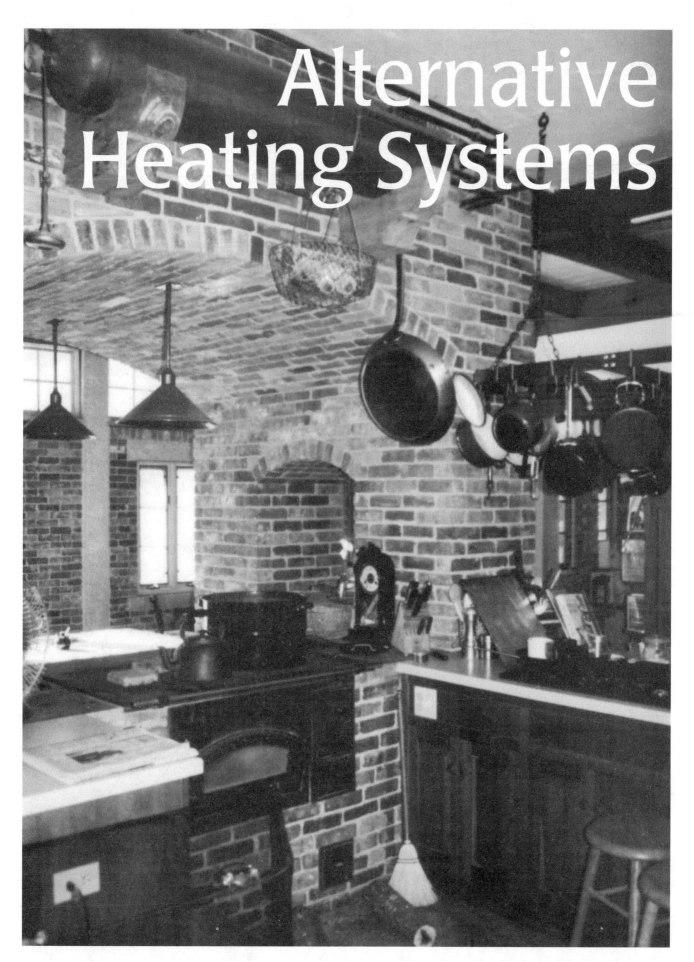

Alternative
Heating Systems

Alternative Heating Systems

Some of these technologies are new; some are ancient. Masonry heaters have evolved over thousands of years, and those available today are more efficient than ever. Emissions are much less than that of woodstoves, and in an average season they can provide the same amount of BTUs using about half the amount of wood. Not only that, but the surface of the stove retains heat and is warm to the touch instead of hot, minimizing the possibility of burns. This also prevents the scorching of dust and airborne particles that can irritate the lungs and nasal cavities.

Solar is still the wave of the future yet to crest. Though it has improved in leaps and bounds, it's still not used as much as it should be. Current systems are more affordable, efficient and available, and if more consumers invested in this type of technology, more

dollars would flow into research and mass production, creating systems that would be much less expensive and much more efficient. It's a case of voting with our dollars.

Radiant heat is another innovative alternative using a system of tubing wound through a grid on the flooring and encased in a lightweight concrete to provide a highly conductive thermal mass. The finished floor is generally hardwood or carpeting, but the beauty of the system lies in its function. Rather than heating the uppermost parts of a room, the heat is concentrated closest to the floor, making this an extremely efficient option, especially in open-plan designs with high, vaulted, or uneven ceilings. By heating objects instead of air, and at more normal temperatures, there's not only a 30 to 50% savings in energy costs, but

substantial health benefits as well. Because the floor heat uses only 80 to 95 degree water to heat the house, a boiler and chimney is unnecessary. A small gas heater can handle the job. Solar hot water is also an ideal compliment to this system.

This section contains suppliers, designers and installation professionals for many different sources of heat and heat recovery. They're listed by state to make it easier to find the closest suppliers, but some of these companies may do the design work "in-house", and have field technicians and installation professional in various regions. Many of the architects and consultants in the *Design and Planning* section may also be of great assistance, so if you're looking for someone closer to home, be sure to check there.

Masonry Heaters

Connecticut

New England Hearth and Soapstone
127 North Street
Goshen, CT 06756
Tel: (860) 491-3091
Fax: same
Hand-crafted masonry heaters, fireplaces, countertops and more in soapstone and other materials, also parts.
E-mail: nehearth@bigfoot.com
Web site: http://mha-net.org/users/nehs/

Illinois

S. Patzer & Co.
3N743 Rt. 31
St. Charles, IL 60174
Tel: (630) 584-1081
Mason contractor specializing in unusual fireplaces, masonry heaters, and ovens.

Maine

Maine Wood Heat Co, Inc
RFD 1, Box 640
Norridgewock, ME 04957
Tel: (207) 696-5442
Fax: (207) 696-5856
Masonry heaters, cookstoves and ovens. Construction, hardware, books, plans, design. Hands-on workshops.

Timberstone Builders
RR 1 Box 3125
Freedom, ME 04941
Tel: (207) 589-4675, Fax: same
We specialize in chink-style log buildings and Rumford fireplaces.

Brick Stove Works
15 Nelson Ridge South
Washington, ME 04574
Tel: (207) 845-2440, Fax: same
20 years experience designing and building masonry heaters. Will travel.
E-mail: jpmanly@midcoast.com

Michigan

Sackett Brick Company
1303 Fulford St.
Kalamazoo, MI 49001
Tel: (800) 848-9440, (616) 381-4757
Fax: (616) 381-2684
Masonry heaters: sales, design, consult, build. Importers of Tulikivi and dealers for most Heater Core kits.

Minnesota

D. Larsen Masonry Construction
10801 Jackpine Road NW
Bemidji, MN 56661
Tel: (218) 751-0523
Specialize in masonry heaters, fireplaces and chimney relining.

Montana

Cornerstone Masonry Distributing, Inc.
PO Box 83
Pray, MT 59065
Tel: (406) 333-4383
Fax: same
Specializing in Tulikivi soapstone masonry heaters, bakeovens, and cookstoves.
E-mail: radiant@alpinet.com
Web site: http://www.tulikivi.com

New York

Alternate Energy Systems
PO Box 344
Peru, NY 12972
Tel: (518) 643-0805
Fax: (518) 643-2012
Masonry heaters–timber frame and log homes–a natural blend–call.

North Carolina

Vesta Masonry Stove, Inc.
373 Old 7 Mile Ridge Road
Burnsville, NC 28714
Tel: (704) 675-5666, (800) 473-5240
Fireplace masons specializing in masonry heater sales, construction and design. Saunas, cooker & bake ovens.

Ohio

Superior Clay Corporation
PO Box 352, 6566 Superior Road SE
Uhrichsville, OH 44683
Tel: (614) 922-4122, Fax:(614) 922-6626
Clay flue lining, Rumford fireplace components, clay chimney pots, ground fired clay.
E-mail: mcclave@tusconet.com
Web site: rumford.com

Top Hat Chimney Sweeps D.B.A. TNT Masonry Heaters
12380 Tinker's Creek Road
Cleveland, OH 44125
Tel: (216) 524-5431
Wood-fired masonry heaters, bake ovens, and cookstoves.
Web site: http://mha-net.org/users/tnt/index.htm

Heartwood Timber Frames
6660 Heartwood Place
Swanton, OH 43558
Tel: (419) 875-5500, Fax: same
Crafting beautiful timber frames, panel homes, and masonry heaters.

Oregon

Kachelofen Unlimited
1407 Caves Camp Road
Williams, OR 97544
Tel: (503) 846-6196
Hand-crafted ceramic tile stoves, a source of healthy, radiant heat. Creates a healthy room climate.

Pennsylvania

Mid-Atlantic Masonry Heat, Inc.
PO Box 277
Emigsville, PA 17318-0277
Tel: (800) 213-0903
Fax: (717) 854-1373
Mid-Atlantic and southeastern regional distributor Tulikivi natural soapstone fireplaces, bake ovens, cookstoves, heater benches, floor and wall tile.

Utah

Blofire, Inc.
3220 Melbourne
Salt Lake City, UT 84106
Tel: (801) 486-0266
Fax: (801) 486-8100
Increased quality of life through efficient, wonderful, natural heating.

Virginia

Masonry Heater Association Of North America
11490 Commerce Pk. Dr., Suite 300
Reston, VA 20191
Tel: (703) 620-3171
Fax: (703) 620-3928
Association of builders, designers & researchers of masonry heaters.
Web site: http://mha-net.org/

Tulikivi U.S.
PO Box 7825
Charlottesville, VA 22906-7825
Tel: (804) 977-5500
Fax: (804) 977-5164
Tulikivi (two-lee-kee-vee) soapstone fireplaces, bake ovens, cookstoves—efficient radiant heat.

Washington

Dietmeyer, Ward & Stroud, Inc.
PO Box 323, 12027 SW Wesleyan Way
Vashon, WA 98070
Tel: (206) 463-3722
Fax: (206) 463-6335
Manufacturer of modular masonry heater kits, the Envirotech radiant fireplace.

Ontario

Temp-Cast Enviroheat Ltd.
PO Box 94059, 3332 Yonge St.
Toronto, Ontario, Canada M4N 3R1
Tel: (416) 322-6084
Fax: (416) 486-3624
Fully modular masonry heaters–quick and easy assembly–wood or gas.
E-mail: staywarm@tempcast.com
Web site: http://www.tempcast.com

Masonry heater firebox sized to heat a 6,000 square foot workshop in Canterbury, New Hampshire, by Maine Wood Heat Company, Inc..

Masonry

Illinois

S. Patzer & Co.
3N743 Rt. 31
St. Charles, IL 60174
Tel: (630) 584-1081
Mason contractor specializing in unusual fireplaces, masonry heaters, and ovens.

Maine

Maine Wood Heat Company, Inc.
RFD 1, Box 640
Norridgewock, Maine 04957
Tel: (207) 696-5442, or 696-8800
Fax: (207) 696-5856
Masonry wood heat services, construction anywhere in N.A., Workshops, plans, custom design, supplies, kits and materials.

Brick Stove Works
15 Nelson Ridge South
Washington, ME 04574
Tel: (207) 845-2440
Fax: same
20 years experience designing and building masonry heaters. Will travel.
E-mail: jpmanly@midcoast.com

Minnesota

D. Larsen Masonry Construction
10801 Jackpine Road NW
Bemidji, MN 56661
Tel: (218) 751-0523
Specialize in masonry heaters, fireplaces and chimney relining.

New Hampshire

Wolf's Rock Farm
PO Box 298
Bradford, NH 03221
Tel: (603) 938-5344
Building stone delivered, wholesale prices. Complete period reproduction, restoration services. Rumford fireplaces.

New York

Barkeater Design Build Company
35 Wellington Street
Malone, NY 12953
Tel: (518) 483-5282
Fax: same
Designer/builders specializing in stone slipform construction. Workshops available
E-mail: barkeatr@slic.com

Ontario

Alderaan Stone/Timber Homes
PO Box 313, 6-14845 Yonge Street
Aurora, Ontario, Canada L4G 6H8
Tel: (905) 713-0001
Fax: (905) 713-0134
Traditional materials and craftsmanship. Comprehensive custom reproductions of early Canadian homes.
Web site: www.craftsman-book.com

Renewable Energy

Real Goods
555 Leslie St.
Ukiah, CA 95482
Tel: (707) 468-9292
Fax: (707) 462-9394
Solar, wind, hydro, efficient lighting, water, catalogs, books and institute.

Solar Energy International
PO Box 715
Carbondale, CO 81623
Tel: (970) 963-8855
Fax: (970) 963-8866
Hands-on workshops on renewable energy and environmental building technologies.
E-mail: sei@solarenergy.org
Web site: http://www.solarenergy.org

Elemental Resources
PO Box 21, 1320 E. 94th St. South
Haysville, KS 67060
Tel: (316) 788-3678
Fax: same
Renewable energy. Specializing in design & installation of photovoltaic & wind hybrid systems.
E-mail: cvdow@aol

Solar Energy

California

Alternative Energy Engineering, Inc.
PO Box 339
Redway, CA 95560
Tel: (800) 777-6609
Fax: (707) 923-3009
Energy from solar, wind or water power. Photovoltaics, lighting, solar fans, fridges and books. 112 page catalog for $3.

Integral Energy Systems
109 Argall Way
Nevada City, CA 95959
Tel: (800) 517-6527, Fax: (916) 265-6151
Solar water pumping, electric systems and hot water. Propane appliances. Full spectrum lighting.

Real Goods Renewables
555 Leslie St.
Ukiah, CA 95482
Tel: (800) 919-2400, Fax: (707) 462-4807
Photovoltaic and other renewable energy system consultation, design, and sales.

Sierra Solar Systems
109-MC Argall Way
Nevada City, CA 95959
(800) 517-6527, (916) 265-6151
Solar electric, pumping, hot water, wind, hydropower and energy efficient lighting. Catalog $5.
E-mail: solarjon@oro.net
Web site: http://www.sierrasolar.com

Idaho

Backwoods Solar Electric Systems
8530 Rapid Lightning Creek Road
Sandpoint, ID 83864
(208) 263-4290
All the equipment with lower than usual prices.
Catalog $3.

Maine

Talmage Solar Engineering, Inc.
18 Stone Road
Kennebunkport, ME 04046
Tel: (207) 967-5945
Fax: (207) 967-5754
Design and sale of solar electric components
for off-grid or utility interface.
E-mail: tse@talmagesolar.com
Web site: www.talmagesolar.com

Massachusetts

New England Solar Electric, Inc.
PO Box 435
Worthington, MA 01098
Tel: (413) 238-5974
$3 for 64 page catalog/design guide, solar
electric kits, components, gas refrigerators,
other appliances and information you need to
live independently with solar electricity.

Montana

Sunelco
PO Box 1499
Hamilton, MT 59840
Tel: (406) 363-6924, (800) 338-6844
Complete source for solar modules, batteries,
inverters, water pumps, energy effecient
lights, and propane appliances. Catalog
$4.95.

North Carolina

Enertia Building Systems, Inc.
13312 Garffe Sherron Road
Wake Forest, NC 27587
Tel: (919) 556-0177
Fax: (919) 556-1135
Design/prefabrication of solid wood solar/
geothermal environmental homes.

Vermont

Vermont Sun Structures, Inc.
42 Walker Hill Road
Williston, VT 05495
Tel: (802) 879-6645
Glulam timber framed sunrooms & green-
houses, fully "weeped" & water tight!

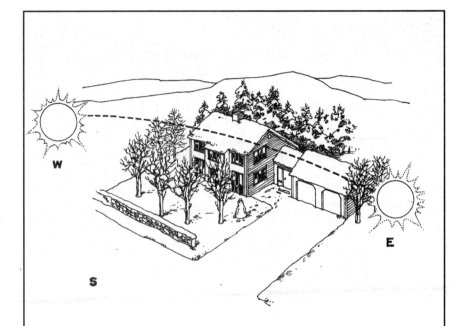

The Solar Slab and Basic Solar Design

Heating-system designers think in terms of heat transfer from warmer to cooler. The typical home furnace warms air to 140°, and the warm air is delivered to the various rooms in the home via ducts. When the thermostat reads 72° or another desired setting, the furnace shuts off. Heat has been transferred from the warmer body (the furnace at 140°) to the cooler body (the house at 72°). The design of a conventional heating system represents a straightforward problem which has a direct solution: determine the heat loss of the building then size the furnace and duct work in order to provide a continual or "on-demand" supply of replacement heat.

Active systems are easy to visualize–boilers, ductwork, pies, and radiators–whereas the elements of a passive heat collection and storage system may be almost "invisible." When faced with the problem of designing a solar home, early solar designers tried to assimilate the elements of an active, furnace-based system. Exterior solar collectors were utilized to build up high temperatures using water or air. This heat was then stored in a high temperature "heat sink" using beds of rocks or tanks of water ("heat sink" is a physics term for a medium that absorbs and stores heat–for example, water, concrete, or masonry, in particular arrays). Ducts or pipes transported the heat back and forth from the sun-exposed exterior collector components to the interior storage components of the system. Such active systems are complicated; they tend to require added-on costs to the home, and are sometimes difficult to justify financially. Further, some of them simply didn't work well or were plagued with mechanical problems, especially over time, necessitating continuous oversight and maintenance.

From *The Passive Solar Home*, by James Kachadorian, Chelsea Green Publishing Co.

Notes & Numbers

Interior Finishes

Interior Finishes

Because home owners have such a wide variety of tastes, needs and health considerations, we've included many different options and categories in this sections. Individual regions may vary in climate, aesthetics, cultural influences, building codes and myriad other factors.

Doors & windows are extremely important, not only in functionality and energy efficiency, but they must also fit the design of the home, whether it's a new house, or restoration project, whether it's located in a warm, dry climate or a damp, cold environ-ment. Skylights can brighten any home, reducing the need for lighting, and in some cases even the need for anti-depressives.

Asthma has increased dramatically over the last twenty years, and many people have become acutely sensitive to chemicals in the environment, as well as those used in the manufacturing process for indoor products. Low toxic paints & finishes, are essential in maintaining healthy Indoor Air Quality. Natural carpeting of wool or seagrass are chemical-free, and there is nontoxic linoleum available. There are several eco-hardware stores that provide both local and mail order service. Some of these items may also be found in the sections on *Natural Building Products and Services, Specialty Products and Services,* or *Catalogs.*

Flooring and architectural millwork from recycled or sustainable sources help to keep the planet as beautiful as the insides of our homes. Recycled woodwork including mouldings, wide plank flooring, wainscotting, wood panel walls and various other treasures can be found in recycling centers that are burgeoning into a multi-billion dollar sector of the economy.

Doors & Windows

California

Maxwell Pacific
PO Box 4127
Malibu, CA 90264
Tel: (310) 457-4533
Douglas fir, redwood, pine, cedar, barnwood,
used and new.

Urban Ore, Inc.
1333 Sixth St.
Berkeley, CA 94710
Tel: (510) 559-4460
Fax: (510) 528-1540
Buy, sell, trade good used lumber, doors,
windows, fixtures, hardware.

Connecticut

Shuttercraft, Inc.
282 Stepstone Hill
Guilford, CT 06437
Tel: (203) 453-1973
Fax: (203) 245-5969
Exterior and interior wood shutters for
authentic restoration, hinges, holdbacks.
E-mail: shutter@iconn.net
Web site: http://www.galaxymall.com/shops/
shuttercraft.html

Roto Frank Of America, Inc.
PO Box 599, Research Park
Chester, CT 06412-0599
Tel: (860) 243-0893
Fax: (860) 526-3785
World's best roof window: Roto designs and
manufactures innovative skylights.

Idaho

Alternative Timber Structures
1054 Rammel Mt. Rd.
Tetonia, ID 83452
Tel: (208) 456-2711
Fax: same
Custom door manufacturer, custom sizes,
interior & exterior—Davis Frame rep—

Stein & Collett
PO Box 4065, 201 South Mission Street
McCall, ID 83638
Tel: (208) 634-5374
Fax: (208) 634-8228
Beams, flooring, doors, stair systems. Both
new and recycled woods custom architectural
millwork. Unique and unusual species are our
specialty.

Massachusetts

Architectural Detail In Wood
41 Parker Road
Shirley, MA 01404
Tel: (508) 425-9026
Reproduction windows, traditional joinery,
matched profiles, all heartwood, any glazing.

Amherst Woodworking & Supply, Inc.
30 Industrial Drive
Northampton, MA 01061
Tel: (800) 532-9110
Fax: (413) 582-0164
Moldings–doors–stair parts–plank flooring–
20+species hardwood lumber.
E-mail: amwooco@copperbeech.com
Web site: www.copperbeech.com

Architectural Components, Inc.
26 North Leverett Road
Montague, MA 01351
Tel: (413) 367-9441
Fax: (413) 367-9461
Architectural components, Inc. specializes in
reproducing historic doorways, doors &
windows.
E-mail: arch.components.inc@worldnet.att.net

Maine

Sun Architectural Woodworks, Inc.
RR 1 Box 8080
West Baldwin, ME 04091
Tel: (207) 625-7000
Custom design and fabrication of sash,
windows, window-walls, palladian windows,
and doors & entrances. 18th century design
and construction a "specialty".

Montana

Specialty Woodworks Company
PO Box 1450
Hamilton, MT 59840
Tel: (406) 363-6353
Fax: (406) 363-6373
Established 1981. Manufactures custom
hand-crafted doors and cabinets. Specializing
in unique blue stain pine, knotty pine, and
other rustic hardwoods. Catalog $7.

New Hampshire

Lamson-Taylor Custom Doors
Tucker Road
South Acworth, NH 03607
Tel: (603) 835-2992
Fax: same
Insulated wood doors, entrances: arched
work, art glass.

Pella Windows & Doors
Maine & New Hampshire Distributor
Tel: (800)859-0512,
Fax: (603) 692-4192
Windows, doors & skylights built to impossibly
high standards.

Wisconsin

Hurd Millwork Company
575 S. Wheelen Ave.
Medford, WI 54451
Tel: (715) 748-2011
Fax: (715) 748-6043
Wood, aluminum-clad wood and vinyl
windows and patio doors.
Web site: http://www.hurd.com

Skylights

Roto Frank Of America, Inc.
PO Box 599, Research Park
Chester, CT 06412-0599
Tel: (860) 243-0893
Fax: (860) 526-3785
World's best roof window: Roto designs and
manufactures innovative skylights.

Shutters

Kestrel Shutters
PO Box 12, 3250 St. Peters Road
St. Peters, PA 19470-0012
Tel: (800) 494-4321, (610) 409-6444
Fax: (610) 469-6881
Custom sized, pegged mortise & tenon
shutters available assembled and D.I.Y.
E-mail: kestrel@fast.net
Web site: http://www.diyshutters.com

Shuttercraft, Inc.
282 Stepstone Hill
Guilford, CT 06437
Tel: (203) 453-1973
Fax: (203) 245-5969
Exterior and interior wood shutters for
authentic restoration, hinges, holdbacks.
E-mail: shutter@iconn.net
Web site: http://www.galaxymall.com/shops/
shuttercraft.html

Architectural Millwork

Arkansas

Charles R. Bailey Cabinetmakers
HC 62, Box 29
Flippin, AR 72634
Tel: (501) 453-3245
Fax: Same
All natural custom furniture and cabinetry from
solid American hardwoods.

California

Jefferson Recycled Woodworks
PO Box 696, 1104 Firenze Ave.
McCloud, CA 96057
Tel: (916) 964-2740
Fax: (916) 964-2745
Reclaimed timbers, lumber and millwork.
Milled to your specifications.
E-mail: goodwood@telis.org
Web site: http://www.ecowood.com

Connecticut

Shuttercraft, Inc.
282 Stepstone Hill
Guilford, CT 06437
Tel: (203) 453-1973
Fax: (203) 245-5969
Exterior and interior wood shutters for
authentic restoration, hinges, holdbacks.
E-mail: shutter@iconn.net
Web site: http://www.galaxymall.com/shops/
shuttercraft.html

Chestnut Specialists, Inc.
PO Box 217, 365 Harwinton Ave.
Plymouth, CT 06782
Tel: (860) 283-4209
Fax: same
Remanufactured flooring from reclaimed
antique lumber. Dimensional antique lumber.

Idaho

Stein & Collett
PO Box 4065, 201 South Mission Street
McCall, ID 83638
Tel: (208) 634-5374
Fax: (208) 634-8228
Beams, flooring, doors, stair systems. Both
new and recycled woods custom architec-
tural millwork. Unique and unusual species
are our specialty.

Massachusetts

New England Preservation Services
95 West Squantum Street, Suite 705
Quincy, MA 02171
Tel: (617) 472-8934
Fax: (617) 770-8934
Restoration of 18th & 19th century homes and
barns.
E-mail: 74131.1254@Compuserve.com

Architectural Detail In Wood
41 Parker Road
Shirley, MA 01404
Tel: (508) 425-9026
Reproduction windows, traditional joinery,
matched profiles, all heartwood, any glazing.

Amherst Woodworking & Supply, Inc.
30 Industrial Drive
Northampton, MA 01061
Tel: (800) 532-9110, Fax: (413) 582-0164
Moldings-doors-stair parts-plank flooring-
20+species hardwood lumber
E-mail: amwooco@copperbeech.com
Web site: www.copperbeech.com

Architectural Components, Inc.
26 North Leverett Road
Montague, MA 01351
Tel: (413) 367-9441, Fax: (413) 367-9461
Architectural Components, Inc. specializes in
reproducing historic doorways, doors &
windows.
E-mail: arch.components.inc@worldnet.att.net

Forester Moulding & Lumber
152 Hamilton St.
Leominster, MA 01453
Tel: (978) 840-3100
Fax: (978) 534-8356
Manufacturer of 1800 hardwood mouldings in
22+ wood species.
Web site: http://www.forestermoulding.com

Maine

Sun Architectural Woodworks, Inc.
RR 1 Box 8080
West Baldwin, ME 04091
Tel: (207) 625-7000
"High end" custom design and fabrication;
doors & entrances, windows, panel walls &
wainscot, stairs. Also, 18th century
reproductions. Hand-planed moldings.

Missouri

Woodmaster Tools
1431 N. Topping Ave.
Kansas City, MO 64120
Tel: (816) 483-7203
Make mirror-smooth custom molding with the
Woodmaster planer/molder.

North Carolina

Woodhouse, Inc.
PO Box 7336, 105 Creek Street
Rocky Mount, NC 27804
Tel: (919) 977-7336
Fax: (919) 641-4477
French oak, chestnut, antique heart pine solid
or laminate flooring.

The Joinery Co.
PO Box 518, 1600 Western Blvd.
Tarboro, NC 27886
Tel: (919) 823-3306
Fax: (919) 823-0818
Antique heart pine, engineered solid wood
flooring, stair parts, mouldings, beams.

New Hampshire

Dan Dustin-Custom Hand-Hewing
1107 Penacook Road
Contoocook, NH 03229
Tel: (603) 746-5683
Expert adze and broadaxe work-your material-
my yard.

New York

New Energy Works Of Rochester, Inc.
1755 Pioneer Road
Shortsville, NY 14548
Tel: (716) 289-3220
Fax: (716) 289-3221
Timber frame production, reclaimed wood
milling; interior woodworks and design.
E-mail: jononewt@aol.com

Oregon

Confluence Design & Construction
PO Box 1258, 1013 NW Taylor
Corvallis, OR 97339
Tel: (514) 757-0511, Fax: (541) 753-4916
"Where thinking and doing are still one."
Design, frames, consultation.

South Carolina

Southern Breeze Timberworks
PO Box 635
Travelers Rest, SC 29690
Tel: (864) 834-3706
Quality hand-wrought joinery.

Texas

Precision Woodworks
507 E. Jackson St.
Burnet, TX 78611
Tel: (512) 756-6950, Fax: same
New products from antique longleaf pine and
other used timbers.

Virginia

Vintage Pine Co.
PO Box 85
Prospect, VA 23960
Tel: (804) 574-6531, Fax: (804) 574-2401
Antique heart pine flooring and stair parts.

Vermont

Belgian Woodworks
1068 Ireland Road
Starksboro, VT 05487
Tel: (802) 453-4787
Custom mouldings, banisters and newels in
sustainably harvested northern hardwoods.

Washington

The G.R. Plume Company
1373 West Smith Road, Suite 1-A
Ferndale, WA 98248
Tel: (360) 384-2800, Fax: (360) 384-0335
Architectural timber millwork fabricated from
reclaimed Douglas fir.

Stairbuilding

Sun Architectural Woodworks, Inc.
RR 1 Box 8080
West Baldwin, ME 04091
Tel: (207) 625-7000
Custom stairs & design a specialty.
Exceptional quality with large circular stairs.
All components & millwork are fabricated in
"our" own shop.

Southern Breeze Timberworks
PO Box 635
Travelers Rest, SC 29690
Tel: (864) 834-3706
Quality hand-wrought joinery

Cabinets & Furniture

Charles R. Bailey Cabinetmakers
HC 62, Box 29
Flippin, AR 72634
Tel: (501) 453-3245
Fax: same
All natural custom furniture and cabinetry from solid American hardwoods.

Karp Woodworks
136 Fountain Street
Ashland, MA 01721
Tel: (508) 881-7000
Fax: (508) 881-7084
Sustainably harvested certified tropical & domestic woods. "Furnature", an organic, sustainable and chemical-free line of upholstered furniture. "Certified Serenity", a line of comfortable and colorful sunroom/patio furniture from certified sustainable sources.

Sandro's Woodshed
20018 486th Ave.
Hendricks, MN 56136
Tel: (605) 479-3875
Custom timber frames. Cabinetry & furniture built with all natural materials–no plywood or particle board–non-toxic finishes available.

Flooring

California

Hendricksen Naturlich Flooring-Interiors
PO Box 1677
Sebastopol, CA 95473
Tel: (707) 824-0914
Fax: (800) 329-9398
Flooring for your health and the planet's. Wool carpet, jute, true linoleum. $10 introductory kit and catalog.

Connecticut

Chestnut Specialists, Inc.
PO Box 217, 365 Harwinton Ave
Plymouth, CT 06782
Tel: (860) 283-4209
Fax: same
Remanufactured flooring from reclaimed antique lumber. Dimensional antique lumber.

Kansas

Design Materials, Inc.
241 S 55th St.
Kansas City, KS 66106
Tel: (800) 654-6451
Fax: (913) 342-9826
"Carpets grown by nature." Jute, wool, seagrass.

Massachusetts

Cataumet Sawmill
494 Thomas Landers Road
E. Falmouth, MA 02536
Tel: (508) 457-9239
Fax: (508) 540-3626
Antique heart pine flooring "for a home of distinction".

Green River Lumber, Inc.
PO Box 329
Gt. Barrington, MA 01230
Tel: (413) 528-9000
Fax: (413) 528-2379
Manufacturer of certified and non-certified plank hardwood flooring.

Maryland

Vintage Lumber Co., Inc.
PO Box 104, 1 Council
Woodsboro, MD 21798
Tel: (800) 499-7859
Fax: (301) 845-6475
Reclaimed, remilled and remarkable tongue and groove antique wood flooring.
E-mail: woodfloors@vintagelumber.com
Web site: www.vintagelumber.com

New Hampshire

Carlisle Restoration Lumber
HCR 32 Box 556C
Stoddard, NH 03464
Tel: (800) 595-9663
Fax: (603) 446-3540
Traditional wide plank flooring custom milled up to 20" wide.
Web site: www.wideplankflooring.com

New Mexico

Plaza Hardwood, Inc.
5 Enebro Court
Santa Fe, NM 87505
Tel: (800) 662-6306
Fax: (505) 466-0456
Distributor of wood flooring and lumber from certified sustainable forest resources.

Rhode Island

South County Post & Beam
521 Liberty Lane
West Kingston, RI 02892
Tel: (401) 783-4415
Fax: (401) 783-4494
A full service timber frame company, wide pine flooring distributor.

Virginia

Vintage Pine Co.
PO Box 85
Prospect, VA 23960
Tel: (804) 574-6531
Fax: (804) 574-2401
Antique heart pine flooring and stair parts.

Mountain Lumber Co.
PO Box 289, 6812 Spring Hill Road
Ruckersville, VA 22968
Tel: (804) 985-3646
Fax: (804) 985-4105
Flooring, moldings, and stair parts milled from reclaimed wood.
E-mail: sales@mountainlumber.com
Web site: http://www.mountainlumber.com

Washington

Resource Woodworks
627 E. 60th Street
Tacoma, WA 98404
Tel: (206) 474-3757
Fax: (206) 474-1139
Custom milling & planing of reclaimed Douglas fir timbers, also flooring & trim package available. We ship anywhere.

Carpet

Hendricksen Naturlich Flooring-Interiors
PO Box 1677
Sebastopol, CA 95473
Tel: (707) 824-0914
Fax: (800) 329-9398
Flooring for your health and the planet's. Wool carpet, jute, true linoleum. $10 introductory kit and catalog.

Design Materials, Inc.
241 S 55th St.
Kansas City, KS 66106
Tel: (800) 654-6451, Fax: (913) 342-9826
"Carpets grown by nature." Jute, wool, seagrass.

Building for Health Materials Center
PO Box 113
Carbondale, CO 81623
Tel: (970) 963-0437
Fax: (970) 963-3318
Created to provide a central supplier for healthy, environmentally sound building products to meet your building material needs and requirements.
E-mail: crose@rof.net

Hardware

Colorado

Planetary Solutions
2030 17th Street
Boulder, CO 80302
Tel: (303) 442-6228, (303) 444-3730
Fax: (303) 442-6474
Natural hardware store.

Florida

The Healthy Home Center
1403 A Cleveland St.
Clearwater, FL 34615
Tel: (813) 447-4454
Fax: (813) 447-0140
Paints & stains, flooring, insulation, air
purification, cleaning supplies...

The Eco Store, Inc.
2441 Edgewater Drive
Orlando, FL 32804
Tel: (407) 426-9949
Energy savers, household products, paints,
varnishes, solar, cleaning products.

Massachusetts

Old Sturbridge Village
One Old Sturbridge Village Road
Sturbridge, MA 01566
Tel: (508) 347-3362
Fax: (508) 347-0369
Hand-forged wrought iron hinges, latches and
more.

Tremont Nail Co.
PO Box 111, 8 Elm St.
Wareham, MA 02571
Tel: (508) 295-0038
Fax: (508) 295-1365
Manufacturer of restoration pattern steel cut
nails; colonial hardware distributor.
E-mail: cutnails@aol.com

Konceptual
Architectural Hardware
PO Box 99
North Quincy, MA 02171-0099

Minnesota

The Woodworkers' Store
4365 Willow Dr.
Medina, MN 55340
Tel: (800) 279-4441
Fax: (612) 478-8395
Woodworking hardware, wood, tools and
know-how.
E-mail: rocklerl@pclink.com
Web site: www.woodworkerstore.com

New Hampshire

Scott Northcott Woodturning
RR#1 Box 624
Walpole, NH 03608
Tel: (603) 756-4204
Hardwood pegs for timber framing.

Woodstock Soapstone Co., Inc.
66 Airpark Road
W. Lebanon, NH 03784
Tel: (603) 298-5955

New York

Lee Valley Tools Ltd.
PO Box 178012 East River St.
Ogdensburg, NY 13669-0490
Tel: (800) 871-8158
Fax: (800) 513-7885
Our 236-page full-color catalog has the widest
selection of woodworking hand tools in the
market.
Web site: http://www.leevalley.com

Historic Housefitters Co.
Dept. 6027 Farm to Market Road
Brewster, NY 10509
Tel: (914) 278-2427
Hand-wrought hardware and lighting.

Crosscut Saw Company
PO Box 7871
Seneca Falls, NY 13148
(315) 568-5755

Ohio

Lehman's
Box 41
Kidron, OH 44636
How the Amish live without electricity. Over
2,500 items including stoves, refrigerators,
lights, appliances, woodworking and garden
tools.

Pennsylvania

Kestrel Shutters
PO Box 12, 3250 St. Peters Road
St. Peters, PA 19470-0012
Tel: (800) 494-4321, (610) 409-6444
Fax: (610) 469-6881
Custom sized, pegged mortise & tenon
shutters available assembled and D.I.Y.
E-mail: kestrel@fast.net
Web site: http://www.diyshutters.com

Simply Natural
RR#2, Box 136
Tamaqua, PA 18252
Tel: (503) 222-3881
Products that are natural, healthy, and earth-
friendly.

Tennessee

Cumberland General Store
#1 Highway 68
Crossville, TN 38555
One of a kind old time mercantile and
hardware company.

Vermont

Bethel Mills, Inc.
PO Box 61, 1 North Main
Bethel, VT 05032
Tel: (800) 234-9951
Fax: (802) 234-5631
Retail lumber, building materials, and tools for
the serious contractor.
E-mail: bml@sover.net
Web site: bethelmills.com

West Virginia

Woodcraft Supply
PO Box 1686, 210 Wood County Industrial
Park
Parkersburg, WV 26102
Tel: (800) 225-1153
Fax: (304) 428-8271
Quality woodworking tools, books, hardware,
hardwoods; plus tool sharpening service.
E-mail: custserv@woodcraft.com
Web site: www.woodcraft.com

Low Toxic Paints & Finishes

Environmental Home Center
1724 4th Ave. South
Seattle, WA 98134
Tel: (800) 281-8275, (206) 682-8275
Retail/wholesale—environmentally respon-
sible building materials and decorating
supplies.
E-mail: info@enviresource.com
Web site: www.enviresource.com

The Healthy Home Center
1403 A Cleveland St.
Clearwater, FL 34615
Tel: (813) 447-4454, Fax: (813) 447-0140
Paints & stains, flooring, insulation, air
purification, cleaning supplies...

The Eco Store, Inc.
2441 Edgewater Drive
Orlando, FL 32804
Tel: (407) 426-9949
Energy savers, household products, paints,
varnishes, solar, cleaning products.

Environmental Building Supplies
1314 NW Northrup St.
Portland, OR 97209
Tel: (503) 222-3881
Low-toxic, renewable and recycled materials.
Hardwood floors, carpet, linoleum, tile, paint,
finishes.

American Formulating & Manufacturing
350 W Ash St., Suite 700
San Diego, CA 92101
Tel: (619) 239-0321
Fax: (619) 239-0565
Quality paints, stains, cleaners and sealers formulated without the toxic chemicals commonly used. Designed to prevent or alleviate indoor air pollution.

Earth Studio
6761 Sebastopol Ave., Suite 8
Sebastopol, CA 95472
Tel: (707) 823-2569
Petroleum-free & biodegradable natural paints and finishes. Free Catalog.

Building for Health Materials Center
PO Box 113
Carbondale, CO 81623
Tel: (970) 963-0437
Fax: (970) 963-3318
Created to provide a central supplier for healthy, environmentally sound building products to meet your building material needs and requirements.
E-mail: crose@rof.net

Eco Design Co.
1365 Rufina Circle
Santa Fe, NM 87505
Tel: (800) 621-2591, (505) 438-3448
Fax: (505) 438-0199
The Natural Choice. Natural paints, stains & healthy home products catalog.

Restoration

California

Urban Ore, Inc.
1333 Sixth St.
Berkeley, CA 94710
Tel: (510) 559-4460
Fax: (510) 528-1540
Buy, sell, trade good used lumber, doors, windows, fixtures, hardware.

Idaho

Jeff Pedersen—Logsmith
PO Box 788, Hwy. 93 North
Challis, ID 83226
Tel: (208) 879-4211
Fax: (208) 879-5574
Traditional broadax-hewn dovetail and round log scribe-fit log homes. Broadax-hewn and round log timber frames.
E-mail: jplogs@cyberhighway.net

Illinois

Windlass Timber Framing, Inc.
137 N. Center St.
Naperville, IL 60540
Tel: (630) 355-1788
Fax: same
Timber frame barn removal, repair, erection and sales.

Midway Village & Museum Center
6799 Guilford Road
Rockford, IL 61107
Tel: (815) 397-9112
Fax: (815) 397-9156
Turn-of-the-century village and Rockford area history center.

Massachusetts

New England Preservation Services
95 West Squantum Street, Suite 705
Quincy, MA 02171
Tel: (617) 472-8934
Fax: (617) 770-8934
Restoration of 18th & 19th century homes and barns.
E-mail: 74131.1254@Compuserve.com

Berkshire House Publishers
480 Pleasant Street, Suite 5
Lee, MA 01238
Tel: (800) 321-8526
Fax: (413) 243-0303
Explore colonial barn lore with master restorer Richard Babcock.

Architectural Components, Inc.
26 North Leverett Road
Montague, MA 01351
Tel: (413) 367-9441
Fax: (413) 367-9461
Architectural Components, Inc. specializes in reproducing historic doorways, doors & windows.
E-mail: arch.components.inc@worldnet.att.net

Colonial Restorations
26 Main St.
Brookfield, MA 01506
Tel: (508) 867-4400
Structural restoration/repair of post & beam homes or barns.

Tremont Nail Co.
PO Box 111, 8 Elm St.
Wareham, MA 02571
Tel: (508) 295-0038
Fax: (508) 295-1365
Manufacturer of restoration pattern steel cut nails; colonial hardware distributor.
E-mail: cutnails@aol.com

Forester Moulding & Lumber
152 Hamilton St.
Leominster, MA 01453
Tel: (978) 840-3100
Fax: (978) 534-8356
Manufacturer of 1800 hardwood mouldings in 22+ wood species.
Web site: www.forestermoulding.com

Old-House Journal (Dovetail Publishers)
2 Main St.
Gloucester, MA 01930
Tel: (508) 283-3200
Fax: (508) 283-4629
Bimonthly magazine about restoring, maintaining, and decorating pre-1940's houses.

Old-House Journal Directory (Dovetail Publishers)
2 Main St.
Gloucester, MA 01930
Tel: (508) 283-3200
Fax: (508) 283-4629
Annual sourcebook for suppliers of reproduction hardware, lighting, building materials.

Maine

Connolly & Co. Timber Frame Homes & Barns
10 Atlantic Highway
Edgecomb, ME 04556
Tel: (207) 882-4224
Fax: (207) 882-4247
Custom timber frame homes & barns built to last. Traditional oak pegged mortise and tenon joinery. Design services. Project management. Frames to complete projects. Visit our facility in Maine and observe our commitment to excellence.
E-mail: connolly@lincoln.midcoast.com

Authentic Timberframes
Route 302, RR 2 Box 698
Bridgton, ME 04009
Tel: (207) 647-5720
Timber frame homes, barns, cottages, camps and signs. Traditional joinery, hand-crafted frames.
E-mail: tenon@maine.com
Web site: http://timberframe.maine.com

Barnstormers
RR1 Box 566, North Rochester Road
East Lebanon, ME 04027-9730
Tel: (207) 658-9000
The barn recycling specialists. Antique barns resourced, restored, shipped & reassembled nationwide. Authentic timber framing. Vintage lumber.

North Carolina

Woodhouse, Inc.
PO Box 7336, 105 Creek Street
Rocky Mount, NC 27804
Tel: (919) 977-7336
Fax: (919) 641-4477
French oak, chestnut, antique heart pine solid or laminate flooring.

The Joinery Co.
PO Box 518, 1600 Western Blvd.
Tarboro, NC 27886
Tel: (919) 823-3306, Fax: (919) 823-0818
Antique heart pine, engineered solid wood flooring, stair parts, mouldings, beams.

New Hampshire

Great Northern Barns
PO Box 912E, RFD2
Canaan, NH 03741
Tel: (603) 523-7134
Fax: (603) 523-7134 *51
Great northern barns dismantles and erects antique barn frames.
E-mail: ejl@endor.com
Web site: www.greatnorthernbarns.com

Specialty Timberworks
PO Box 261, Brownfield Road
Eaton, NH 03832
Tel: (603) 447-5625, Fax: same
Designers & fabricators of new and reconstruction of antique timber frames. 3-D CAD services.

New York

Tea House Design, Inc.
PO Box 99, 11 Benedict Road
Waccabuc, NY 10597
Tel: (914) 763-3078
Fax: (914) 763-6165
27 years experience. 100 mile radius NYC.
Innovative and diligent.

Eastfield Village
PO Box 539, 104 Mud Pond Road
Nassau, NY 12062
Tel: (518) 766-2422
Fax: same
School of historic preservation and early
American trades.

M. Fine Lumber Co., Inc.
175 Varick Ave.
Brooklyn, NY 11231
Tel: (718) 381-5200
Fax: (718) 366-8907
Buyer & seller of reusable lumber, timber &
flooring available.
E-mail: MerritF@Fine-Lumber.com
Web site: www.Fine-Lumber.com/Lumber.html

Rondout Woodworking, Inc.
29 Terra Road
Saugerties, NY 12477
Tel: (914) 246-5879, Fax: (914) 246-5845
Restoration specialist. Agricultural–industrial,
waterwheels, windmills, barns, timber
frames.

Texas

What Its Worth, Inc.
PO Box 162135
Austin, TX 78716
Tel: (512) 328-8837, Fax: same
Recycled heart pine. Timbers, planks,
custom flooring, cabinet, door and moulding
stock. Sold by piece or truck load. Virgin
tidewater cypress mined from south
Louisiana waterway, cut wet to spec. Or sold
in log form.

Vermont

Trow & Holden Co.
45 So. Main St.
Barre, VT 05641
Tel: (800) 451-4349
Fax: (802) 476-7025
Stone carving and splitting tools, mortar-
removal tools.
E-mail: trowco@aol.com

Second Harvest Salvage & Demo
PO Box 194-E, RR1
Jeffersonville, VT 05464
Tel: (802) 644-8169
Specializing in hand hewn frames and antique
flooring and lumbers.

North Woods Joinery
PO Box 1166
Burlington, VT 05402-1166
Tel: (802) 644-5667
Fax: (802) 644-2509
Traditional post and beam construction:
homes, barns, steeples, bridges, towers.

Wisconsin

Abatron Inc.
5501-95th Ave.
Kenosha, WI 53144
Tel: (414) 653-2000
Fax: (414) 653-2019
Wood, concrete, metal restoration products;
adhesives; moldmaking compounds.
E-mail: info@abatron.com
Web site: http://www.abatron.com

Standard Tar Products Co., Inc.
2456 West Cornell St.
Milwaukee, WI 53209-6294
Tel: (800) 825-7650
Fax: (414) 873-7737
"Organiclear" protective wood coatings &
finishes for log homes & restoration.

Nova Scotia

Acorn Timber Frames, Ltd.
RR 1
Hantsport, Kings County, NS,
Canada B0P 1P0
Tel: (902) 684-9708, Fax: same
Traditional joinery: homes, churches, farm/
garden/tourism/vacation structures, great
rooms, restorations. Serving Canada and
alluring locations with your requirements since
1978

The Look and Feel of Tradition

RESTORATION® **&RENOVATION**™

**Sheraton Washington Hotel and
Convention Center
January 28-30, 1999
Washington, DC**

**LA Convention Center
December 2-3, 1998
Los Angeles, California**

Whether you are the building owner, homeowner or client — or the professeional hired to restore or recreate that look and feel of tradition...RESTORATION&RENOVATION is the most comprehensive exhibition and conference designed to help you make the right planning and purchasing decisions.

❖ See and touch the growing array of products in traditional design and craft, in both residential and commercial spheres

❖ Learn about the latest materials, methods and techniques for maintaining, preserving and re-creating traditional or historical exteriors, interiors, gardens/landscapes and collections

❖ If your plans include restoration, rehabilitation, reconstruction, remodeling or incorporating older styles and craftsmanship into new construction, you will find specific solutions to your project problems at RESTORATION&RENOVATION!

For more information, contact:
EGI Exhibitions, Inc.
129 Park Street, North Reading, MA 01864 USA
978.664.6455, fax 978.664.5822, e-mail: show@egiexhib.com
Visit our web site at www.egiexhib.com

RESTORATION® is a registered trademark of EGI Exhibitions, Inc. RESTORATION&RENOVATION™ is a trademark of EGI Exhibitions, Inc

Notes & Numbers

Notes & Numbers

Natural Building Products & Services

Natural Building Products & Services

Throughout most of the history of humankind, the primary sources of building materials were natural. We evolved in structures built of breathable, nontoxic and indigenous materials. As knowledge and craftsmanship grew over the last few millennia, our creativity blossomed, resulting in the vast reservoir of architectural and engineering data available today.

During the last century or so, home building has taken on a whole new approach. No longer in the hands of prospective homeowners, banks, government and the construction industry have taken control. Cement, steel, vinyl, fiberglass, urethane, etc., mass-produced in various forms, have become the standard, and despite the fact that they have proven themselves no more viable, they've been adopted by the home building industry almost to the exclusion of natural materials. In fact, those natural materials that are acceptable, are most often reconstituted into composites or manufactured units.

And now, at the supposed cusp of architectural ingenuity, many find themselves in the preposterous position of having to revalidate building systems that have been in use for thousands of years. This, despite the fact that current standards precipitate shoddy building practices (as demonstrated in the aftermath of hurricane Andrew), use toxic materials that can cause serious illness through off-gassing, con-tribute to local and worldwide pollution through manufacturing processes, and deplete resources through a profit-oriented assembly line of corporations.

Nevertheless, a new breed of builders and prospective howeowners is emerging with a preference for quality construction, healthy homes and sustainable building practices. In most cases, locally available natural materials can be incorporated into the building process, with maximum comfort in the home and minimal impact on the environment. The listings in this section provide information and sources for bamboo, clay, thatch, wheat straw panels, hemp products, strawbale, workshops and more.

Bamboo

Bamboo-Smiths
PO Box 1801
Nevada City, CA 95959
Tel: (916) 292-9449
Fax: (916) 292-9460
Bamboo items in traditional Japanese or adapted styles. Specialty tools and classes available.

Bamboo Fencer
31 Germania St.
Jamaica Plain, MA 02130-2314
Tel: (617) 524-6137
Fax: (617) 524-6100
Manufactures and imports fences, gates, and other products.
E-mail: Dave@bamboofencer.com
Web site: http://www.bamboofencer.com

Smith & Fong Company
2121 Bryant Street, Suite 203
San Francisco, CA 94110
Tel: (415) 285-4889
Fax: (415) 285-8230
Plyboo, natural or amber. The first US distributor of bamboo flooring; horizontally laminated strips (3-ply).

Bamboo Hardwoods Mfg. Co.
PO Box 20069
Seattle, WA 99102
Tel: (206) 223-0658
Fax: (206) 223-0659
Bamboo Hardwood Flooring. Produced in Viet Nam. Vertically laminated strips.

Bamboo Flooring International Corp.
20120 Paseo Del Prado, Suite E
Walnut, CA 91789
Tel: (800) 827-9261
Fax: (909) 594-6938
Sun Brand Bamboo Flooring. 3-ply horizontal lamination.

Amati Bambu Ltd.
350 Steelcase Road W
Markham, Ontario, Canada L3R 1B3
Tel: (905) 477-8899
Fax: (905) 477-5208
3-ply: horizontally lanimated, with thin vertically laminated strips in center ply.

Mintec Corp.
100 E. Pennsylvania Avenue
Towson, MD 21286
Tel: (888) 964-6832
Fax: (410) 296-6693
Bamtex Bamboo Flooring. 2-ply or 3-ply with horizontal laminations, or vertically laminated 1/2".

Floorworks
115 Dupont Street
Toronto, Ontario, Canada M5R 1V4
Tel: (416) 961-6891
Fax: (416) 961-3881
Rishi Bamboo flooring. Available with both vertically and horizontally laminated strips.

Plyboo America, Inc.
745 Chestnut Ridge Road
Kirkville, NY 13082
Tel: (315) 687-3270
Fax: (315) 687-5177
Plyboo bamboo flooring. Horizontally laminated strips.

Clay

Maine

Proclay
c/o Fox Maple
PO Box 249
Brownfield, ME 04010
Tel: (207) 935-3720
Fax: (207) 935-4575
Light-clay infill techniques, clay & lime plasters, clay building materials, workshops and consulting.
E-mail: foxmaple@nxi.com

Ohio

Superior Clay Corporation
PO Box 352, 6566 Superior Road SE
Uhrichsville, OH 44683
Tel: (614) 922-4122
Fax: (614) 922-6626
Clay flue lining, Rumford fireplace components, clay chimney pots, ground fired clay.
E-mail: mcclave@tusconet.com
Web site: rumford.com

Natural Homesteads
13182 N. Boone Road
Columbia Station, OH 44028
Tel: (440) 236-3344
Natural building design/consultation; slide presentations; straw-bale and cob workshops.

Quikspray, Inc.
PO Box 327
Port Clinton, OH 43452-9485
Tel: (419) 732-2611, (419) 732-2601
Fax: (419) 734-2628
Spray guns for clay & plaster.

Oregon

Cob Cottage Co.
PO Box 123
Cottage Grove, OR 97424
Tel: (541) 942-2005
Fax: (541) 942-3021
Information and workshops on building with cob (sand, clay, straw).
Web site: http://www.deatech.com/cobcottage

Frank Andresen, a German clay builder, applying clay plaster to compressed straw panels on the walls of office at Fox Maple.

Germany

Uelzener Maschinenfabrik
Friedrich Maurer Gmbh
D-65843 Sulzbach/Ts.
Wiesenstrasse 18
Germany
Tel: 06196-05840
Fax: 06196-71273
Professional German-made clay construction equipment.

Dust Control

Dust Door & Wall System
524 Green St.
Boylston, MA 01505
Modular zipper doors & wall panels which attach with no damage.

Building Schools

Arizona

The Canelo Project
HCL Box 324
Elgin, AZ 85611
Tel: (520) 455-5548
Fax: (520) 455-9360
Straw bale building/earthen floors and plasters, workshops, resources, consulting.
E-mail: absteen@dakotacom.net
Web site: http://www.deatech.com/canelo

Arcosanti
HC 74, Box 4136
Mayer, AZ 86333
Tel: (520) 632-7135
Fax: (520) 632-6229
E-mail: arcosanti@aol.com

California

Real Goods
555 Leslie St.
Ukiah, CA 95482
Tel: (707) 468-9292, Fax: (707) 462-9394
Solar, wind, hydro, efficient lighting, water, catalogs, books and institute.

Cal-Earth Institute
10225 Baldy Lane
Hesperia, CA 92345
Tel: (619) 244-0614, (619) 956-7533
Fax: (619) 244-2201
E-mail: calearth@aol.com

Eos Institute
580 Broadway, Suite 200
Laguna Beach, CA 92651
Tel: (714) 497-1896, Fax: (714) 497-7861
Educational nonprofit for the study of sustainable living. Resources, consulting, and programs on ecological community design. Library, lectures, workshops.
E-mail: eos@igpc.org

Colorado

Solar Energy International
PO Box 715
Carbondale, CO 81623
Tel: (970) 963-8855, Fax: (970) 963-8866
Hands-on workshops in solar home design, straw bale, rammed earth, adobe, photovoltaics, wind, hydro, solar cooking & consulting.
E-mail: sei@solarenergy.org

DC, Washington

Sandra Leibowitz
Eco-Building Schools
3220 N Street NW #218
Washington, DC 20007
$7 ($6 + $1 postage) for Eco-Building Schools: A directory of alternative educational resources in environmentally sensitive design. Detailed info on 35 eco-building schools across the U.S.
Web site: http://www.ecodesign.org/edi/eden

Florida

International Institute for Bau-Biologie
1401 A Cleveland St.
Clearwater, FL 34615
Tel: (813) 461-4371
Holistic education in the creation of homes & offices that are harmonious and healthy to the occupants and have no adverse effect on the environment.
E-mail: baubiologie@earthlink.net
Web site: http://www.bau-biologieusa.com

Massachusetts

The Heartwood School
Johnson Hill Road
Washington, MA 01235
Tel: (413) 623-6677
Fax: (413) 623-0277
Workshops in homebuilding, timber framing, woodworking, and more.
E-mail: info@heartwoodschool.com
Web site: www.heartwoodschool.com

Maine

Fox Maple School of Traditional Building
PO Box 249, Corn Hill Road
Brownfield, ME 04010
Tel: (207) 935-3720
Fax: (207) 935-4575
Workshops for introductory & advanced timber framing. Other workshops available in the areas of thatch, clay and alternative building systems. Fox Maple strives for quality craftsmanship, with a view towards a sustainable future.
E-mail: foxmaple@nxi.com
Web site: http://www.nxi.com/WWW/joinersquarterly

Minnesota

Energy Efficient Building Association
2950 Metro Drive #108
Minneapolis, MN 55425
Tel: (612) 851-9940
Fax: (612) 851-9507
EEBA produces & presents training based on the "systems approach".
E-mail: EEBANews@aol.com
Web site: http://www.eeba.org

New Mexico

Natural Building Resources
Star Rt. 2, Box 119
Kingston, NM 88042
Tel: (505) 895-5652
Fax: (505) 895-3326
Books and videos on natural building. Host–Natural Building Colloquium.
E-mail: blackrange@zianet.com
Web site: www.zianet.com/blackrange

Natural House Building Center
2300 West Alameda, A5
Santa Fe, NM 87501
Tel: (505) 471-5314
Fax: (505) 471-3714
Hands-on workshops: timber framing, straw-clay construction, earth floors & plastering.

Southwest Solaradobe School
PO Box 153
Bosque, NM 87006
Tel: (505) 861-1255
Fax: (505) 861-1304

New York

Eastfield Village
PO Box 539, 104 Mud Pond Road
Nassau, NY 12062
Tel: (518) 766-2422
Fax: same
School of historic preservation and early American trades.

Barkeater Design Build Company
35 Wellington Street
Malone, NY 12953
Tel: (518) 483-5282
Fax: same
Designer/builders specializing in stone slipform construction. Workshops available.
E-mail: barkeatr@slic.com
Web site: www.xlic.com/~barkeatr/home.html

Earthwood Building School
366 Murtagh Hill Road
West Chazy, NY 12992
Tel: (518) 493-7744
Fax: same, phone first
Teaches cordwood masonry and underground housing. Books, videos and workshops.
Web site: http://www.interlog.com/newood

Oregon

Cob Cottage Co.
PO Box 123
Cottage Grove, OR 97424
Tel: (541) 942-2005
Fax: (541) 942-3021
Information and workshops on building with cob (sand, clay, straw).
Web site: http://www.deatech.com/cobcottage

Groundworks
PO Box 381
Murphy, OR 97533
Tel: (541) 471-3470
Workshops and handbook available on cob (hand-sculpted earth) construction.
Web site: http://www.cpros.com/~sequoia

Pennsylvania

Feng Shui Institute
160 Hopwood Road
Collegeville, PA 19426
Tel: (610) 489-2684
Education to develop the capacity to heal environments and transform lives. Geomancy, color, Medicine Wheel, land healing & landscaping.

Texas

Owner Builder Center At Houston Community College
PO Box 7849, 4141 Costa Rica
Houston, TX 77092
Tel: (713) 956-1178, Fax: (713) 956-7413
Non credit instructional program for residential building–hands-on and lecture classes.

Vermont

Yestermorrow Design/Build School
RR 1 Box 97-5
Warren, VT 05674
Tel: (802) 496-5545
Fax: (802) 496-5540
Offers hands-on courses in residential design
and "green" construction.
E-mail: ymschool@aol.com
Web site: www.yestermorrow.org

Washington

Greenfire Institute
PO Box 1040
Winthrop, WA 98862
Tel: (509) 996-3593
Fax: same
Straw bale construction training, consultation
and design.
E-mail: greenfire@igc.org
Web site: www.balewolf.com

Healthy Homes, Bau-Biologie

Institute For Bau-Biologie (IBE)
PO Box 387, 1401A Cleveland St.
Clearwater, FL 33757
Tel: (813) 461-4371
Fax: (813) 441-4373
Home study courses, seminars, consulting
on "healthy homes and offices"

Renaissance Developments
10704 Oviatt Road
Honor, MI 49640
Tel: (616) 326-4009
Sustainable building, healthy creative
dreamspaces, bau-biologie, owner-builder
involvement welcome.

Hemp

Industrial AG Innovations
2725 N. Westwood Blvd, Suite 7
Poplar Bluff, MO 63901
Tel: (573) 785-3355
Fax: (573) 785-3059
Hemp fiberboard products. 100% hemp
particles and a typical UF resin.

The Ohio Hempery, Inc.
7002 State Route 329
Guysville, OH 45735
Tel: (614) 662-4367
Fabric, paper, oil, clothes, shoes, skin & body
care, twine, seeds, stalks, sliver, yarn and
hurds manufactured from hemp. Free catalog.

*Timber frame and straw bale
enclosure constructed in the spring
1996 workshops series at Fox Maple.*

Strawbale

Arizona

The Canelo Project
HCL Box 324
Elgin, AZ 85611
Tel: (520) 455-5548
Fax: (520) 455-9360
Straw bale building/earthen floors and
plasters, workshops, resources, consulting.
E-mail: absteen@dakotacom.net
Web site: http://www.deatech.com/canelo

The Last Straw
PO Box 42000
Tucson, AZ 85733
Tel: (520) 882-3848
The Last Straw: the quarterly journal of straw-
bale construction.
E-mail: thelaststraw@igc.apc.org
Web site: http://www.netchaos.com/+ls

Out On Bale By Mail
1039 E. Linden St.
Tucson, AZ 85719
Tel: (520) 624-1673
Fax: (520) 299-9099
Educational materials for straw bale building.
Help for owner builders.
E-mail: outonbale@aol.com

Sustainable Systems Support
PO Box 318
Bisbee, AZ 85603
Tel: (520) 432-4292
Offers books and videos on plastered straw
bale construction, including an excellent 90
min. "how-to" video with a 62 page manual.
Wall raising workshops and consultations.

Colorado

Solar Energy International
PO Box 715
Carbondale, CO 81623
Tel: (970) 963-8855Fax: (970) 963-8866
Hands-on workshops on renewable energy
and environmental building technologies.
E-mail: sei@solarenergy.org
Web site: http://www.solarenergy.org

Massachusetts

Greenspace Collaborative
PO Box 107
Ashfield, MA 01330
Tel: (413) 369-4905
Buildings of straw bales and other natural
materials detailed for the northeastern
climate.

Maine

Wentworth Timberframes
PO Box 1116, 45 Mason Street
Bethel, ME 04217
Tel: (207) 824-4237
25 years experience. Hewn, rough-sawn, or
hand-planed timbers. Mortise and tenon
joinery. Owner friendly

Proclay
c/o Fox Maple
PO Box 249
Brownfield, ME 04010
Tel: (207) 935-3720
Fax: (207) 935-4575
Light-clay infill techniques, clay & lime
plasters, clay building materials, workshops
and consulting.
E-mail: foxmaple@nxi.com

Minnesota

Community Eco-Design Network
PO Box 6241, 3151-29th Ave. S, #103
Minneapolis, MN 55406
Tel: (612) 306-2326
Super-insulated construction planbook, design services, northern climate strawbale building system.
E-mail: erichart@mtn.org
Web site: http://www.umn.edu/n/home/m037/kurtdand/cen

New Hampshire

Straw Works
152 West Main St.
Conway, NH 03818
Tel: (603) 447-1701, Fax: (603) 447-6412
Design for those wishing to walk lightly upon the earth.
E-mail: Straw-Works@juno.com

Ohio

Natural Homesteads
13182 N. Boone Road
Columbia Station, OH 44028
Tel: (440) 236-3344
Natural building design / consultation; slide presentations; straw-bale and cob workshops.

Oregon

Sustainable Architecture
PO Box 696, 910 Glendale Ave.
Ashland, OR 97520
Tel: (541) 482-6332, Fax: (541) 488-8299
Architectural services integrating full spectrum of healthy, holistic building.

Aprovecho Research Center
80574 Hazelton Road
Cottage Grove, OR 97424
Tel: (541) 942-8198, Fax: (541) 942-0302
Demonstration research and education center for sustainable living.
E-mail: apro@efn.org/~apro
Web site: http://www.efn.org/~apro

Gringo Grip
4951 Netarts Hwy. W. #2041
Tillamook, OR 97141
Tel: (800) 734-8091, Fax: (800) 734-8071
A simple thru-the-bale anchor for fastening cabinets, interior wall sections, electrical boxes, fixtures, and pipe to straw-bale walls.

Vermont

Yestermorrow Design/Build School
RR 1 Box 97-5
Warren, VT 05674
Tel: (802) 496-5545, Fax: (802) 496-5540
Offers hands-on courses in residential design and "green" construction.
E-mail: ymschool@aol.com
Web site: www.yestermorrow.org

Organic Oat Straw
RR#1 Box 520
Orleans, VT 05860
Tel: (802) 754-2028
Straw bales for building.

Washington

Greenfire Institute
PO Box 1040
Winthrop, WA 98862
Tel: (509) 996-3593
Fax: same
Straw bale construction training, consultation and design.
E-mail: greenfire@igc.org
Web site: www.balewolf.com

Thatch

Fox Maple School of Traditional Building
PO Box 249, Corn Hill Road
Brownfield, ME 04010
Tel: (207) 935-3720
Fax: (207) 935-4575
Workshops in timber framing, thatching, straw clay and alternative building systems. Researce into appropriate uses of traditional building systems. Demonstration projects.
E-mail: foxmaple@nxi.com
Web site: http://www.nxi.com/WWW/joinersquarterly

Custom Roof Thatching & Supplies
PO Box 62054
Cincinnati, OH 45262
Tel: (513) 772-4979
Fax: (513) 772-6313
Has thatched in U.S. since 1986. A guide to roof thatching in the U.S. $6.00
web site: http://www.roofthatch.com

Thatching Advisory Services, Ltd.
Faircross Offices
Stratfield Saye,
Reading, Berks
United Kingdom RG7 2BT
Tel: 01256 880828, Fax: 01256 880866
Complete thatching services: design, thatching crews worldwide, materials, tools, supplies, books and publications.

Wheat Straw Panels

Agriboard Industries
PO Box 645
Fairfield, IA 52556
Tel: (515) 472-0363
Complete, OSB laminated, compressed wheat straw panel building systems.
E-mail: agriboard@lisco.com

Wood Roofing

Liberty Cedar
535 Liberty Lane
W. Kingston, RI 02892
Tel: (800) 882-3327, (401) 789-6626
Fax: (401) 789-0320
Naturally decay-resistant exterior wood products specializing in wood roofing.

Wheat straw panel installation on the shop at Fox Maple. Stramit, U.S.A., produced compressed wheat straw panels from a new plant in Texas, using technology developed by the mother company in England, where they have been producing panels for over 50 years. Their Texas plant stands idle at this time due to their inability to establish a sufficient market.

Thatching

There is something innately appealing about the way a thatched roof softens the impact of a building on a site— thatch is welcoming, and speaks to the part of us that yearns to live in harmony with nature. Thatch is indeed the "warm roof" it appears to be, in insulating qualities as well as charm.

An unbroken tradition for thousands of years in parts of the world where the need for roofing materials is best met with available, renewable, cost-free vegetation, thatching's demise in the U.S. about two hundred years ago was due to its poor track record in association with heating with wood... In postwar Britain, newer materials supplanted the use of labor intensive thatch. Ironically it is the mechanization of harvesting and bundling straw and reed that has revitalized thatching in Europe. The strawbale revolution is fueling American developments in natural building systems and materials. The rediscovery of the excellent insulating properties of thatch, an un-exploited sustainable resource, may enable the beauty of thatch to grace this country again. Several factors need to be addressed for thatch to become a viable natural roofing option on this continent:

1. Fire hazard: the fire safety hurdle has been surmounted in England. *Thatching Advisory Services* (TAS), a professional thatchers' company organized on a franchise basis, are US distributors for 'environmentally friendly fire retardants' designed and rated for use on thatch. A barrier foil product can also be laid under thatch, with added benefits of increasing the insulating value of the roof, and creating a weather-proof covering for the building while thatching. Fire insurance for buildings meeting TAS maintenance and fireproofing guidelines is available at rates competitive with those for conventionally roofed structures.

2. Thatchers: thatching is both an art and a craft, requiring sensitive skills, a deep understanding of natural materials, and years of arduous toil to achieve proficiency. Competent thatchers are few and far between in America. TAS has offered high quality craftsmanship to a specialty market of US clients for about 15 years.

3. Thatch: to rely on European-grown materials is not sustainable, although Americans have gone this route to guarantee a reliable roof. Many available plants can be utilized: reed, straws, sedge, heather and flax. Straw, a by-product of grain production, has a roof-life about half that of reed, a wild wetland plant. To research harvesting the common reed, *phragmites australis*, a locally growing thatch material known in England as Norfolk reed, we queried the Maine Dept. of Environmental Protection. They consider it a nuisance, competing to the exclusion of other plants; it's encroachment in saltmarsh and coastal wetlands is creeping north, and some towns want to eradicate it. Care should be exercised to prevent its arbitrary introduction into wetlands where it is not already growing. Harvesting thatch can be helpful in maintaining wetlands, by reducing the build-up of decomposing old stalks which fill in and dry up marshes. Cutting should be done in winter or early spring, prior to the emergence of new shoots. A weed-whacker with a woody-type blade will work! In Europe, a Danish tractor-like harvester both cuts and bundles. Standard bundles measure 12" in diameter. An acre will yield up to 400 bundles.

Reed is laid in overlapping courses, secured by horizontal rods called sways. Butt ends are beaten with a 'legget' up under the sways to the correct slope. Ridging is done in sedge or long straw secured by spars, and it is here that a thatcher's creativity has free reign, shaping and dressing with ligger and cross-rod decorations to hold it in place. -*Janot Mendler*

A. Ligger and cross-rod decorations, fixed along eaves & barges (A) of a thatched roof.

Building Suppliers

Environmental Building Supplies
1314 NW Northrup St.
Portland, OR 97209
Tel: (503) 222-3881
Low-toxic, renewable and recycled materials.
Hardwood floors, carpet, linoleum, tile, paint,
finishes.

Certified Erection Crews

Hearthstone Log & Timberframe Homes
120 Carriage Drive
Macon, GA 31210
Tel: (800) 537-7931
Fax: (912) 477-6535
21 years experience, CADD design,
professional erection and dry-in services.
E-mail: hearthstonehomes@mindspring.com
Web site: www.mindspring.com/
~hearthstonehomes

Crane Service

Acorn Crane Service
PO Box 68, Main Road
Huntington, VT 05462
Tel: (800) 990-1953
14 ton national crane, 76' tip height, Ford
9000 flatbed.

Cupolas

Allen Woodworking And Cupolas
2242 Bethel Road
Lansdale, PA 19446
Tel: (215) 699-8100
Fax: same
Custom redwood, cedar, poplar cupolas;
portable sawmill with backhoe services.

Custom Sawing

Timber Frame Systems, Inc.
PO Box 458, 28 Main St.
Frankford, DE 19945
Tel: (302) 732-9428
Fax: (302) 537-4971
Manufacturer of custom post & beam frame
kits.

Framing Connectors

TIBVITSS Unlimited, LLC
PO Box 267, 35500 East Colfax Avenue
Watkins, CO 80137
Tel: (303) 261-7775
Fax: (303) 261-7778
Innovative metal connectors for simple yet
strong continuous load paths

Hot Tubs

Snorkel Stove Company
4216 6th Avenue S.
Seattle, WA 98108
Tel: (206) 340-0981
Fax: (206) 340-0982
Cedar, wooden hot tubs heated with
underwater stoves–available in kits.
E-mail: hottubs@snorkel.com
Web site: www.snorkel.com

Humidors, Wine Cellars

Ellison Timberframes
20 Six Penny Lane
Harwichport, MA 02646
Tel: (508) 430-0407
Award-winning design/build company. No
steel connections used. Humidors, wine
cellars

Pegs

Scott Northcott Woodturning
RR#1 Box 624
Walpole, NH 03608
Tel: (603) 756-4204
Hardwood pegs for timber framing.

Pipe Tracing

Easy Heat, Inc.
31977 US 20 E.
New Carlisle, IN 46552
Tel: (219) 654-3144
Fax: (219) 654-7739
Electrical radiant heating cable solutions.
E-mail: mgb~1@msn.com
Web site: www.easyheat.com

Slate

The New England Slate Company
RD 1, Box 1181, Burr Pond Road
Sudbury, VT 05733
Tel: (802) 247-8809
Fax: (802) 247-0089
Quality roofing slate for repair work,
restorations, and new construction.

Hilltop Slate, Inc.
PO Box 201
Middle Granville, NY 12849
Tel: (518) 642-2270
Fax: (518) 642-1220
Hilltop Slate has been a leading supplier of
roofing and structural slate since 1948.

Slate International
15106 Marlboro Pike
Upper Marlboro, MD 20772
Tel: (800) 343-9785, (301) 952-0120
Fax: (301) 952-0295
Slate International is a nationwide supplier of
high grade roofing slate and slate ridge vents.

Soapstone

Woodstock Soapstone Co., Inc.
66 Airpark Road
W. Lebanon, NH 03784
Tel: (603) 298-5955

Tool Sharpening

Miller's Sharpening Service
11301 N. Webb
Alliance, OH 44601
Tel: (330) 821-6240

Trusses

Pacific Post & Beam
PO Box 13708
San Luis Obispo, CA 93406
Tel: (805) 543-7565
Fax: (805) 543-1287
Full service timber frame and truss design and
build.

Wood Foundations

Woodmaster Foundations, Inc.
PO Box 66, 845 Dexter St.
Prescott, WI 54021
Tel: (715) 262-3655
Fax: (715) 262-5079
Permanent wood foundations, earth sheltered
structures and wall building panels.
E-mail: woodmstr@pressenter.com
Web site: www.pressenter.com/~woodmstr/

Wood Siding

Johnson Clapboard Mill
134 Wendell Road
Shutesbury, MA 01072
Tel: (413) 259-1271
Fax: same
Manufacturer of restoration quality clapboard
siding.

Liberty Cedar
535 Liberty Lane
W. Kingston, RI 02892
Tel: (800) 882-3327, (401) 789-6626
Fax: (401) 789-0320
Naturally decay-resistant exterior wood
products specializing in wood roofing.

Education &
Information

"It would be part of my scheme of physical education that every youth in the state should learn to do something finely and thoroughly with his hand, so as to let him know what touch meant...Let him once learn to take a straight shaving off a plank, or draw a fine curve without faltering, or lay a brick level in its mortar; and he has learned a multitude of other matters..."

—John Ruskin

Books & Publications

Alaska

Alaska Craftsman Home Program, Inc.
PO Box 241647
Anchorage, AK 99524-1647
Tel: (907) 258-2247 (ACHP)
Fax: (907) 258-5352
Education and research advanced cold climate home building techniques.
E-mail: achp@alaska.net
Web site: http://www.alaska.net/~achp

Arizona

The Canelo Project
HCL Box 324
Elgin, AZ 85611
Tel: (520) 455-5548
Fax: (520) 455-9360
Straw bale building/earthen floors and plasters, workshops, resources, consulting.
E-mail: absteen@dakotacom.net
Web site: http://www.deatech.com/canelo

Sustainable Systems Support
PO Box 318
Bisbee, AZ 85603
Tel: (520) 432-4292
Offers books and videos on plastered straw bale construction, including an excellent 90 min. "how-to" video with a 62 page manual. Wall raising workshops and consultations.

Out On Bale By Mail
1039 E. Linden St.
Tucson, AZ 85719
Tel: (520) 624-1673
Fax: (520) 299-9099
Educational materials for straw bale building. Help for owner builders.
E-mail: outonbale@aol.com

California

Craftsman Book Company
6058 Corte Del Cedro
Carlsbad, CA 92009
Tel: (800) 829-8123
Fax: (760) 438-0398
Professional construction books that solve actual problems in the builder's office and in the field.

Building with Nature Newsletter
P.O. Box 4417
Santa Rosa, CA 95402-4417
Tel: (707) 579-2201
Quarterly Newsletter focusing on natural building issues.

Connecticut

Fine Homebuilding Magazine
PO Box 5506, 63 S. Main Street
Newtown, CT 06470-5506
Tel: (203) 426-8171
Fax: (203) 270-6751
Homebuilders share tips, techniques and reviews of tools and materials.
E-mail: fh@taunton.com
Web site: http://www.taunton.com

Illinois

Frog Tool Co., Ltd.
2169 IL Rt. 26
Dixon, IL 61021
Tel: (800) 648-1270
Fax: (815) 288-3919
Timber framing and handling tools, hand woodworking tools, books. Catalog $5.

Kansas

Cappers
Ogden Publications
1503 SW 42nd Street
Topeka, KS 66609-1265
Tel: (785) 274-4330
Fax: (785) 274-4305
A family-oriented publication providing readers with "good news".
E-mail: cappers@kspress.com
Web site: www.cappers.com

Grit
Ogden Publications
1503 SW 42nd Street
Topeka, KS 66609-1265
Tel: (785) 274-4330
Fax: (785) 274-4305
Publication that preserves the best of family life and traditions.
E-mail: grit@kspress.com
Web site: www.oweb.com/grit

Massachusetts

Berkshire House Publishers
480 Pleasant Street, Suite 5
Lee, MA 01238
Tel: (800) 321-8526
Fax: (413) 243-0303
Explore colonial barn lore with master restorer Richard Babcock.

Old-House Journal Directory (Dovetail Publishers)
2 Main St.
Gloucester, MA 01930
Tel: (508) 283-3200
Fax: (508) 283-4629
Annual sourcebook for suppliers of reproduction hardware, lighting, building materials.

Maryland

NAHB Research Center
400 Prince George's Blvd.
Upper Marlboro, MD 20774-8731
Residential building research including innovative/alternative materials and systems.
E-mail: pyost@nahbrc.org
Web site: http://www.nahbrc.com

Maine

Fox Maple Press, Inc.
PO Box 249, Corn Hill Road
Brownfield, ME 04010
Tel: (207) 935-3720, Fax: (207) 935-4575
Publisher of Joiners' Quarterly, *The Journal of timber Framing & Traditional Building*. JQ is dedicated to blending modern technology with traditional craftsmanship, bringing innovative ideas for a sustainable future to the forefront. Books, workshops and education.
E-mail: foxmaple@nxi.com
Web site: http://www.nxi.com/WWW/ joinersquarterly

North Carolina

Country Workshops
90 Mill Creek Road
Marshall, NC 28753
Tel: (704) 656-2280
Tools, books and instruction in traditional woodworking with hand tools.
E-mail: langsner@countryworkshops.org
Web site: countryworkshops.org

New Mexico

Natural Building Resources
Star Rt. 2, Box 119
Kingston, NM 88042
Tel: (505) 895-5652
Fax: (505) 895-3326
Books and videos on natural building. Host—Natural Building Colloquium.
E-mail: blackrange@zianet.com
Web site: www.zianet.com/blackrange

New York

Lofty Branch Bookstore
PO Box 512
Victor, NY 14564
Tel: (716) 742-2607
Fax: (716) 289-3221
Over 350 timber framing, construction, design and woodworking books/videos.
E-mail: loftybooks@aol.com
Web site: http://members.aol.com.loftybooks

Earthwood Building School
366 Murtagh Hill Road
West Chazy, NY 12992
Tel: (518) 493-7744
Fax: same, phone first
Teaches cordwood masonry and underground housing. Books, videos and workshops.
Web site: http://www.interlog.com/newood

Lee Valley Tools Ltd.
PO Box 178012 East River St.
Ogdensburg, NY 13669-0490
Tel: (800) 871-8158, Fax: (800) 513-7885
Our 236-page full-color catalog has the widest selection of woodworking hand tools on the market.
Web site: http://www.leevalley.com

Donald J. Berg, AIA
150 Harvard Avenue
Rockville Centre, NY 11570
Tel: (516) 766-5585, Fax: (516) 536-4081
Editor of American Barns and Backbuildings
Catalog. Author of American Country
Building Design. Historical research. Building
plans available.
E-mail:XCBR70A@prodigy.com

Ohio

Custom Roof Thatching & Supplies
PO Box 62054
Cincinnati, OH 45262
Tel: (513) 772-4979
Fax: (513) 772-6313
Has thatched in U.S. since 1986. A guide to
roof thatching in the U.S. $6.00.
Web site: http://www.roofthatch.com

Oregon

Iris Communications, Inc.
PO Box 5920
Eugene, OR 97405
Tel: (541) 484-9353, Fax: (541) 484-1645
Carefully selected books, videos and
software for green construction.
E-mail: iris@oikos.com
Web site: www.oikos.com

Groundworks
PO Box 381
Murphy, OR 97533
Tel: (541) 471-3470
Workshops and handbook available on cob
(hand-sculpted earth) construction.
Web site: http://www.cpros.com/~sequoia

Pennsylvania

American Woodworker
22 S. 2nd Street
Emmaus, PA 18098-0099
Tel: (610) 967-8315
Fax: (610) 967-7692
American Woodworker provides information &
ideas for serious woodworkers.

Vermont

JLC Bookstore
PO Box 2050, West Main St.
Richmond, VT 05477
Tel: (800) 859-3669, Fax: (802) 434-4467
Hard to find books for
construction professionals.
Web site: bgibooks.com

Tree Talk
PO Box 426, 431 Pine Street
Burlington, VT 05402
Tel: (802) 865-1111
Fax: (802) 863-4344
Multimedia cd-rom on wood. 900 species.
Database. Video. Pictures. Maps.
E-mail: wow@together.net
Web site: www.woodweb.com/~treetalk/
home.html

Chelsea Green Publishing Company
PO Box 428
White River Junction, VT 05001
Tel: (802) 295-6300
Fax: (802) 295-6444
Publisher of quality books, specializing in
alternative, natural & traditional homes for
the owner/builder.

West Virginia

Woodcraft Supply
PO Box 1686, 210 Wood County Industrial
Park
Parkersburg, WV 26102
Tel: (800) 225-1153
Fax: (304) 428-8271
Quality woodworking tools, books, hardware,
hardwoods; plus tool sharpening service.
E-mail: custserv@woodcraft.com
Web site: www.woodcraft.com

Catalogs

California

Craftsman Book Company
6058 Corte Del Cedro
Carlsbad, CA 92009
Tel: (800) 829-8123
Fax: (760) 438-0398
Professional construction books that solve
actual problems in the builder's office and in
the field.

Bailey's
PO Box 550, 44650 Hwy. 101
Laytonville, CA 95454
Tel: (800) 322-4539
Fax: (707) 984-8115
Free catalog: world's largest mail order
woodsman supplies company.
E-mail: baileys@bbaileyscom
Web site: http://www.bbaileys.com

Alternative Energy Engineering, Inc.
PO Box 339
Redway, CA 95560
Tel: (800) 777-6609
Fax: (707) 923-3009
Energy from solar, wind or water power.
Photovoltaics, lighting, solar fans, fridges and
books. 112 page catalog for $3.

Real Goods
555 Leslie St.
Ukiah, CA 95482
Tel: (707) 468-9292
Fax: (707) 462-9394
Solar, wind, hydro, efficient lighting, water,
catalogs, books and institute.

Sierra Solar Systems
109-MC Argall Way
Nevada City, CA 95959
Tel: (800) 517-6527
Fax: (916) 265-6151
Solar electric, pumping, hot water, wind,
hydropower and energy efficient lighting.
Catalog $5.
E-mail: solarjon@oro.net
Web site: www.sierrasolar.com

Earth Studio
6761 Sebastopol Ave., Suite 8
Sebastopol, CA 95472
Tel: (707) 823-2569
Petroleum-free & biodegradable natural paints
and finishes. Free Catalog.

Florida

International Tool Corporation
2590 Davie Road
Davie, FL 33317
Tel: (800) 338-3384
Fax: (954) 792-3560
Woodworking & construction power tools at
the guaranteed lowest prices.
Web site: http://www.internationaltool.com

Idaho

Woodhouse
PO Box 801
Ashton, ID 83420
Tel: (208) 652-3608
Fax: (208) 652-3628
Supplying all specialized tools and materials
for log-timber construction. Providing owner
and/or professional with largest selection of
quality products available.

Backwoods Solar Electric Systems
8530 Rapid Lightning Creek Road
Sandpoint, ID 83864
Tel: (208) 263-4290
All the equipment with lower than usual prices.
Catalog $3.

Illinois

Frog Tool Co., Ltd.
2169 IL Rt. 26
Dixon, IL 61021
Tel: (800) 648-1270
Fax: (815) 288-3919
Timber framing and handling tools, hand
woodworking tools, books. Catalog $5.

Davis Caves Construction, Inc.
PO Box 69
Armington, IL 61721
Tel: (309) 392-2574
Fax: (309) 392-2578
We will design and build to your specific floorplan, or choose from our 80 page planbook.
E-mail: earthome@daviscaves.com
Web site: www.daviscaves.com/builder.htm

Indiana

Wood-Mizer Products, Inc.
8180 W. 10th Street
Indianapolis, IN 46214
Tel: (317) 271-1542
Fax: (317) 273-1011
Transportable sawmills and accessories: lowers lumber costs and improves quality.
E-mail: adindy@woodmizer.com
Web site: http://www.woodmizer.com

Massachusetts

Old Sturbridge Village
One Old Sturbridge Village Road
Sturbridge, MA 01566
Tel: (508) 347-3362
Fax: (508) 347-0369
Hand-forged wrought iron hinges, latches and more.

Tremont Nail Co.
PO Box 111, 8 Elm St.
Wareham, MA 02571
Tel: (508) 295-0038
Fax: (508) 295-1365
Manufacturer of restoration pattern steel cut nails; colonial hardware distributor.
E-mail: cutnails@aol.com

Old-House Journal Directory (Dovetail Publishers)
2 Main St.
Gloucester, MA 01930
Tel: (508) 283-3200
Fax: (508) 283-4629
Annual sourcebook for suppliers of reproduction hardware, lighting, building materials.

New England Solar Electric, Inc.
PO Box 435
Worthington, MA 01098
Tel: (413) 238-5974
$3 for 64 page catalog/design guide, solar electric kits, components, gas refrigerators, other appliances and information you need to live independently with solar electricity.

Maine

Natural Knees
281 Hartland Road
St. Albans, ME 04971
Tel: (207) 938-2380
Natural grown knees for timber frame construction and boat building.
E-mail: kneeman@somtel.com

Barn Masters, Inc.
PO Box 258
Freeport, ME 04032
Tel: (207) 865-4169, Fax: (207) 865-6169
Makita tools for timber framing: chain mortisers, stationary routers, chisel mortisers, groove cutters, circular saws, 6" x 12" planers, tenon cutters. Free brochure.

Minnesota

Tools On Sale Div.
Of Seven Corners Hdwr., Inc.
216 West 7th Street
St. Paul, MN 55102
Tel: (800) 328-0457
Fax: (612) 224-8263
496 page catalog of power tools and related accessories featuring the most respected brands in the business.

Montana

Specialty Woodworks Company
PO Box 1450
Hamilton, MT 59840
Tel: (406) 363-6353
Fax: (406) 363-6373
Established 1981. Manufactures custom hand-crafted doors and cabinets. Specializing in unique blue stain pine, knotty pine, and other rustic hardwoods. Catalog $7.

Sunelco
PO Box 1499
Hamilton, MT 59840
Tel: (406) 363-6924, (800) 338-6844
Complete source for solar modules, batteries, inverters, water pumps, energy effecient lights, and propane appliances. Catalog $4.95.

North Carolina

Harmony Exchange
Route 2, Box 843-A
Boone, NC 28607
Tel: (800) 968-9663
Antique, reclaimed & new growth. Flooring, timber trusses, decking, exposed beam systems, siding & more. Catalog.

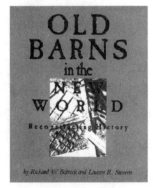

Klingspor's Sanding Catalogue
PO Box 3737
Hickory, NC 28603-3737

North Dakota

Tool Crib Of The North
PO Box 14040, 1603 12th Ave. N
Grand Forks, ND 58206-4040
Tel: (701) 780-2882
Fax: (701) 746-2869
96 color pages of woodworking tools and
accessories, free!
E-mail: kcolman@corpcomm.net
Web site: www.toolcribofthenorth.com

New Mexico

Eco Design Co.
1365 Rufina Circle
Santa Fe, NM 87505
Tel: (800) 621-2591, (505) 438-3448
Fax: (505) 438-0199
The natural choice. Natural paints, stains &
healthy home products catalog.

New York

Lofty Branch Bookstore
PO Box 512
Victor, NY 14564
Tel: (716) 742-2607
Fax: (716) 289-3221
Over 350 timber framing, construction,
design and woodworking books/videos.
E-mail: loftybooks@aol.com
Web site: http://members.aol.com.loftybooks

Lok-N-Logs, Inc.
PO Box 677, Route 12
Sherburne, NY 13460
Tel: (800) 343-8928, (607) 674-4447
Fax: (607) 674-6433
Producer of top quality, pre-cut log home
packages—lifetime limited warranty!
E-mail: lnlinfo@loknlogs.com
Web site: http://www.loknlogs.com
Catalog: $12.95

Ohio

Lehman's
Box 41
Kidron, OH 44636
How the Amish live without electricity. Over
2,500 items including stoves, refrigerators,
lights, appliances, woodworking and garden
tools.

The Ohio Hempery, Inc.
7002 State Route 329
Guysville, OH 45735
Tel: (614) 662-4367
Fabric, paper, oil, clothes, shoes, skin & body
care, twine, seeds, stalks, sliver, yarn and
hurds manufactured from hemp. Free catalog.

Tennessee

Cumberland General Store
#1 Highway 68,
Crossville, TN 38555
Tel: (800) 334-4640
Items include everything from windmills to
woodstoves, Victorian baths to tonics,
handpumps to gristmills, Alladin kerosene
lamps to buggies and harness. 288 page
catalog for $4.
Web site: www.gatewayad.com/cumber.html

*Dave Carlon and Jack Sobon workshop raising at
Hancock Shaker Village, Pittsfield, MA.*

Vermont

JLC Bookstore
PO Box 2050, West Main St.
Richmond, VT 05477
Tel: (800) 859-3669
Fax: (802) 434-4467
Hard to find books for construction
professionals.
Web site: bgibooks.com

Yestermorrow Design/Build School
RR 1 Box 97-5
Warren, VT 05674
Tel: (802) 496-5545
Fax: (802) 496-5540
Offers hands-on courses in residential design
and "green" construction.
E-mail: ymschool@aol.com
Web site: www.yestermorrow.org

Real Log Homes
PO Box 202, National Information Center
Hartland, VT 05048
Tel: (800) 732-5564
Fax: (802) 436-2150
Pre-cut log home packages over 19,000
worldwide since 1963. Catalog $10.
Web site: http://www.realloghomes.com

Chelsea Green Publishing Company
PO Box 428
White River Junction, VT 05001
Tel: (802) 295-6300
Fax: (802) 295-6444
Publisher of quality books, specializing in
alternative, natural & traditional homes for
the owner/builder.

Washington

Environmental Home Center
1724 4th Ave. South
Seattle, WA 98134
Tel: (800) 281-8275, (206) 682-8275
Retail / wholesale—environmentally respon-
sible building materials and decorating
supplies.
E-mail: info@enviresource.com
Web site: www.enviresource.com

Systimatic
12530 135th Ave. NE
Kirkland, WA 98034
Tel: (800) 426-0035, Fax: (425) 821-0801
Manufacturer of carbide tipped circular saw
blades.

Timbercraft Homes, Inc.
85 Martin Road
Port Townsend, WA 98368
Tel: (360) 385-3051, Fax: (360) 385-7745
Since 1979, high quality timber frame
structures, components, and architectural
engineering.
E-mail: info@timbercraft.com
Web site: http://www.timbercraft.com

Building Schools

Arizona

The Canelo Project
HCL Box 324
Elgin, AZ 85611
Tel: (520) 455-5548
Fax: (520) 455-9360
Straw bale building/earthen floors and
plasters, workshops, resources, consulting.
E-mail: absteen@dakotacom.net
Web site: http://www.deatech.com/canelo

Arcosanti
HC 74, Box 4136
Mayer, AZ 86333
Tel: (520) 632-7135
Fax: (520) 632-6229
E-mail: arcosanti@aol.com

California

Real Goods
555 Leslie St.
Ukiah, CA 95482
Tel: (707) 468-9292
Fax: (707) 462-9394
Solar, wind, hydro, efficient lighting, water,
catalogs, books and institute.

Cal-Earth Institute
10225 Baldy Lane
Hesperia, CA 92345
Tel: (619) 244-0614, (619) 956-7533
Fax: (619) 244-2201
E-mail: calearth@aol.com

Eos Institute
580 Broadway, Suite 200
Laguna Beach, CA 92651
Tel: (714) 497-1896
Fax: (714) 497-7861
Educational nonprofit for the study of
sustainable living. Resources, consulting, and
programs on ecological community design.
Library, lectures, workshops.
E-mail: eos@igpc.org

Colorado

Solar Energy International
PO Box 715
Carbondale, CO 81623
Tel: (970) 963-8855
Fax: (970) 963-8866
Hands-on workshops in solar home design,
straw bale, rammed earth, adobe, photovolta-
ics, wind, hydro, solar cooking & consulting.
E-mail: sei@solarenergy.org

DC, Washington

Sandra Leibowitz
Eco-Building Schools
3220 N Street NW #218
Washington, DC 20007
$7 ($6 + $1 postage) for Eco-Building
Schools: A directory of alternative educational
resources in environmentally sensitive design.
Detailed info on 35 eco-building schools
across the U.S.
Web site: http://www.ecodesign.org/edi/eden

Florida

International Institute for Bau-Biologie
1401 A Cleveland St.
Clearwater, FL 34615
Tel: (813) 461-4371
Holistic education in the creation of homes &
offices that are harmonious and healthy to
the occupants and have no adverse effect on
the environment.
E-mail: baubiologie@earthlink.net
Web site: http://www.bau-biologieusa.com

Massachusetts

The Heartwood School
Johnson Hill Road
Washington, MA 01235
Tel: (413) 623-6677
Fax: (413) 623-0277
Workshops in homebuilding, timber framing,
woodworking, and more.
E-mail: info@heartwoodschool.com
Web site: www.heartwoodschool.com

Maine

Fox Maple School Of Traditional Building
PO Box 249, Corn Hill Road
Brownfield, ME 04010
Tel: (207) 935-3720, Fax: (207) 935-4575
Introductory & advanced timber framing
workshops. Other workshops available in
alternative building systems—thatch, straw/
clay, etc.— using natural, local materials.
Quality in design and craftsmanship
paramount, with a view towards a sustainable future. E-mail: foxmaple@nxi.com
Web site:
http://www.nxi.com/WWW/joinersquarterly

Workshop and yard at Fox Maple School, Spring 1997.

Minnesota

Energy Efficient Building Association
2950 Metro Drive #108
Minneapolis, MN 55425
Tel: (612) 851-9940, Fax: (612) 851-9507
EEBA produces & presents training based on the "systems approach".
E-mail: EEBANews@aol.com
Web site: http://www.eeba.org

New Mexico

Natural Building Resources
Star Rt. 2, Box 119
Kingston, NM 88042
Tel: (505) 895-5652, Fax: (505) 895-3326
Books and videos on natural building. Host– Natural Building Colloquium.
E-mail: blackrange@zianet.com
Web site: www.zianet.com/blackrange

Natural House Building Center
2300 West Alameda, A5
Santa Fe, NM 87501
Tel: (505) 471-5314
Fax: (505) 471-3714
Hands-on workshops: timber framing, straw-clay construction, earth floors & plastering.

Southwest Solaradobe School
PO Box 153
Bosque, NM 87006
Tel: (505) 861-1255
Fax: (505) 861-1304

New York

Eastfield Village
PO Box 539, 104 Mud Pond Road
Nassau, NY 12062
Tel: (518) 766-2422, Fax: same
School of historic preservation and early American trades.

Barkeater Design Build Company
35 Wellington Street
Malone, NY 12953
Tel: (518) 483-5282, Fax: same
Designer/builders specializing in stone slipform construction. Workshops available.
E-mail: barkeatr@slic.com
Web site: www.xlic.com/~barkeatr/home.html

Earthwood Building School
366 Murtagh Hill Road
West Chazy, NY 12992
Tel: (518) 493-7744, Fax: same, phone first
Teaches cordwood masonry and underground housing. Books, videos and workshops.
Web site: http://www.interlog.com/newood

Oregon

Cob Cottage Co.
PO Box 123
Cottage Grove, OR 97424
Tel: (541) 942-2005, Fax: (541) 942-3021
Information and workshops on building with cob (sand, clay, straw).
Web site: http://www.deatech.com/cobcottage

Groundworks
PO Box 381
Murphy, OR 97533
Tel: (541) 471-3470
Workshops and handbook available on cob (hand-sculpted earth) construction.
Web site: http://www.cpros.com/~sequoia

Pennsylvania

Feng Shui Institute
160 Hopwood Road
Collegeville, PA 19426
Tel: (610) 489-2684
Education to develop the capacity to heal environments and transform lives. Geomancy, color, Medicine Wheel, land healing & landscaping.

Texas

Owner Builder Center At Houston Community College
PO Box 7849, 4141 Costa Rica
Houston, TX 77092
Tel: (713) 956-1178, Fax: (713) 956-7413
Non credit instructional program for residential building–hands-on and lecture classes.

Center For Maximum Potential Building Systems
8604 FM 969
Austin, TX 78724
Tel: (512) 928-4786, Fax: (512) 926-4418
E-mail: max_pot@txinfinet.com
Web site: http://www.maxpot.com/maxpot

Vermont

Yestermorrow Design/Build School
RR 1 Box 97-5
Warren, VT 05674
Tel: (802) 496-5545, Fax: (802) 496-5540
Offers hands-on courses in residential design and "green" construction.
E-mail: ymschool@aol.com
Web site: www.yestermorrow.org

Washington

Greenfire Institute
PO Box 1040
Winthrop, WA 98862
Tel: (509) 996-3593, Fax: same
Straw bale construction training, consultation and design.
E-mail: greenfire@igc.org
Web site: www.balewolf.com

Museums

Hancock Shaker Village
PO Box 927, Rtes. 20 & 41
Pittsfield, MA 01202
Tel: (413) 443-0188, Fax: (413) 447-9357
200 year-old original Shaker site, crafts demonstrations, working farm.
E-mail: info@hancockshakervillage
Web site: http://www.hancockshakervillage.org

Frank Andresen demonstrates the technique of mixing straw/light clay in a traditional German clay building workshop at Fox Maple School of Traditional Building. The 'slip' is made by mixing clay and water to a consistency of thick syrup. Clay slip is mixed with straw so that it is lightly coated. The result is a fire proof and efficient insulating wall building material. Right: Adjustable slip form suitable for straw/light clay and woodchip/light clay.

Magazines/Newsletters

American Woodworker
22 S. 2nd Street
Emmaus, PA 18098-0099
Tel: (610) 967-8315
Fax: (610) 967-7692
American Woodworker provides information &
ideas for serious woodworkers.

Building With Nature Newsletter
PO Box 4417
Santa Rosa, CA 95402
Tel: (707) 579-2201
Information and inspiration about healthful,
ecologically responsible spirited building.

Canadian Workshop
130 Spy Court
Markham, Ontario, Canada L3R 0W5
Tel: (905) 475-8440
Fax: (905) 475-9560
Canadian magazine for the home woodworker
and do-it-yourself home improvement
enthusiast.
E-mail: letters@canadianworkshop.ca
Web site: http://www.canadianworkshop.ca

**Center For Resourceful
Building Technology**
PO Box 100, 516 S. Orange
Missoula, MT 59806
Tel: (406) 549-7678
Fax: (406) 549-4100
Non-profit educating the public on environ-
mentally responsible construction practices.

Colonial Homes
1790 Broadway, 14th Floor
New York, NY 10019
Tel: (212) 830-2910
Fax: (212) 586-3455
Colonial Homes is the authority on America's
design heritage.
E-mail: aberman@hearst.com

*Learning is understanding the subtle nuances.
Teaching is being able to say, "I've made that mistake
before."*

Construction Business & Computing
PO Box 2050, West Main St.
Richmond, VT 05477
Tel: (800) 375-5981
Fax: (802) 434-4467
Monthly newsletter on computer applications
and business techniques for construction
professionals.
E-mail: cbc@bginet.com
Web site: www.bginet.com

Country Journal
4 High Ridge Park
Stamford, CT 06905
Tel: (203) 321-1778, Fax: (203) 322-1966
Magazine serving readers who live in rural
areas.

Early American Life
Cowles History Group
6405 Flank Dr.
Harrisburg, PA 17112
Tel: (717) 540-6711
Artcles on restoration, replicas, historic paints,
fence patterns, period furniture, gardens,
recipes and many other Early American
interests.

Environmental Building News
RR 1, Box 161
Brattleboro, VT 05301
Tel: (802) 257-7300, Fax: (802) 257-7304
The leading publication on environmentally
responsible design and construction.
E-mail: ebn@ebuild.com
Web site: http://www.ebuild.com

Environ
PO Box 2204
Fort Collins, CO 80522
A national voice for environmental health and
lifestyles.

GCR Publishing Group, Inc.
1700 Broadway
New York, NY 10019
Tel: (212) 541-7100
Fax: (212) 245-1241
Publisher of Timber Homes Illustrated
magazine

Joiners' Quarterly
PO Box 249
Brownfield, ME 04010
Tel: (207) 935-3720, Fax: (207) 935-4575
The Journal of Timber Framing & Traditional Building. Blending modern technology with traditional craftsmanship, bringing innovative ideas for a sustainable future to the forefront.
E-mail: foxmaple@nxi.com
Web site: http://www.nxi.com/WWW/ joinersquarterly

Journal Of Light Construction
RR 2 Box 146, West Main St.
Richmond, VT 05477
Tel: (800) 375-5981, Fax: (802) 434-4467
Leading monthly magazine written by builders for builders.
Web site: www.bginet.com

Living History
Box 202
West Hurley, NY 12491
Dutch Barn Society. Information on local history.

NAHB Research Center
400 Prince George's Blvd.
Upper Marlboro, MD 20774-8731
Residential building research including innovative/alternative materials and systems.
E-mail: pyost@nahbrc.org
Web site: http://www.nahbrc.com

Old-House Journal (Dovetail Publishers)
2 Main St.
Gloucester, MA 01930
Tel: (508) 283-3200, Fax: (508) 283-4629
Bimonthly magazine about restoring, maintaining, and decorating pre-1940's houses.

Preservation Magazine
1785 Massachusetts Avenue NW
Washington, DC 20036
Tel: (202) 588-6068
Fax: (202) 588-6172
To go beyond old houses and historic sites.
Web site: www.nationaltrust.org

The Last Straw
PO Box 42000
Tucson, AZ 85733
Tel: (520) 882-3848
The Last Straw: the quarterly journal of straw-bale construction.
E-mail: thelaststraw@igc.apc.org
Web site: http://www.netchaos.com/+ls

Scantlings/Timber Framing
PO Box 1075
Bellingham, WA 98227-1075
Tel: (360) 733-4001, Fax: (360) 733-4002
Magazine of the Timber Framers Guild of North America

Timber Frame Homes Magazine
4200-T Lafayette Center Drive
Chantilly, VA 22021
Tel: (800) 850-7279 X128
Elegance & new ideas in timber framing four times a year.

Today's Woodworker Magazine
4365 Willow Dr.
Medina, MN 55340
Tel: (800) 610-0883
Woodworking projects, tips and techniques.
E-mail: editor@todayswoodworker.com
Web site: todayswoodworker.com

Tools of The Trade
PO Box 2001, West Main St.
Richmond, VT 05477
Tel: (800) 375-5981
Fax: (802) 434-4467
The only magazine devoted exclusively to tools for construction professionals.
Web site: www.bginet.com

Workshop frame raising at Heartwood Owner Builder School, Washington, MA.

Shaving tenons. A requisite part of a workshop raising.

Clay plaster being worked into straw bales in a bale and clay building workshop.

Publishers

Cappers
Ogden Publications
1503 SW 42nd Street
Topeka, KS 66609-1265
Tel: (785) 274-4330, Fax: (785) 274-4305
A family-oriented publication providing readers with "good news".
E-mail: cappers@kspress.com
Web site: www.cappers.com

Chelsea Green Publishing Company
PO Box 428
White River Junction, VT 05001
Tel: (802) 295-6300, Fax: (802) 295-6444
Publisher of quality books, specializing in alternative, natural & traditional homes for the owner/builder.

Construction Business & Computing
PO Box 2050, West Main St.
Richmond, VT 05477
Tel: (800) 375-5981, Fax: (802) 434-4467
Monthly newsletter on computer applications and business techniques for construction professionals.
E-mail: cbc@bginet.com
Web site: www.bginet.com

Craftsman Book Company
6058 Corte Del Cedro
Carlsbad, CA 92009
Tel: (800) 829-8123, Fax: (760) 438-0398
Professional construction books that solve actual problems in the builder's office and in the field.

Fine Homebuilding Magazine
PO Box 5506, 63 S. Main Street
Newtown, CT 06470-5506
Tel: (203) 426-8171, Fax: (203) 270-6751
Homebuilders share tips, techniques and reviews of tools and materials.
E-mail: fh@taunton.com
Web site: http://www.taunton.com

GCR Publishing Group, Inc.
1700 Broadway
New York, NY 10019
Tel: (212) 541-7100, Fax: (212) 245-1241
Publisher of Timber Homes Illustrated magazine.

Grit
Ogden Publications
1503 SW 42nd Street
Topeka, KS 66609-1265
Tel: (785) 274-4330, Fax: (785) 274-4305
Publication that preserves the best of family life and traditions.
E-mail: grit@kspress.com
Web site: www.oweb.com/grit

Iris Communications, Inc.
PO Box 5920
Eugene, OR 97405
Tel: (541) 484-9353, Fax: (541) 484-1645
Carefully selected books, videos and software for green construction.
E-mail: iris@oikos.com
Web site: www.oikos.com

JLC Bookstore
PO Box 2050, West Main St.
Richmond, VT 05477
Tel: (800) 859-3669, Fax: (802) 434-4467
Hard to find books for construction professionals.
Web site: bgibooks.com

Fox Maple Press, Inc.
PO Box 249, Corn hill Road
Brownfield, ME 04010
Tel: (207) 935-3720, Fax: (207) 935-4575
Publishing Joiners' Quarterly and books about traditional building methods and systems. Traditional building crafts a primary focus, while bringing innovative ideas for a sustainable future to the forefront.
E-mail: foxmaple@nxi.com
Web site: http://www.nxi.com/WWW/joinersquarterly

Journal Of Light Construction
RR 2 Box 146, West Main St.
Richmond, VT 05477
Tel: (800) 375-5981, Fax: (802) 434-4467
Leading monthly magazine written by builders for builders.
Web site: www.bginet.com

Tools Of The Trade
PO Box 2001, West Main St.
Richmond, VT 05477
Tel: (800) 375-5981, Fax: (802) 434-4467
The only magazine devoted exclusively to tools for construction professionals.
Web site: www.bginet.com

Building with Nature Newsletter
P.O. Box 4417
Santa Rosa, CA 95402-4417
Tel: (707) 579-2201
Information and inspiration about healthful, ecologically responsible spirited building.

Education & Information

Research

A & K Technical Services
PO Box 22
Anola, MB, Canada R0E 0A0
Tel: (204) 866-3262, Fax: (204) 866-3287
Structural engineering in wood. "Stackwall"
house construction design, consulting,
manual.
E-mail: krisdick@mb.sympatico.ca

Alaska Craftsman Home Program, Inc.
PO Box 241647
Anchorage, AK 99524-1647
Tel: (907) 258-2247 (ACHP),
Fax: (907) 258-5352
Education and research advanced cold
climate home building techniques.
E-mail: achp@alaska.net
Web site: http://www.alaska.net/~achp

Aprovecho Research Center
80574 Hazelton Road
Cottage Grove, OR 97424
Tel: (541) 942-8198
Fax: (541) 942-0302
Demonstration research and education center
for sustainable living.
E-mail: apro@efn.org/~apro
Web site: http://www.efn.org/~apro

Berkshire House Publishers
480 Pleasant Street, Suite 5
Lee, MA 01238
Tel: (800) 321-8526
Fax: (413) 243-0303
Explore colonial barn lore with master
restorer Richard Babcock.

Carroll, Franck & Associates
1357 Highland Parkway
St. Paul, MN 55116
Tel: (612) 690-9162
Fax: (612) 690-9156
Engineering of architectural structures,
traditional joinery and concealed steel
connections.
E-mail: carrfran@gold.tc.umn.edu

Community Eco-Design Network
PO Box 6241, 3151-29th Ave. S, #103
Minneapolis, MN 55406
Tel: (612) 306-2326
Super-insulated construction planbook, design
services, northern climate strawbale building
system.
E-mail: erichart@mtn.org
Web site: http://www.umn.edu/n/home/m037/
kurtdand/cen

Energy Efficient Building Association
2950 Metro Drive #108
Minneapolis, MN 55425
Tel: (612) 851-9940
Fax: (612) 851-9507
EEBA produces & presents training based on
the "systems approach".
E-mail: EEBANews@aol.com
Web site: http://www.eeba.org

Journal Of Light Construction
RR 2 Box 146, West Main St.
Richmond, VT 05477
Tel: (800) 375-5981
Fax: (802) 434-4467
Leading monthly magazine written by builders
for builders.
Web site: www.bginet.com

Midway Village & Museum Center
6799 Guilford Road
Rockford, IL 61107
Tel: (815) 397-9112
Fax: (815) 397-9156
Turn-of-the-century village and Rockford area
history center.

NAHB Research Center
400 Prince George's Blvd.
Upper Marlboro, MD 20774-8731
Residential building research including
innovative/alternative materials and systems.
E-mail: pyost@nahbrc.org
Web site: http://www.nahbrc.com

ORNL Buildings Technology Center
PO Box 2008, 1 Bethel Valley Road
Oak Ridge, TN 37831
Tel: (423) 574-4345
Fax: (423) 574-9338
Whole wall & roof R-value measurements.
E-mail: jef@ornl.gov
Web site: www.ornl.gov/roofs+walls

Software

Tree Talk
PO Box 426, 431 Pine Street
Burlington, VT 05402
Tel: (802) 865-1111, Fax: (802) 863-4344
Multimedia CD-ROM on wood. 900 species.
Database. Video. Pictures. Maps.
E-mail: wow@together.net
Web site: www.woodweb.com/~treetalk/
home.html

Passive Solar Industries Council
1511 K Street, Suite 600
Washington, DC 20005
Tel: (202) 628-7400, Fax: (202) 393-5043
PSIC independent nonprofit advancing climate
responsive buildings.
E-mail: PSICouncil@aol.com
Web site: http://www.psic.org

Videos

Alaska Craftsman Home Program, Inc.
PO Box 241647
Anchorage, AK 99524-1647
Tel: (907) 258-2247 (ACHP)
Fax: (907) 258-5352
Education and research advanced cold
climate home building techniques.
E-mail: achp@alaska.net
Web site: http://www.alaska.net/~achp

Bailey's
PO Box 550, 44650 Hwy. 101
Laytonville, CA 95454
Tel: (800) 322-4539
Fax: (707) 984-8115
Free catalog: world's largest mail order
woodsman supplies company.
E-mail: baileys@bbaileyscom
Web site: http://www.bbaileys.com

Canterbury Shaker Village
288 Shaker Road
Canterbury, NH 03224
Tel: (603) 783-9511
Fax: (603) 783-9152
From tree to beam–hand-hewing with Dan
Dustin. 58 minutes.
E-mail: shakervillage@mv.mv.com

Cob Cottage Co.
PO Box 123
Cottage Grove, OR 97424
Tel: (541) 942-2005
Fax: (541) 942-3021
Information and workshops on building with
cob (sand, clay, straw).
Web site: http://www.deatech.com/cobcottage

Earthwood Building School
366 Murtagh Hill Road
West Chazy, NY 12992
(518) 493-7744
Fax: same, phone first
Teaches cordwood masonry and underground
housing. Books, videos and workshops.
Web site: http://www.interlog.com/newood

Fine Homebuilding Magazine
PO Box 5506, 63 S. Main Street
Newtown, CT 06470-5506
Tel: (203) 426-8171
Fax: (203) 270-6751
Homebuilders share tips, techniques and
reviews of tools and materials.
E-mail: fh@taunton.com
Web site: http://www.taunton.com

Freedom Builders
1013 Naples Drive
Orlando, FL 32804
Tel: (407) 647-5849
Fax: (407) 645-5652
Internet informational & advertising site—log &
t.f. design—video productions.
E-mail: freedom@magicnet.net
Web site: www.magicnet.net/freedom

Workshop Raising

Goldec International Equipment, Inc.
6760 65 Ave.
Red Deer, Alberta, Canada T4R 1G5
Tel: (403) 343-6607
Fax: (403) 340-0640
De-bark logs with our chainsaw attachment.
The amazing Log Wizard!
E-mail: goldec@telusplanet.net
Web site: goldec.com

Iris Communications, Inc.
PO Box 5920
Eugene, OR 97405
Tel: (541) 484-9353
Fax: (541) 484-1645
Carefully selected books, videos and
software for green construction.
E-mail: iris@oikos.com
Web site: www.oikos.com

Lofty Branch Bookstore
PO Box 512
Victor, NY 14564
Tel: (716) 742-2607
Fax: (716) 289-3221
Over 350 timber framing, construction,
design and woodworking books/videos.
E-mail: loftybooks@aol.com
Web site: http://members.aol.com.loftybooks

Lok-N-Logs, Inc.
PO Box 677, Route 12
Sherburne, NY 13460
Tel: (800) 343-8928, (607) 674-4447
Fax: (607) 674-6433
Producer of top quality, pre-cut log home
packages–lifetime limited warranty!
E-mail: lnlinfo@loknlogs.com
Web site: http://www.loknlogs.com
Catalog: $12.95

Natural Building Resources
Star Rt. 2, Box 119
Kingston, NM 88042
Tel: (505) 895-5652
Fax: (505) 895-3326
Books and videos on natural building. Host—
Natural Building Colloquium.
E-mail: blackrange@zianet.com
Web site: www.zianet.com/blackrange

Out On Bale By Mail
1039 E. Linden St.
Tucson, AZ 85719
Tel: (520) 624-1673
Fax: (520) 299-9099
Educational materials for straw bale building.
Help for owner builders.
E-mail: outonbale@aol.com

Sustainable Systems Support
PO Box 318
Bisbee, AZ 85603
Tel: (520) 432-4292
Offers books and videos on plastered straw
bale construction, including an excellent 90
min. "how-to" video with a 62 page manual.
Wall raising workshops and consultations.

The Canelo Project
HCL Box 324
Elgin, AZ 85611
Tel: (520) 455-5548
Fax: (520) 455-9360
Straw bale building/earthen floors and
plasters, workshops, resources, consulting.
E-mail: absteen@dakotacom.net
Web site: http://www.deatech.com/canelo

Workshops & Conferences

Country Workshops
90 Mill Creek Road
Marshall, NC 28753
Tel: (704) 656-2280
Tools, books and instruction in traditional
woodworking with hand tools
E-mail: langsner@countryworkshops.org
Web site: countryworkshops.org

Alaska Craftsman Home Program, Inc.
PO Box 241647
Anchorage, AK 99524-1647
Tel: (907) 258-2247 (ACHP)
Fax: (907) 258-5352
Education and research advanced cold
climate home building techniques
E-mail: achp@alaska.net
Web site: http://www.alaska.net/~achp

**Construction Business & Technology
Conference**
PO Box 2010, West Main St.
Richmond, VT 05477
Tel: (800) 375-5981, Fax: (802) 434-4467
Unique conference and expo featuring
practical information and hands-on learning
opportunities.
E-mail: cbtc@bginet.com
Web site: www.bginet.com

Internet Web Sites & E-mail Addresses

The internet has become an increasingly valuable tool, not only in bringing new products and ideas to the world, but as an efficient and cost-effective form of communication, a very inexpensive means of advertising, and a forum for companies and individuals to express their goals and initiatives to the global marketplace. With more than 50 million users already online, and an average of 40,000 more added every day, it's obvious that it will soon become a necessary function of business, and a mainstay in most households in the near future. Web sites are becoming increasingly easier to create—there's no longer any need to learn HTML—and plenty of programs are already available that are little more complicated than word-processing programs. Many come with thousands of images to make pages both professional and informative. Encrypting devices have made instant fiscal transactions secure and reliable. As the following list of individuals and companies makes evident, the benefits of the internet are currently online and operational.

However, the technology of the World Wide Web is constantly evolving. Because of this, many websites move frequently, flocking to servers that offer lower rates at faster speeds. Therefore, while the URLs listed below are current, it won't be long before many of them have moved to other locations, and these addresses will become obsolete. Seasoned internet aficionados may know how to search out the company's listed in the following pages regardless of any changes that may come about. For those who are new to the web, sites can often be located by keying in the primary word or symbol sequence of the URL address into any one of the many search engines available. If this fails, keying in the company name will often turn up the web site—if they still have one. Most successful sites are linked to many more of the same interest group. The odds are good, no matter what changes may come about, that many of the listings in the following pages will maintain links with each other for a long time to come.

The listings that appear in the following section are categorized by product type as supplied by the companies listed. Listings may be duplicated if they offer more than one product or service that fell into categories listed in our initial product selections questionnaire.

Designing & Planning

Passive Solar Industries Council
E-mail: PSICouncil@aol.com
Web site: http://www.psic.org

Community Eco-Design Network
E-mail: erichart@mtn.org
Web site: http://www.umn.edu/n/home/m037/
kurtdand/cen

Straw Works
E-mail: Straw-Works@juno.com

Hugh Lofting Timber Framing, Inc.
E-mail: hlofting@aol.com

Center For Maximum Potential Building
Systems
E-mail: max_pot@txinfinet.com
Web site: http://www.maxpot.com/maxpot

Richard Berg, Architect
E-mail: rberg@olympus.net

Jean Steinbrecher Architects
E-mail: jsa@whidbey.com

Greenbuilder
E-mail:
Web site: http://www.greenbuilder.com

The Canelo Project
E-mail: absteen@dakotacom.net
Web site: http://www.deatech.com/canelo

Eos Institute
E-mail: eos@igpc.org

Freedom Builders
E-mail: freedom@magicnet.net/freedom
Web site: http://www.magicnet.net/freedom

Upper Loft Design, Inc.
Web site: http://www.upperloft@stc.net

Elemental Resources
E-mail: cvdow@aol.com

The Raven River Co., Inc.
E-mail: ravenriver@kitt.net

Bamboo Fencer
E-mail: dave@bamboofencer.com
Web site: http://www.bamboofencer.com

Talmage Solar Engineering, Inc.
E-mail: tse@talmagesolar.com
Web site: http://www.talmagesolar.com

Connolly & Co. Timber Frame Homes & Barns
E-mail: connolly@lincoln.midcoast.com

Fox Maple School of Trad. Building
E-mail: foxmaple@nxi.com
Web site: http://www.nxi.com/WWW/
joinersquarterly

Carroll, Franck & Associates
E-mail: carrfran@gold.tc.umn.edu

Goshen Timber Frames, Inc.
E-mail: goshen@dnet.net
Web site: http://www.timberframemag.com

Barkeater Design Build Company
E-mail: barkeater@slic.com
Web site: http://www.xlic.com/~barkeater/
home.html

Terry F. Johnson Building Design
E-mail: sarah@peak.org

Memphremagog Heat Exchangers, Inc.
E-mail: info@mhevt.com
Web site: http://www.mhevt.com

Environmental Building News
E-mail: ebn@ebuild.com
Web site: http://www.ebuild.com

Greenfire Institute
E-mail: greenfire@agc.org
Web site: http://www.balewolf.com

A & K Technical Services
E-mail: krisdick@mb.sympatico.ca

Northern Timberhouse, Ltd.
E-mail: nortim@halhinet.on.ca

International Institute for Bau-Biologie
E-mail: baubiologie@earthlink.net
Web site: http://www.bau-biologieusa.com

Timber Framing

Hearthstone Log & Timberframe Homes
(Macon, GA)
E-mail: hearthstonehomes@mindspring.com
Web site: http://www.mindspring.com/-
hearthstonehomes

Upper Loft Design, Inc.
Web site: http://www.upperloft@stc.net

Jeff Pedersen–Logsmith
E-mail: jplogs@cyberhighway.net

The Edge Woodworks
E-mail: edgewrks@gtec.com

The Raven River Co., Inc.
E-mail: ravenriver@kitt.net

New England Preservation Services
E-mail: 74131.1254@Compuserve.com

The Timber Framers Guild of North America
E-mail: mccarty@top.monad.net
Web site: http://tfguild.org

The Heartwood School
E-mail: info@heartwoodschool.com
Web site: http://www.heartwoodshcool.com

Connolly & Co. Timber Frame Homes & Barns
E-mail: connolly@lincoln.midcoast.com

Authentic Timberframes
E-mail: tenon@nxi.com
Web site: http://timberframe.maine.com

Fox Maple School of Traditional Building
E-mail: foxmaple@nxi.com
Web site: http://www.nxi.com/WWW/
joinersquarterly

Mountain Construction Enterprises
E-mail: Mtnconst@skybest.com
Web site: http://blowingrock.com/nc/
timberframe

Goshen Timber Frames, Inc.
E-mail: goshen@dnet.net
Web site: http://www.timberframemag.com

Timberpeg
E-mail: info@timberpeg.com
Web site: http://www.timberpeg.com

Great Northern Barns
E-mail: ejl@endor.com
Web site: http://www.greatnorthernbarns.com

New Energy Works of Rochester, Inc.
E-mail: jononewt@aol.com

Hugh Lofting Timber Framing, Inc.
E-mail: hlofting@aol.com

Pocono Mt. Timber Frames
E-mail: etreible@ptd.net
Web site: http://www.pmtf.com

Bruce Cowie Timber Frames
E-mail: bruce220@juno.com

Hearthstone, Inc. (Dandridge, Tennessee)
E-mail: sales@hearthstonehomes.com
Web site: http://www.hearthstonehomes.com

Kondor Post & Beam
E-mail: kondor@sover.net
Web site: http://www.kondorinc.com

Vermont Frames
E-mail: foamlam@sover.net
Web site: http://www.sover.net/~foamlam

Richard Berg, Architect
E-mail: rberg@olympus.net]

Timbercraft Homes, Inc.
E-mail: info@timbercraft.com
Web site: http://www.timbercraft.com

Alderaan Stone/Timber Homes
Web site: http://www.craftsman-book.com

Northern Timberhouse, Ltd.
E-mail: nortim@halhinet.on.ca

Log Homes

Freedom Builders
E-mail:freedom@magicnet.net
Web site: http://www.magicnet.net/freedom

Hearthstone Log & Timberframe Homes
E-mail: hearthstonehomes@mindspirng.com
Web site: http://www.mincspring.com/
~hearthstonehomes

Jeff Pedersen–Logsmith
E-mail: jplogs@cyberhighway.net

Northern Land & Lumber Co.
E-mail: nlandl@up.net
Web site: http://www.deltami.org/nlandl

Mountain Construction Enterprises
E-mail: Mtnconst@skybest.com
Web site: http://blowingrock.com/nc/
timberframe

Timberfab, Inc.
E-mail: tfab@coastalnet.com
Web site: http://www4.coastalnet.com/
timberfab

Lok-N-Logs, Inc.
E-mail: lnlinfo@loknlogs.com
Web site: http://www.loknlogs.com

Hearthstone, Inc. (Dandridge, TN)
E-mail: sales@hearthstonehomes.com
Web site: http://www.hearthstonehomes.com

Real Log Homes
Web site: http://www.realloghomes.com

Timbercraft Homes, Inc.
E-mail: info@timbercraft.com
Web site: http://www.timbercraft.com

Goldec International Equipment, Inc.
E-mail: goldec@telusplanet.net
Web site: http://www.goldec.com

Northern Timberhouse, Ltd.
E-mail: nortim@halhinet.on.ca

Boatbuilding
The Center For Wooden Boats
E-mail:cwboats@eskimo.com/~cwboats

Strawbale Construction

The Canelo Project
E-mail: absteen@dakotacom.net
Web site: http://www.deatech.com/canelo

The Last Straw
E-mail: thelaststraw@igc.apc.org
Web site: http://www.netchaos.com/+ls

Out On Bale By Mail
E-mail: outonbale@aol.com

Solar Energy International
E-mail: sei@solarenergy.org
Web site: http://www.solarenergy.org

Proclay
E-mail: foxmaple.nxi.com
Web site: http://www.nxi.com/WWW/
joinersquarterly

Community Eco-Design network
E-mail: erichart@mtn.org
Web site: http://www.umn.edu/n/home/m037/
kurtdand/cen

Straw Works
E-mail:
Web site: http://Straw-Works@juno.com

Aprovecho Research Center
E-mail: apro@efn.org/~apro
Web site: http://www/efn.org/~apro

Yestermorrow Design/Build School
E-mail: ymschool@aol.com
Web site: http://www.yestermorrow.org

Greenfire Institute
E-mail: greenfire@igc.org
Web site: http://www.balewolf.com

Sustainable Building

The Last Straw
E-mail: thelaststraw@igc.apc.org
Web site: http://www.netchaos.com/+ls

Solar Energy International
E-mail: sei@solarenergy.org
Web site: http://www.psic.org

Eco-Building Schools (Sandra Leibowitz)
Web site: http://www.ecodesign.org/edi/eden

Lite-Form International
E-mail: liteform@pionet.net
Web site: http://www.pionet.net/~liteform/
index.html

Agriboard Industries
E-mail: agriboard@lisco.com

The Heartwood School
E-mail: info@heartwoodshcool.com
Web site: http://www.heartwoodschool.com

Talmage Solar Engineering, Inc.
E-mail: tse@talmagesolar.com
Web site: http://www.talmagesolar.com

Fox Maple of Traditional Building
E-mail: foxmaple@nxi.com
Web site: http://www.nxi.com/WWW/
joinersquarterly

Cob Cottage Co.
Web site: http://www.deatech.com/cobcottage

Terry F. Johnson Building Design
E-mail: sarah@peak.org

Aprovecho Research Center
E-mail: apro@efn.org/~apro
Web site: http://www.efn.org/~apro

Center For Maximum Potential Building
Systems
E-mail: max_pot@txinfinet.com
Web site: http://www.maxpot.com/maxpot

Groundworks
Web site: http://www.cpros.com/~sequoia

Hugh Lofting Timber Framing, Inc.
E-mail: hlofting@aol.com

ORNL   Buildings Technology Center
E-mail: jef@oml.gov
Web site: http://www.oml.gov/roofs+walls

Masonry Heater Association of North America
Web site: http://mha-net.org/

Yestermorrow Design/Build School
E-mail: ymschool@aol.com
Web site: http://www.yestermorrow.org

Environmental Building News
E-mail: ebn@ebuild.com
Web site: http://www.ebuild.com

Alternative Building Systems

Pumice-Crete Building Systems
E-mail: machardy@newmex.com
Web site: www.taosnet.com/pumice-crete/
index.html

Advanced Earthen Construction Technologies,
Inc.
E-mail: vwehman@connecti.com

A & K Technical Services.
E-mail: krisdick@mb.sympatico.ca

Davis Caves Construction, Inc.
E-mail: earthome@daviscaves.com
Web site: www.daviscaves.com/builder.htm

Center For Maximum Potential Building
Systems
E-mail: max_pot@txinfinet.com
Web site: http://www.maxpot.com/maxpot

Wood/Timbers

Sirocco Trading Company
E-mail: eeh3@sedona.net

Granberg International
E-mail: granberg@aol.com
Web site: http://www.granberg.com

Michael Evenson Natural Resources
E-mail: evenson@igc.apc.org

Hull Forest Products
Web site: http://www.HullForest.com

Tropical American Tree Farms
E-mail: tatfsa.sol.racsa.co.cr

Vintage Lumber Co., Inc.
E-mail: woodfloors@vintagelumber.com
Web site: http://www.vintagelumber.com

Natural Knees
E-mail: kneeman@somtel.com

Northern Land & Lumber Co.
E-mail: nlandl@up.net
Web site: http://www.deltami.org/nlandl

Great Northern Barns
E-mail: ejl@endor.com
Web site: http://www.greatnorthernbarns.com

M. Fine Lumber Co., Inc.
E-mail: merritf@fine-lumber.com
Web site: http://www.fine-lumber.com/
lumber.html

Conklin's Authentic Barnwood
E-mail: conklins@epix.net
Web site: http://www.conklinsbarnwood.com

Pocono Mt. Timber Frames
E-mail: etreible@ptd.net
Web site: http://www.pmtf.com

Hearthstone, Inc. (Dandridge, TN)
E-mail: sales@hearthstonehomes.com
Web site: http://www.hearthstonehomes.com

Trestlewood
(A Division Of Cannon Structures, Inc.)
E-mail: bradnat@burgoyne.com

Recycled Lumber

Sirroco Trading Company
E-mail: eeh3@sedona.net

Michael Evenson Natural Resources
E-mail: evenson@igc.apc.org

Jefferson Recycled Woodworks
E-mail: goodwood@telis.org
Web site: http://www.ecowood.com

Vintage Lumber Co., Inc.
E-mail: woodfloors@vintagelumber.com
Web site: http://www.vintagelumber.com

Carlisle Restoration Lumber
Web site: http://www.wideplankflooring.com

New Energy Works of Rochester, Inc.
E-mail: jononewt@aol.com

M. Fine Lumber Co., Inc.
E-mail: merritf@fine-lumber.com
Web site: http://www.fine-lumber.com/
lumber.html

Conklin's Authentic Barnwood
E-mail: conkilns@epix.net
Web site: http://www.conklinsbarnwood.com

Trestlewood
E-mail: bradnate@burgoyne.com

Mountain Lumber Co.
E-mail: sales@mountainlumber.com
Web site: http://www.mountainlumber.com

Sustainable/Certified Wood Suppliers

Michael Evenson Natural Resources
E-mail: evenson@igc.apc.org

Jefferson Recycled Woodworks
E-mail: goodwood@telis.org
Web site: http://www.ecowood.com

Natural Knees
E-mail: kneeman@somtel.com

Bamboo Fencer
E-mail: Dave@bamboofencer.com
Web site: http://www.bamboofencer.com

Northern Land & Lumber Co.
E-mail: nlandl@up.net
Web site: http://www.deltami.org.nlandl

The Woodworkers' Store
E-mail: rocklerl@pclink.com
Web site: http://www.woodworkerstore.com

Midwest Hardwood Corp.
E-mail: MWHWD@ix.netcom.com

Conklin's Authentic Barnwood
E-mail: conklins@epix.net
Web site: http://conklinsbarnwood.com

Tree Talk
E-mail: wow@together.net
Web site: http://www.woodweb.com/~treetalk/
home.html

Environmental Home Center
E-mail: info@enviresource.com
Web site: http://www.enviresource.com

Tools

Bailey's
E-mail: baileys@bbaileys.com
Web site: http://www.bbaileys.com

Granberg International
E-mail: granberg@aol.com
Web site: http://www.granberg.com

International Tool Corporation
Web site: http://www.internationaltool.com

Estwing Mfg. Co.
E-mail: estwing@estwing.com
Web site: http://www.estwing.com

Wood-Mizer Products, Inc.
E-mail: adindy@woodmizer.com
Web site: http://www.woodmizer.com

Lie-Nielsen Toolworks, Inc.
E-mail: toolworks@lie-nielsen.com
Web site: http://www.lie-nielsen.com

The Woodworkers' Store
E-mail: rocklerl@pclink.com
Web site: http://www.woodworkerstore.com

Country Workshops
E-mail: langsner@countryworkshops.org
Web site: http://www.countryworkshops.org

Tool Crib of the North
E-mail: kcolman@corpcomm.net
Web site: http://www.toolcribofthenorth.com

Lee Valley Tools
Web site: http://www.leevalley.com

Martin J. Donnelly Antique Tools
E-mail: MJDtools@servtech.com

Trow & Holden Co.
E-mail: trowco@aol.com

Tools of the Trade
Web site: http://www.bginet.com

Bethel Mills, Inc.
E-mail: bml@sover.net
Web site: http://bethelmills.com

Woodcraft Supply
E-mail: custserv@woodcraft.com
Web site: http://www.woodcraft.com

Portable Sawmills/ Machinery

Wilke Machinery Co.
Web site: http://www.wilkemach.com

Sawmill Exchange
E-mail: nml@mindspring.com
(Note: letter preceding @ is an "L")
Web site: http://www.sawmill-exchange.com/

Granberg International
E-mail: granberg@aol.com
Web site: http://www.granberg.com

The Edge Woodworks
E-mail: edgewrks@gtec.com

Wood-Mizer Products, Inc.
E-mail: adindy@woodmizer.com
Web site: http://www.woodmizer.com

Norwood Industries, Inc.
E-mail: norwood@norwoodindustries.com
Web site: http://www.norwoodindustries.com

Pocono Mt. Timber Frames
E-mail: etreible@ptd.net
Web site: http://www.pmtf.com

Goldec International Equipment, Inc.
E-mail: goldec@TelusPlanet.net
Web site: http://goldec.com

Natural Enclosure Systems

Clay

Proclay
E-mail: foxmaple@nxi.com
Web site: http://www.nxi.com/WWW/ joinersquarterly

Superior Clay Corporation
E-mail: mcclave@tusconet.com
Web site: http://www.rumford.com

Cob Cottage Company
Web site: http://www.deatech.com/cobcottage

Strawbale
See Strawbale Construction (under Building Methods & Systems)

Thatch

Custom Roof Thatching & Supplies
Web site: http://www.roofthatch.com

Wheat Straw Panels

Agriboard Industries
E-mail: agriboard@lisco.com

Structural Panel Systems

Upper Loft Design, Inc.
Web site: http://www.upperloft.com

AFM Corporation
E-mail: afmcorp@worldnet.att.net
Web site: http://www.afmcorp-spsfoam.com

Foard Panel
E-mail: shippees@sover.net

Insulating Concrete Forms

Lite-Form International
E-mail: liteform@pionet.net
Web site: http://www.pionet.net/~liteform/ index.html

Mechanical Systems

Air Exchangers

Memphremagog Heat Exchangers, Inc.
E-mail: info@mhevt.com
Web site: http://www.mhevt.com

Passive Solar Industries Council
E-mail: PSICouncil@aol.com
Web site: http://www.psic.org

Radiant Heat

New England and Soapstone
E-mail: nehearth@bigfoot.com
Web site: http://mha-net.org/users/nehs

Easy Heat, Inc.
E-mail: mgb~1@msn.com
Web site: http://www.easyheat.com

Maxxon Corporation
E-mail: debi@maxxon.com
Web site: http://www.maxxon.com

Cornerstone Masonry Distributing, Inc.
E-mail: radiant@alpinet.com
Web site: http://www.tulikivi.com

Radiant Technology
E-mail: radtech2@usa.pipeline.com
Web site: http://www.radiant-tech.com

Top Hat Chimney Sweeps D.B.A. TNT Masonry Heaters
Web site: http://mha-net.org/users/tnt/ index.htm

Masonry Heater Association of North America
Web site: http://mha-net.org/

Alternative Heating Systems

Masonry Heaters

New England Hearth and Soapstone
E-mail: nehearth@bigfoot.com
Web site: http://mha-net.org/users/nehs/

Brick Stove Works
E-mail: jpmanly@midcoast.com

Cornerstone Masonry Distributing, Inc.
E-mail: radiant@alpinet.com
Web site: http://www.tulikivi.com

Superior Clay Corporation
E-mail: mcclave@tusconet.com
Web site: http://rumford.com

Top Hat Chimney Sweeps D.B.A. TNT Masonry Heaters
Web site: http://mha-net.org/users/tnt/ index.htm

Masonry Heater Association of North America
Web site: http://mha-net.org/

Temp-Cast Enviroheat Ltd.
E-mail: staywarm@tempcast.com
Web site: http://www.tempcast.com

Renewable Energy

Solar Energy International
E-mail: sei@solarenergy.org
Web site: http://www.solarenergy.org

Elemental Resources
E-mail: cvdow@aol.com

Solar Energy

Sierra Solar Systems
E-mail: solarjon@oro.net
Web site: http://www.sierrasolar.com

Talmage Solar Engineering, Inc.
E-mail: tse@talmagesolar.com
Web site: http://www.talmagesolar.com

Architectural Millwork

Jefferson Recycled Woodworks
E-mail: goodwood@telis.org
Web site: http://www.ecowood.com

Shuttercraft, Inc.
E-mail: shutter@iconn.net
Web site: http://www.galaxymall.com/shops/ shuttercraft.html

New England Preservation Services
E-mail: 74131.1254@Compuserve.com

Amherst Woodworking & Supply, Inc.
E-mail: amwooco@copperbeech.com
Web site: http://www.copperbeech.com

Architectural Components, Inc.
E-mail: arch.components.inc@worldnet.att.net

Forester Moulding & Lumber
Web site: http://www.forestermoulding.com

New Energy Works of Rochester
E-mail: jononewt@aol.com

Flooring

Vintage Lumber Co., Inc.
E-mail: woodfloors@vintagelumber.com
Web site: http://www.vintagelumber.com

Carlisle Restoration Lumber
Web site: http://www.wideplankflooring.com

Mountain Lumber Co.
E-mail: sales@mountainlumber.com
Web site: http://www.mountainlumber.com

Hardware

Tremont Nail Co.
E-mail: cutnails@aol.com

The Woodworkers' Store
E-mail: rocklerl@pclink.com
Web site: http://www.woodworkerstore.com

Lee Valley Tools
Web site: http://www.leevalley.com

Kestrel Shutters
E-mail: kestrel@fast.net
Web site: http://www.diyshutters.com

Bethel Mills, Inc.
E-mail: bml@sover.net
Web site: http://www.bethelmills.com

Woodcraft Supply
E-mail: custserv@woodcraft.com
Web site: http://www.woodcraft.com

Natural, Low Toxic Paints & Finishes

Environmental Home Center
E-mail: info@enviresource.com
Web site: http://www.enviresource.com

Shutters

Shuttercraft, Inc.
E-mail: shutter@iconn.net
Web site: http://www.galaxymall.com/shops/shuttercraft.html

Kestrel Shutters
E-mail: kestrel@fast.net
Web site: http://www.diyshutters.com

Windows & Doors

Amherst Woodworking & Supply, Inc.
E-mail: amwooco@copperbeech.com
Web site: http://www.copperbeech.com

Architectural Components, Inc.
E-mail: arch.components.inc@worldnet.att.net

Hurd Millwork Company
Web site: http://www.hurd.com

Restoration

Jeff Pedersen–Logsmith
E-mail: jplogs@cyberhighway.net

New England Preservation Services
E-mail: 74131.1254@Compuserve.com

Architectural Components, Inc.
E-mail: arch.components.inc@worldnet.att.net

Tremont Nail Co.
E-mail: cutnails@aol.com

Forester Moulding & Lumber
Web site: http://www.forestermoulding.com

Connolly & Co. Timber Frame Homes & Barns
E-mail: connolly@lincoln.midcoast.com

Authentic Timberframes
E-mail: tenon@nxi.com
Web site: http://timberframe.maine.com

Great Northern Barns
E-mail: ejl@endor.com
Web site: http://www.greatnorthernbarns.com

M. Fine Lumber Co., Inc.
E-mail: merritf@fine-lumber.com
Web site: http://www.fine-lumber.com/lumber.html

Trow & Holden Co.
E-mail: trowco@aol.com

Abatron, Inc.
E-mail: info@abatron.com
Web site: http://www.abatron.com

Specialty Products & Services

Bamboo Fencer
E-mail: Dave@bamboofencer.com
Web site: http://www.bamboofencer.com

International Institute for Bau-Biologie
E-mail: baubiologie@earthlink.net
Web site: http://www.bau-biologieusa.com

Hearthstone Log & Timberframe Homes
E-mail: hearthstonehomes@mindspring.com
Web site: http://www.mindspring.com/~hearthstonehomes

Sandra Leibowitz
Eco-Building Schools
Web site: http://www.ecodesign.org/edi/eden

Construction Business & Technology Conference
E-mail: cbtc@bginet.com
Web site: http://www.bginet.com

Snorkel Stove Company
E-mail: hottubs@snorkel.com
Web site: http://www.snorkel.com

Lite-Form International
E-mail: liteform@pionet.net
Web site: http://www.pionet.net/~liteform/index.html

Environmental Home Center
E-mail: info@enviresource.com
Web site: http://www.enviresource.com

Wilke Machinery Co.
Web site: http://www.wilkemach.com

Hancock Shaker Village
E-mail: info@hancockshakervillage
Web site: http://www.hancockshakervillage.org

Easy Heat, Inc.
E-mail: mgb~1@msn.com
Web site: http://www.easyheat.com

Shuttercraft, Inc.
E-mail: shutter@iconn.net
Web site: http://www.galaxymall.com/shops/shuttercraft.html

Kestrel Shutters
E-mail: kestrel@fast.net
Web site: http://www.diyshutters.com

Tree Talk
E-mail: wow@together.net
Web site: http://www.woodweb.com/~treetalk/home.html

Passive Solar Industries Council
E-mail: PSICouncil@aol.com
Web site: http://www.psic.org

A & K Technical Services.
E-mail: krisdick@mb.sympatico.ca

Carroll, Franck & Associates
E-mail: carrfran@gold.tc.umn.edu

Agriboard Industries
E-mail: agriboard@lisco.com

Woodmaster Foundations, Inc.
E-mail: woodmstr@pressenter.com
Web site: http://www.pressenter.com/~woodmstr/

Country Workshops
E-mail: langsner@countryworkshops.org
Web site: http://www.countryworkshops.org

Alaska Craftsman Home Program, Inc.
E-mail: achp@alaska.net/~achp
Web site: http://www.alaska.net/~achp

Custom Roof Thatching & Supplies
Web site: http://www.roofthatch.com

Abatron, Inc.
E-mail: info@abatron.com
Web site: http://www.abatron.com

Education & Information

Books & Publications

Alaska Craftsman Home Program, Inc.
E-mail: achp@alaska.net/~achp
Web site: http://www.alaska.net/~achp

The Canelo Project
E-mail: absteen@dakotacom.net
Web site: http://www.deatech.com/canelo

Out On Bale By Mail
E-mail: outonbale@aol.com

Fine Homebuilding Magazine
E-mail: tf@taunton.com
Web site: http://www.taunton.com

Cappers
E-mail: cappers@kspress.com
Web site: http://www.cappers.com

Grit
E-mail: grit@kspress.com
Web site: http://www.oweb.com/grit

NAHB Research Center
E-mail: pyost@nahbrc.org
Web site: http://www.nahbrc.com

Joiners' Quarterly
E-mail: foxmaple@nxi.com
Web site: http://www.nxi.com/WWW/joinersquarterly

Country Workshops
E-mail: langsner@countryworkshops.org
Web site: http://www.countryworkshops.org

Natural Building Resources
E-mail: blackrange@zianet.com
Web site: http://www.zianet.com/blackrange

Lofty Branch Bookstore
E-mail: loftybooks@aol.com
Web site: http://members.aol.com.loftybooks

Earthwood Building School
Web site: http://www.interlog.com/newood

Lee Valley Tools Ltd.
Web site: http://www.leevalley.com

Custom Roof Thatching & Supplies
Web site: http://www.roofthatch.com

Iris Communications, Inc.
E-mail: iris@oikos.com
Web site: http://www.oikos.com

Groundworks
Web site: http://www.cpros.com/~sequoia

JLC Bookstore
Web site: http://www.bgibooks

Tree Talk
E-mail: wow@together.net
Web site: http://www.woodweb.com/~treetalk/home.html

Woodcraft Supply
E-mail: custserv@woodcraft.com
Web site: http://www.woodcraft.com

Canadian Workshop
E-mail: letters@canadianworkshop.ca
Web site: http://www.canadianworkshop.ca

Colonial Homes
E-mail: aberman@hearst.com

Construction Business & Computing
E-mail: cbc@bginet.com
Web site: http://www.bginet.com

Environmental Building News
E-mail: ebn@ebuild.com
Web site: http://www.ebuild.com

Hancock Shaker Village
E-mail: info@hancockshakervillage
Web site: http://www.hancockshakervillage.org

Journal of Light Construction
Web site: http://www.bginet.com

Preservation Magazine
Web site: http://www.nationaltrust.org

The Last Straw
E-mail: thelaststraw@igc.apc.org
Web site: http://www.netchaos.com/+ls

Today's Woodworker
E-mail: editor@todayswoodworker.com
Web site: http://www.todayswoodworker.com

Tools of the Trade
Web site: http://www.bginet.com

Catalogs

Bailey's
E-mail: baileys@bbaileys.com
Web site: http://www.bbaileys.com

Sierra Solar Systems
E-mail: solarjon@oro.net
Web site: http://www.sierrasolar.com

International Tool Corporation
Web site: http://www.internationaltool.com

Wood-Mizer Products, Inc.
E-mail: adindy@woodmizer.com
Web site: http://www.woodmizer.com

Tremont Nail Co.
E-mail: cutnails@aol.com

Natural Knees
E-mail: kneeman@somtel.com

Tool Crib of the North
E-mail: kcolman@corpcomm.net
Web site: http://www.toolcribothenorth.com

Lofty Branch Bookstore
E-mail: loftybooks@aol.com
Web site: http://members.aol.com.loftybooks

Lok-N-Logs, Inc.
E-mail: lnlinfo@loknlogs.com
Web site: http://www.loknlogs.com

The Cumberland General Store
Web site: http://www.gatewayad.com/cumber.html

JLC Bookstore
Web site: http://www.bgibooks@aol.com

Yestermorrow Design/Build School
E-mail: ymschool@aol.com
Web site: http://www.yestermorrow.org

Real Log Homes
Web site: http://www.realloghomes.com

Environmental Home Center
E-mail: info@enviresource.com
Web site: http://www.enviresource.com

Timbercraft Homes, Inc.
E-mail: info@timbercraft.com
Web site: http://www.timbercraft.com

Building Schools/ Workshops

The Canelo Project
E-mail: absteen@dakotacom.net
Web site: http://www.deatech.com/canelo

Arcosanti
E-mail: arcosanti@aol.com

Cal-Earth Institute
E-mail: calearth@aol.com

Solar Energy International
E-mail: sei@solarenergy.org
Web site: http://www.solarenergy.org

Sandra Leibowitz
Eco-Building Schools
Web site: http://www.ecodesign.org/edi/eden

International Institute for Bau-Biologie
E-mail: baubiologie@earthlink.net
Web site: http://www.bau-biologieusa.com

The Heartwood School
E-mail: info@heartwoodschool.com
Web site: http://www.heartwoodshcool.com

Fox Maple School of Traditional Building
E-mail: foxmaple@nxi.com
Web site: http://www.nxi.com/WWW/joinersquarterly

Energy Efficient Building Association
E-mail: EEBANews@aol.com
Web site: http://www.eeba.org

Natural Building Resources
E-mail: blackrange@zianet.com
Web site: http://www.zianet.com/blackrange

Barkeater Design Build Company
E-mail: barkeatr@slic.com
Web site: http://www.xlic.com/~barkeatr/home.html

Earthwood Building School
Web site: http://www.interlog.com/newood

Cob Cottage Company
Web site: http://www.deatech.com/cobcottage

Groundworks
Web site: http://www.cpros.com/~sequoia

Yestermorrow Design/Build School
E-mail: ymschool@aol.com
Web site: http://www.yestermorrow.org

Greenfire Institute
E-mail: greenfire@igc.org
Web site: http://www.balewolf.com

Publishers

Ogden Publications
E-mail: cappers@kspress.com
Web site: www.cappers.com

JLC Bookstore
Web site: http://www.bgibooks@aol.com

Taunton Press
E-mail: tf@taunton.com
Web site: http://www.taunton.com

Fox Maple Press
E-mail: foxmaple@nxi.com
Web site: http://www.nxi.com/WWW/joinersquarterly

Iris Communications, Inc.
E-mail: iris@oikos.com
Web site: http://www.oikos.com

Research

A & K Technical Services.
E-mail: krisdick@mb.sympatico.ca

Alaska Craftsman Home Program, Inc.
E-mail: achp@alaska.net/~achp
Web site: http://www.alaska.net/~achp

Aprovecho Research Center
E-mail: apro@efn.org/~apro
Web site: http://www/efn.org/~apro

Carroll, Franck & Associates
E-mail: carrfran@gold.tc.umn.edu

Community Eco-Design Network
E-mail: erichart@mtn.org
Web site: http://www.umn.edu/n/home/m037/kurtdand/cen

Energy Efficient Building Association
E-mail: EEBANews@aol.com
Web site: http://www.eeba.org

Fox Maple School of Traditional Building
E-mail: foxmaple@nxi.com
Web site: http://www.nxi.com/WWW/joinersquarterly

JLC Bookstore
Web site: http://www.bgibooks@aol.com

NAHB Research Center
E-mail: pyost@nahbrc.org
Web site: http://www.nahbrc.com

ORNL Buildings Technology Center
E-mail: jef@oml.gov
Web site: http://www.oml.gov/roofs+walls

Software

Tree Talk
E-mail: wow@together.net
Web site: http://www.woodweb.com/~treetalk/home.html

Passive Solar Industries Council
E-mail: PSICouncil@aol.com
Web site: http://www.psic.org

Notes & Numbers

Subject Listings

The listings in this section are based on subject/product listings. We've included it in this format so that it may be easier to match a company with a known product, or vise versa. The subject headings in this section are based on the subject listings corresponding directly to the questionnaire that was initially filled out for all of the companies listed in the book.

Air Exchangers & Radiant Heat

Allermed Corp.
31 Steel Road
Wylie, TX 75098
Tel: (214) 442-4898
Air exchangers.

American Aldes Ventilation Corporation
Northgate Center Business Park
Sarasota, FL 34234-4864
Tel: (800) 255-7749
Exhausts from several rooms at low economical airflow rates and assures a healthy environment within the home.

Memphremagog
Heat Exchangers, Inc.
PO Box 490
Newport, VT 05855
Tel: (800) 660-5412, Fax: (802) 895-2666
Indoor air quality solutions for tightly built homes since 1982.
E-mail: info@mhevt.com
Web site: www.mhevt.com

The Non-Toxic Hotline
830 Meadow Road
Aptos, CA 95003
Tel: (408) 684-0199
Austin Air, Allermed, Aireox, Foust, Pure Air Systems, Nilfisk Allergy Vaccums, Rainbow Ozone Generators, Ionizers at discount prices.

Ozark Air & Water Service
114 Spring St.
Sulphur Springs, AR 72768
Tel: (800) 835-8908 Fax: (501) 298-3421
Testing, sales, installations and service of air & water equipment.

Passive Solar Industries Council
1511 K Street, Suite 600
Washington, DC 20005
Tel: (202) 628-7400 Fax: (202) 393-5043
PSIC independent nonprofit advancing climate responsive buildings.
E-mail: PSICouncil@ao l.com
Web site: http://www.psic.org

Sanologistics Inc., Environmental Altenatives
7200 West Camino Real, Ste. 102
Boca Raton, FL 33433
Tel: (407) 394-0203 Fax: (407) 394-9421
Water-Air purification systems for POE and POU. Most advanced, utilizing Ozone, UV, & patented exotic multi-media filtering.

Venmar Ces
2525 Wentz Avenue
Saskatoon, SK, Canada S7K 2K9
Tel: (306) 242-3663 Fax: (306) 242-3484
Commercial HRV's (heat recovery ventilators) and ERV's (energy recovery ventilators).

Worldwide Technology, Inc.
PO Box 272302
Tampa, FL 33688
Tel: (813) 855-2443 Fax: (813) 855-2655
Manufacturer of air & water purification systems for residential, commercial and industrial environments.

Connecticut

New England Hearth And Soapstone
127 North Street, Goshen, CT 06756
Tel: (860) 491-3091, Fax: same
Hand-crafted masonry heaters, fireplaces, countertops and more in soapstone and other materials, also parts.
E-mail: nehearth@bigfoot.com
Web site: http://mha-net.org/users/nehs/

Indiana

Easy Heat, Inc.
31977 US 20 E.
New Carlisle, IN 46552
Tel: (219) 654-3144
Fax: (219) 654-7739
Electrical radiant heating cable solutions.
E-mail: mgb~1@msn.com
Web site: www.easyheat.com

Massachusetts

Runtal North America, Inc.
187 Neck Road
Ward Hill, MA 01835
Tel: (508) 373-1666
Fax: (508) 372-7140
Decorative panel radiators, towel radiator.

Minnesota

Maxxon Corporation
PO Box 253, 920 Hamel Road
Hamel, MN 55340
Tel: (612) 478-9600
Fax: (612) 478-2431
Radiant floor heating systems—hot water or electric.
E-mail: debi@maxxon.com
Web site: http://www.maxxon.com

Montana

Cornerstone Masonry Distributing, Inc.
PO Box 83
Pray, MT 59065
Tel: (406) 333-4383 Fax: same
Specializing in Tulikivi soapstone masonry heaters, bakeovens, and cookstoves.
E-mail: radiant@alpinet.com
Web site: http://www.tulikivi.com

New York

Radiant Technology
11A Farber Drive
Bellport, NY 11713
Tel: (800) 784-0234 Fax: (516) 286-0947
E-mail: radtech2@usa.pipeline.com
Web site: http://www.radiant-tech.com

Ohio

Top Hat Chimney Sweeps D.B.A. TNT Masonry Heaters
12380 Tinker's Creek Road
Cleveland, OH 44125
Tel: (216) 524-5431
Wood-fired masonry heaters, bake ovens, and cookstoves.
Web site: http://mha-net.org/users/tnt/index.htm

Pennsylvania

Mid-Atlantic Masonry Heat, Inc.
PO Box 277
Emigsville, PA 17318-0277
Tel: (800) 213-0903 Fax: (717) 854-1373
Mid-Atlantic and southeastern regional distributor Tulikivi natural soapstone fireplaces, bake ovens, cookstoves, heater benches, floor and wall tile.

Virginia

Masonry Heater Association of North America
11490 Commerce Pk. Dr., Suite 300
Reston, VA 20191
Tel: (703) 620-3171
Fax: (703) 620-3928
Association of builders, designers & researchers of masonry heaters.
Web site: http://mha-net.org/

Tulikivi U.S.
PO Box 7825
Charlottesville, VA 22906-7825
Tel: (804) 977-5500
Fax: (804) 977-5164
Tulikivi (two-lee-kee-vee) soapstone fireplaces, bake ovens, cookstoves—efficient radiant heat

Maine

Earthstar Energy Systems
PO Box 626
Waldoboro, ME 04572
Tel: (800) 323-6749, (800) 660-6749 (in Maine)
Complete energy system design & product sales..

Architects

DC, Washington

Passive Solar Industries Council
1511 K Street, Suite 600
Washington, DC 20005
Tel.(202) 628-7400
Fax (202) 393-5043
PSIC independent nonprofit advancing climate responsive buildings.
E-mail: PSICouncil@aol.com
Web site: http://www.psic.org

Massachusetts

Jack A. Sobon: Architect/Builder
PO Box 201, 613 Shaw Road
Windsor, MA 01270-0201
Tel: (413) 684-3223
Fax: same
Specializing in design and construction of sustainable wooden architecture.

Michigan

Millcreek Classic Homes
1009 Parchment Drive SE
Grand Rapids, MI 49546
Tel: (616) 949-3012
Fax: (616) 949-4477
Design and build Riverbend timber frame custom homes.

Minnesota

Community Eco-Design Network
PO Box 6241, 3151-29th Ave. S, #103
Minneapolis, MN 55406
Tel: (612) 306-2326
Super-insulated construction planbook, design services, northern climate strawbale building system.
E-mail: erichart@mtn.org
Web site: http://www.umn.edu/n/home/m037/kurtland/cen

Missouri

Timberland Design/Hearthstone
15444 Clayton Road, Ste. 325-6
St. Louis, MO 63011
Tel: (800) 680-8833, (314) 341-8833
Fax: (314) 341-8833
Architect, Hearthstone distributor, specializing in timber frame/log designs & packages.

New Hampshire

Springpoint Design
2210 Pratt Road
Alstead, NH 03602
Tel: (603) 835-2433
Fax: (603) 835-7825
Architectural design/consulting: health, sustainability, efficiency–timber frames, alternative enclosures.

Straw Works
152 West Main St.
Conway, NH 03818
Tel: (603) 447-1701
Fax: (603) 447-6412
Design for those wishing to walk lightly upon the earth.
E-mail: Straw-Works@juno.com

New York

Gallagher Associates
124-01 20th Ave.
College Point, NY 11356
Tel: (718) 539-6576
Fax: (718) 539-6578
Commercial and residential environmentally friendly architecture and landscape design.

Oregon

Sustainable Architecture
PO Box 696, 910 Glendale Ave.
Ashland, OR 97520
Tel: (541) 482-6332
Fax: (541) 488-8299
Architectural services integrating full spectrum of healthy, holistic building.

Pennsylvania

Hugh Lofting Timber Framing, Inc.
339 Lamborntown Road
West Grove, PA 19390
Tel: (610) 444-5382
Fax: (610) 869-3589
Company dedicated to practicing green architecture with sustainable materials.
E-mail: hlofting@aolcom

Washington

Richard Berg, Architect
727 Taylor St.
Port Townsend, WA 98368
Tel: (360) 379-8090
Fax: (360) 379-8324
Architectural practice specializing in comfortable, energy-efficient, quality timber framed homes.
E-mail: rberg@olympus.net

Jean Steinbrecher Architects
PO Box 788
Langley, WA 98260-0788
Tel: (360) 221-0494
Fax: (360) 221-6594
Log & timber design specialists.
E-mail: jsa@whidbey.com

Architectural Millwork

Arkansas

Charles R. Bailey Cabinetmakers
HC 62, Box 29
Flippin, AR 72634
Tel: (501) 453-3245
Fax: Same
All natural custom furniture and cabinetry from solid American hardwoods.

California

Jefferson Recycled Woodworks
PO Box 696, 1104 Firenze Ave.
McCloud, CA 96057
Tel: (916) 964-2740
Fax: (916) 964-2745
Reclaimed timbers, lumber and millwork. Milled to your specifications.
E-mail: goodwood@telis.org
Web site: http://www.ecowood.com

Connecticut

Shuttercraft, Inc.
282 Stepstone Hill
Guilford, CT 06437
Tel: (203) 453-1973
Fax: (203) 245-5969
Exterior and interior wood shutters for authentic restoration, hinges, holdbacks.
E-mail: shutter@iconn.net
Web site: http://www.galaxymall.com/shops/shuttercraft.html

Chestnut Specialists, Inc.
PO Box 217, 365 Harwinton Ave.
Plymouth, CT 06782
Tel: (860) 283-4209
Fax: same
Remanufactured flooring from reclaimed antique lumber. Dimensional antique lumber.

Idaho

Stein & Collett
PO Box 4065, 201 South Mission Street
McCall, ID 83638
Tel: (208) 634-5374
Fax: (208) 634-8228
Beams, flooring, doors, stair systems. Both new and recycled woods custom architectural millwork. Unique and unusual species are our specialty.

Massachusetts

New England Preservation Services
95 West Squantum Street, Suite 705
Quincy, MA 02171
Tel: (617) 472-8934
Fax: (617) 770-8934
Restoration of 18th & 19th century homes and barns.
E-mail: 74131.1254@Compuserve.com

Architectural Detail In Wood
41 Parker Road
Shirley, MA 01404
Tel: (508) 425-9026
Reproduction windows, traditional joinery, matched profiles, all heartwood, any glazing.

Amherst Woodworking & Supply, Inc.
30 Industrial Drive
Northampton, MA 01061
Tel: (800) 532-9110
Fax: (413) 582-0164
Moldings-doors-stair parts-plank flooring-20+species hardwood lumber
E-mail: amwooco@copperbeech.com
Web site: www.copperbeech.com

Architectural Components, Inc.
26 North Leverett Road
Montague, MA 01351
Tel: (413) 367-9441
Fax: (413) 367-9461
Architectural Components, Inc. specializes in reproducing historic doorways, doors & windows.
E-mail: arch.components.inc@worldnet.att.net

Forester Moulding & Lumber
152 Hamilton St.
Leominster, MA 01453
Tel: (978) 840-3100
Fax: (978) 534-8356
Manufacturer of 1800 hardwood mouldings in 22+ wood species.
Web site: http://www.forestermoulding.com

Maine

Sun Architectural Woodworks, Inc.
RR 1 Box 8080
West Baldwin, ME 04091
Tel: (207) 625-7000
"High end" custom design and fabrication; doors & entrances, windows, panel walls & wainscot, stairs. Also, 18th century reproductions. Hand-planed moldings.

Missouri

Woodmaster Tools
1431 N. Topping Ave.
Kansas City, MO 64120
Tel: (816) 483-7203
Make mirror-smooth custom molding with the Woodmaster planer/molder.

North Carolina

Woodhouse, Inc.
PO Box 7336, 105 Creek Street
Rocky Mount, NC 27804
Tel: (919) 977-7336
Fax: (919) 641-4477
French oak, chestnut, antique heart pine
solid or laminate flooring.

The Joinery Co.
PO Box 518, 1600 Western Blvd.
Tarboro, NC 27886
Tel: (919) 823-3306
Fax: (919) 823-0818
Antique heart pine, engineered solid
wood flooring, stair parts, mouldings,
beams.

New Hampshire

Dan Dustin-Custom Hand-Hewing
1107 Penacook Road
Contoocook, NH 03229
Tel: (603) 746-5683
Expert adze and broadaxe work-your
material-my yard.

New York

New Energy Works Of Rochester, Inc.
1755 Pioneer Road
Shortsville, NY 14548
Tel: (716) 289-3220
Fax: (716) 289-3221
Timber frame production, reclaimed
wood milling; interior woodworks and
design.
E-mail: jononewt@aol.com

Oregon

Confluence Design & Construction
PO Box 1258, 1013 NW Taylor
Corvallis, OR 97339
Tel: (514) 757-0511
Fax: (541) 753-4916
"Where thinking and doing are still one."
Design, frames, consultation.

South Carolina

Southern Breeze Timberworks
PO Box 635
Travelers Rest, SC 29690
Tel: (864) 834-3706
Quality hand-wrought joinery.

Texas

Precision Woodworks
507 E. Jackson St.
Burnet, TX 78611
Tel: (512) 756-6950
Fax: same
New products from antique longleaf pine
and other used timbers.

Virginia

Vintage Pine Co.
PO Box 85
Prospect, VA 23960
Tel: (804) 574-6531
Fax: (804) 574-2401
Antique heart pine flooring and stair
parts.

Vermont

Belgian Woodworks
1068 Ireland Road
Starksboro, VT 05487
Tel: (802) 453-4787
Custom mouldings, banisters and
newels in sustainably harvested
northern hardwoods.

Washington

The G.R. Plume Company
1373 West Smith Road, Suite 1-A
Ferndale, WA 98248
Tel: (360) 384-2800
Fax: (360) 384-0335
Architectural timber millwork fabricated
from reclaimed Douglas fir.

Books

Alaska

Alaska Craftsman Home Program, Inc.
PO Box 241647
Anchorage, AK 99524-1647
Tel: (907) 258-2247 (ACHP)
Fax: (907) 258-5352
Education and research advanced cold
climate home building techniques.
E-mail: achp@alaska.net
Web site: http://www.alaska.net/~achp

Arizona

The Canelo Project
HCL Box 324
Elgin, AZ 85611
Tel: (520) 455-5548
Fax: (520) 455-9360
Straw bale building/earthen floors and
plasters, workshops, resources,
consulting.
E-mail: absteen@dakotacom.net
Web site: http://www.deatech.com/
canelo

Sustainable Systems Support
PO Box 318
Bisbee, AZ 85603
Tel: (520) 432-4292
Offers books and videos on plastered
straw bale construction, including an
excellent 90 min. "how-to" video with a
62 page manual. Wall raising workshops
and consultations.

Out On Bale By Mail
1039 E. Linden St.
Tucson, AZ 85719
Tel: (520) 624-1673
Fax: (520) 299-9099
Educational materials for straw bale
building. Help for owner builders.
E-mail: outonbale@aol.com

California

Craftsman Book Company
6058 Corte Del Cedro
Carlsbad, CA 92009
Tel: (800) 829-8123
Fax: (760) 438-0398
Professional construction books that
solve actual problems in the builder's
office and in the field.

Connecticut

Fine Homebuilding Magazine
PO Box 5506, 63 S. Main Street
Newtown, CT 06470-5506
Tel: (203) 426-8171
Fax: (203) 270-6751
Homebuilders share tips, techniques
and reviews of tools and materials.
E-mail: fh@taunton.com
Web site: http://www.taunton.com

Illinois

Frog Tool Co., Ltd.
2169 IL Rt. 26
Dixon, IL 61021
Tel: (800) 648-1270
Fax: (815) 288-3919
Timber framing and handling tools, hand
woodworking tools, books. Catalog $5.

Kansas

Cappers
Ogden Publications
1503 SW 42nd Street
Topeka, KS 66609-1265
Tel: (785) 274-4330
Fax: (785) 274-4305
A family-oriented publication providing
readers with "good news".
E-mail: cappers@kspress.com
Web site: www.cappers.com

Grit

Ogden Publications
1503 SW 42nd Street
Topeka, KS 66609-1265
Tel: (785) 274-4330
Fax: (785) 274-4305
Publication that preserves the best of
family life and traditions.
E-mail: grit@kspress.com
Web site: www.oweb.com/grit

Massachusetts

Berkshire House Publishers
480 Pleasant Street, Suite 5
Lee, MA 01238
Tel: (800) 321-8526
Fax: (413) 243-0303
Explore colonial barn lore with master
restorer Richard Babcock.

Old-House Journal Directory (Dovetail
Publishers)
2 Main St.
Gloucester, MA 01930
Tel: (508) 283-3200
Fax: (508) 283-4629
Annual sourcebook for suppliers of
reproduction hardware, lighting, building
materials.

Maryland

NAHB Research Center
400 Prince George's Blvd.
Upper Marlboro, MD 20774-8731
Residential building research including
innovative/alternative materials and
systems.
E-mail: pyost@nahbrc.org
Web site: http://www.nahbrc.org

Maine

Fox Maple School Of Traditional
Building
PO Box 249
Brownfield, ME 04010
Tel: (207) 935-3720
Fax: (207) 935-4575
Workshops for introductory & advanced
timber framing. Other workshops
available in the areas of thatch, clay and
alternative building systems. Fox Maple
strives for quality craftsmanship, with a
view towards a sustainable future.
E-mail: foxmaple@nxi.com
Web site: http://www.nxi.com/WWW/
joinersquarterly

Joiners' Quarterly
PO Box 249
Brownfield, ME 04010
Tel: (207) 935-3720
Fax: (207) 935-4575
The timber framer's choice for hard core
information. JQ is also a leader in
blending modern technology with
traditional craftsmanship, bringing
innovative ideas for a sustainable future
to the forefront.
E-mail: foxmaple@nxi.com
Web site: http://www.nxi.com/WWW/
joinersquarterly

North Carolina

Country Workshops
90 Mill Creek Road
Marshall, NC 28753
Tel: (704) 656-2280
Tools, books and instruction in traditional
woodworking with hand tools.
E-mail: langsner@countryworkshops.org
Web site: countryworkshops.org

New Mexico

Natural Building Resources
Star Rt. 2, Box 119
Kingston, NM 88042
Tel: (505) 895-5652
Fax: (505) 895-3326
Books and videos on natural building.
Host—Natural Building Colloquium.
E-mail: blackrange@zianet.com
Web site: www.zianet.com/blackrange

New York

Lofty Branch Bookstore
PO Box 512
Victor, NY 14564
Tel: (716) 742-2607
Fax: (716) 289-3221
Over 350 timber framing, construction,
design and woodworking books/videos.
E-mail: loftybooks@aol.com
Web site: http://
members.aol.com.loftybooks

Earthwood Building School
366 Murtagh Hill Road
West Chazy, NY 12992
Tel: (518) 493-7744
Fax: same, phone first
Teaches cordwood masonry and
underground housing. Books, videos
and workshops.
Web site: http://www.interlog.com/
newood

Lee Valley Tools Ltd.
PO Box 178012 East River St.
Ogdensburg, NY 13669-0490
Tel: (800) 871-8158
Fax: (800) 513-7885
Our 236-page full-color catalog has the
widest selection of woodworking hand
tools on the market.
Web site: http://www.leevalley.com

Ohio

Custom Roof Thatching & Supplies
PO Box 62054
Cincinnati, OH 45262
Tel: (513) 772-4979
Fax: (513) 772-6313
Has thatched in U.S. since 1986. A
guide to roof thatching in the U.S. $6.00.
Web site: http://www.roofthatch.com

Oregon

Iris Communications, Inc.
PO Box 5920
Eugene, OR 97405
Tel: (541) 484-9353
Fax: (541) 484-1645
Carefully selected books, videos and
software for green construction.
E-mail: iris@oikos.com
Web site: www.oikos.com

Groundworks
PO Box 381
Murphy, OR 97533
Tel: (541) 471-3470
Workshops and handbook available on
cob (hand-sculpted earth) construction.
Web site: http://www.cpros.com/
~sequoia

Vermont

JLC Bookstore
PO Box 2050, West Main St.
Richmond, VT 05477
Tel: (800) 859-3669
Fax: (802) 434-4467
Hard to find books for construction
professionals.
Web site: bgibooks@aol.com

Tree Talk
PO Box 426, 431 Pine Street
Burlington, VT 05402
Tel: (802) 865-1111
Fax: (802) 863-4344
Multimedia cd-rom on wood. 900
species. Database. Video. Pictures.
Maps.
E-mail: wow@together.net
Web site: www.woodweb.com/~treetalk/
home.html

Chelsea Green Publishing Company
PO Box 428
White River Junction, VT 05001
Tel: (802) 295-6300
Fax: (802) 295-6444
Publisher of quality books, specializing
in alternative, natural & traditional
homes for the owner/builder.

West Virginia

Woodcraft Supply
PO Box 1686, 210 Wood County
Industrial Park
Parkersburg, WV 26102
Tel: (800) 225-1153
Fax: (304) 428-8271
Quality woodworking tools, books,
hardware, hardwoods; plus tool
sharpening service.
E-mail: custserv@woodcraft.com
Web site: www.woodcraft.com

Publications

American Woodworker
22 S. 2nd Street
Emmaus, PA 18098-0099
Tel: (610) 967-8315
Fax: (610) 967-7692
American Woodworker provides
information & ideas for serious
woodworkers.

Building With Nature Newsletter
PO Box 4417
Santa Rosa, CA 95402
Tel: (707) 579-2201
Information and inspiration about
healthful, ecologically responsible
spirited building.

Canadian Workshop
130 Spy Court
Markham, Ontario, Canada L3R 0W5
Tel: (905) 475-8440
Fax: (905) 475-9560
Canadian magazine for the home
woodworker and do-it-yourself home
improvement enthusiast.
E-mail: letters@canadianworkshop.ca
Web site: http://
www.canadianworkshop.ca

Cappers
Ogden Publications
1503 SW 42nd Street
Topeka, KS 66609-1265
Tel: (785) 274-4330
Fax: (785) 274-4305
A family-oriented publication providing
readers with "good news".
E-mail: cappers@kspress.com
Web site: www.cappers.com

Center For Resourceful Building
Technology
PO Box 100, 516 S. Orange
Missoula, MT 59806
Tel: (406) 549-7678
Fax: (406) 549-4100
Non-profit educating the public on
environmentally responsible
construction practices.

Colonial Homes
1790 Broadway, 14th Floor
New York, NY 10019
Tel: (212) 830-2910
Fax: (212) 586-3455
Colonial Homes is the authority on
America's design heritage.
E-mail: aberman@hearst.com

Construction Business & Computing
PO Box 2050, West Main St.
Richmond, VT 05477
Tel: (800) 375-5981
Fax: (802) 434-4467
Monthly newsletter on computer
applications and business techniques for
construction professionals.
E-mail: cbc@bginet.com
Web site: www.bginet.com

Country Journal
4 High Ridge Park
Stamford, CT 06905
Tel: (203) 321-1778
Fax: (203) 322-1966
Magazine serving readers who live in
rural areas.

Early American Life
Cowles History Group
6405 Flank Dr.
Harrisburg, PA 17112
Tel: (717) 540-6711
Artcles on restoration, replicas, historic
paints, fence patterns, period furniture,
gardens, recipes and many other Early
American interests.

Environmental Building News
RR 1, Box 161
Brattleboro, VT 05301
Tel: (802) 257-7300
Fax: (802) 257-7304
The leading publication on
environmentally responsible design and
construction.
E-mail: ebn@ebuild.com
Web site: http://www.ebuild.com

Environ
PO Box 2204
Fort Collins, CO 80522
A national voice for environmental health
and lifestyles.

GCR Publishing Group, Inc.
1700 Broadway
New York, NY 10019
Tel: (212) 541-7100
Fax: (212) 245-1241
Publisher of Timber Homes Illustrated
magazine

Grit
Ogden Publications
1503 SW 42nd Street
Topeka, KS 66609-1265
Tel: (785) 274-4330
Fax: (785) 274-4305
Publication that preserves the best of
family life and traditions.
E-mail: grit@kspress.com
Web site: www.oweb.com/grit

Hancock Shaker Village
PO Box 927, Rtes. 20 & 41
Pittsfield, MA 01202
Tel: (413) 443-0188
Fax: (413) 447-9357
200 year-old original Shaker site, crafts
demonstrations, working farm.
E-mail: info@hancockshakervillage
Web site: http://
www.hancockshakervilLage.org

Joiners' Quarterly
PO Box 249
Brownfield, ME 04010
Tel: (207) 935-3720
Fax: (207) 935-4575
The timber framer's choice for hard core
information. JQ is also a leader in
blending modern technology and

traditional craftsmanship, bringing
innovative ideas for a sustainable future
to the forefront.
E-mail: foxmaple@nxi.com
Web site: http://www.nxi.com/WWW/
joinersquarterly

Journal Of Light Construction
RR 2 Box 146, West Main St.
Richmond, VT 05477
Tel: (800) 375-5981
Fax: (802) 434-4467
Leading monthly magazine written by
builders for builders.
Web site: www.bginet.com

Living History
Box 202
West Hurley, NY 12491
Dutch Barn Society. Information on local
history.

Lofty Branch Bookstore
PO Box 512
Victor, NY 14564
Tel: (716) 742-2607
Fax: (716) 289-3221
Over 350 timber framing, construction,
design and woodworking books/videos.
E-mail: loftybooks@aol.com
Web site: http://
members.aol.com.loftybooks

NAHB Research Center
400 Prince George's Blvd.
Upper Marlboro, MD 20774-8731
Residential building research including
innovative/alternative materials and
systems.
E-mail: pyost@nahbrc.org
Web site: http://www.nahbrc.com

Old-House Journal (Dovetail
Publishers)
2 Main St.
Gloucester, MA 01930
Tel: (508) 283-3200
Fax: (508) 283-4629
Bimonthly magazine about restoring,
maintaining, and decorating pre-1940's
houses.

Preservation Magazine
1785 Massachusetts Avenue NW
Washington, DC 20036
Tel: (202) 588-6068
Fax: (202) 588-6172
To go beyond old houses and historic
sites.
Web site: www.nationaltrust.org

The Last Straw
PO Box 42000
Tucson, AZ 85733
Tel: (520) 882-3848
The Last Straw: the quarterly journal of
straw-bale construction.
E-mail: thelaststraw@igc.apc.org
Web site: http://www.netchaos.com/+ls

Scantlings/Timber Framing
PO Box 1075
Bellingham, WA 98227-1075
Tel: (360) 733-4001
Fax: (360) 733-4002
Magazine of the Timber Framers Guild
of North America

Timber Frame Homes Magazine
4200-T Lafayette Center Drive
Chantilly, VA 22021
Tel: (800) 850-7279 X128
Elegance & new ideas in timber framing
four times a year.

Today's Woodworker Magazine
4365 Willow Dr.
Medina, MN 55340
Tel: (800) 610-0883
Woodworking projects, tips and
techniques.
E-mail: editor@todayswoodworker.com
Web site: todayswoodworker.com

Tools of The Trade
PO Box 2001, West Main St.
Richmond, VT 05477
Tel: (800) 375-5981
Fax: (802) 434-4467
The only magazine devoted exclusively
to tools for construction professionals.
Web site: www.bginet.com

Boatbuilding

Wooden Boat School
PO Box 78
Brooklin, ME 04616
Tel: (207) 359-4651
Fax: (207) 359-8920

The Atlantic Challenge Foundation
Apprenticeshop of Rockland
Box B
Rockland, ME

Rondout Woodworking, Inc.
29 Terra Road
Saugerties, NY 12477
Tel: (914) 246-5879
Fax: (914) 246-5845
Restoration specialist. agricultural-
industrial, waterwheels, windmills, barns,
timber frames.

International Yacht Restoration
449 Thames Street
Newport, RI 02840
401-848-5777
E-mail: info@iyrs.com

The Center For Wooden Boats
1010 Valley Street
Seattle, WA 98109
Tel: (206) 382-2628
Fax: (206) 382-2699
Traditional wooden boatbuilding
workshops offered. To do is to learn.
E-mail: cwboats@eskimo.com/~cwboats

Cabinets &
Furniture

Charles R. Bailey Cabinetmakers
HC 62, Box 29
Flippin, AR 72634
Tel: (501) 453-3245
Fax: same
All natural custom furniture and
cabinetry from solid American
hardwoods.

Karp Woodworks
136 Fountain Street
Ashland, MA 01721
Tel: (508) 881-7000
Fax: (508) 881-7084
Sustainably harvested certified tropical
& domestic woods. "Furnature," an
organic, sustainable and chemical-free
line of upholstered furniture. "Certified
Serenity", a line of comfortable and
colorful sunroom/patio furniture from
certified sustainable sources.

Sandro's Woodshed
20018 486th Ave.
Hendricks, MN 56136
Tel: (605) 479-3875
Custom timber frames. Cabinetry and
furniture built with all natural materials–
no plywood or particle board–non-toxic
finishes available.

Catalogs

California

Craftsman Book Company
6058 Corte Del Cedro
Carlsbad, CA 92009
Tel: (800) 829-8123
Fax: (760) 438-0398
Professional construction books that
solve actual problems in the builder's
office and in the field.
Bailey's
PO Box 550, 44650 Hwy. 101
Laytonville, CA 95454
Tel: (800) 322-4539
Fax: (707) 984-8115
Free catalog: world's largest mail order
woodsman supplies company.
E-mail: baileys@bbaileyscom
Web site: http://www.bbaileys.com

Alternative Energy Engineering, Inc.
PO Box 339
Redway, CA 95560
Tel: (800) 777-6609
Fax: (707) 923-3009
Energy from solar, wind or water power.
Photovoltaics, lighting, solar fans,
fridges and books. 112 page catalog for
$3.

Real Goods
555 Leslie St.
Ukiah, CA 95482
Tel: (707) 468-9292 Fax: (707) 462-9394
Solar, wind, hydro, efficient lighting,
water, catalogs, books and institute.

Sierra Solar Systems
109-MC Argall Way
Nevada City, CA 95959
Tel: (800) 517-6527 Fax: (916) 265-6151
Solar electric, pumping, hot water, wind,
hydropower and energy efficient lighting.
Catalog $5.
E-mail: solarjon@oro.net
Web site: www.sierrasolar.com

Earth Studio
6761 Sebastopol Ave., Suite 8
Sebastopol, CA 95472
Tel: (707) 823-2569
Petroleum-free & biodegradable natural
paints and finishes. Free Catalog.

Florida

International Tool Corporation
2590 Davie Road
Davie, FL 33317
Tel: (800) 338-3384 Fax: (954) 792-3560
Woodworking & construction power tools
at the guaranteed lowest prices.
Web site: http://
www.internationaltool.com

Idaho

Woodhouse
PO Box 801
Ashton, ID 83420
Tel: (208) 652-3608 Fax: (208) 652-3628
Supplying all specialized tools and
materials for log-timber construction.
Providing owner and/or professional with
largest selection of quality products
available.

Backwoods Solar Electric Systems
8530 Rapid Lightning Creek Road
Sandpoint, ID 83864
Tel: (208) 263-4290
All the equipment with lower than usual
prices. Catalog $3.

Illinois

Frog Tool Co., Ltd.
2169 IL Rt. 26
Dixon, IL 61021
Tel: (800) 648-1270 Fax: (815) 288-3919
Timber framing and handling tools, hand
woodworking tools, books. Catalog $5.

Davis Caves Construction, Inc.
PO Box 69
Armington, IL 61721
Tel: (309) 392-2574
Fax: (309) 392-2578
We will design and build to your specific
floorplan, or choose from our 80 page
planbook.
E-mail: earthome@daviscaves.com
Web site: www.daviscaves.com/
builder.htm

Indiana

Wood-Mizer Products, Inc.
8180 W. 10th Street
Indianapolis, IN 46214
Tel: (317) 271-1542
Fax: (317) 273-1011
Transportable sawmills and accessories:
lowers lumber costs and improves
quality.
E-mail: adindy@woodmizer.com
Web site: http://www.woodmizer.com

Massachusetts

Old Sturbridge Village
One Old Sturbridge Village Road
Sturbridge, MA 01566
Tel: (508) 347-3362
Fax: (508) 347-0369
Hand-forged wrought iron hinges,
latches and more.

Tremont Nail Co.
PO Box 111, 8 Elm St.
Wareham, MA 02571
Tel: (508) 295-0038
Fax: (508) 295-1365
Manufacturer of restoration pattern steel
cut nails; colonial hardware distributor.
E-mail: cutnails@aol.com

Old-House Journal Directory (Dovetail
Publishers)
2 Main St.
Gloucester, MA 01930
Tel: (508) 283-3200
Fax: (508) 283-4629
Annual sourcebook for suppliers of
reproduction hardware, lighting, building
materials.

New England Solar Electric, Inc.
PO Box 435
Worthington, MA 01098
Tel: (413) 238-5974
$3 for 64 page catalog/design guide,
solar electric kits, components, gas
refrigerators, other appliances and
information you need to live
independently with solar electricity.

Maine

Natural Knees
281 Hartland Road
St. Albans, ME 04971
Tel: (207) 938-2380
Natural grown knees for timber frame
construction and boat building.
E-mail: kneeman@somtel.com

Barn Masters, Inc.
PO Box 258
Freeport, ME 04032
Tel: (207) 865-4169
Fax: (207) 865-6169
Makita tools for timber framing: chain
mortisers, stationary routers, chisel
mortisers, groove cutters, circular saws,
6" x 12" planers, tenon cutters. Free
brochure.

Minnesota

Tools On Sale Div. Of Seven Corners
Hdwr., Inc.
216 West 7th Street
St. Paul, MN 55102
Tel: (800) 328-0457 Fax: (612) 224-8263
496 page catalog of power tools and
related accessories featuring the most
respected brands in the business.

Montana

Specialty Woodworks Company
PO Box 1450
Hamilton, MT 59840
Tel: (406) 363-6353 Fax: (406) 363-6373
Established 1981. Manufactures custom
hand-crafted doors and cabinets.
Specializing in unique blue stain pine,
knotty pine, and other rustic hardwoods.
Catalog $7.

Sunelco
PO Box 1499
Hamilton, MT 59840
Tel: (406) 363-6924, (800) 338-6844
Complete source for solar modules,
batteries, inverters, water pumps,
energy effecient lights, and propane
appliances. Catalog $4.95.

North Carolina

Harmony Exchange
Route 2, Box 843-A
Boone, NC 28607
Tel: (800) 968-9663
Antique, reclaimed & new growth.
Flooring, timber trusses, decking,
exposed beam systems, siding & more.
Catalog.

Klingspor's Sanding Catalogue
PO Box 3737
Hickory, NC 28603-3737

North Dakota

Tool Crib Of The North
PO Box 14040, 1603 12th Ave. N
Grand Forks, ND 58206-4040
Tel: (701) 780-2882
Fax: (701) 746-2869
96 color pages of woodworking tools
and accessories, free!
E-mail: kcolman@corpcomm.net
Web site: www.toolcribofthenorth.com

New Mexico

Eco Design Co.
1365 Rufina Circle
Santa Fe, NM 87505
Tel: (800) 621-2591, (505) 438-3448
Fax: (505) 438-0199
The natural choice. Natural paints,
stains & healthy home products catalog.

New York

Lofty Branch Bookstore
PO Box 512
Victor, NY 14564
Tel: (716) 742-2607
Fax: (716) 289-3221
Over 350 timber framing, construction,
design and woodworking books/videos.
E-mail: loftybooks@aol.com
Web site: http://
members.aol.com.loftybooks

Lok-N-Logs, Inc.
PO Box 677, Route 12
Sherburne, NY 13460
Tel: (800) 343-8928, (607) 674-4447
Fax: (607) 674-6433
Producer of top quality, pre-cut log home
packages–lifetime limited warranty!
E-mail: lnlinfo@loknlogs.com
Web site: http://www.loknlogs.com
Catalog: $12.95

Ohio

Lehman's
Box 41
Kidron, OH 44636
How the Amish live without electricity.
Over 2,500 items including stoves,
refrigerators, lights, appliances,
woodworking and garden tools.

The Ohio Hempery, Inc.
7002 State Route 329
Guysville, OH 45735
Tel: (614) 662-4367
Fabric, paper, oil, clothes, shoes, skin &
body care, twine, seeds, stalks, sliver,
yarn and hurds manufactured from
hemp. Free catalog.

Tennessee

Cumberland General Store
#1 Highway 68,
Crossville, TN 38555
Tel: (800) 334-4640
Items include everything from windmills
to woodstoves, Victorian baths to tonics,
handpumps to gristmills, Alladin
kerosene lamps to buggies and harness.
288 page catalog for $4.
Web site: www.gatewayad.com/
cumber.html

Vermont

JLC Bookstore
PO Box 2050, West Main St.
Richmond, VT 05477
Tel: (800) 859-3669 Fax: (802) 434-4467
Hard to find books for construction
professionals.
Web site: bglbooks@aol.com

Yestermorrow Design / Build School
RR 1 Box 97-5
Warren, VT 05674
Tel: (802) 496-5545
Fax: (802) 496-5540
Offers hands-on courses in residential
design and "green" construction.
E-mail: ymschool@aol.com
Web site: www.yestermorrow.org

Real Log Homes
PO Box 202, National Information
Center
Hartland, VT 05048
Tel: (800) 732-5564
Fax: (802) 436-2150
Pre-cut log home packages over 19,000
worldwide since 1963. Catalog $10.
Web site: http://www.realloghomes.com

Chelsea Green Publishing Company
PO Box 428
White River Junction, VT 05001
Tel: (802) 295-6300
Fax: (802) 295-6444
Publisher of quality books, specializing
in alternative, natural & traditional
homes for the owner/builder.

Washington

Environmental Home Center
1724 4th Ave. South
Seattle, WA 98134
Tel: (800) 281-8275, (206) 682-8275
Retail / wholesale–environmentally
responsible building materials and
decorating supplies.
E-mail: info@enviresource.com
Web site: www.enviresource.com

Systimatic
12530 135th Ave. NE
Kirkland, WA 98034
Tel: (800) 426-0035
Fax: (425) 821-0801
Manufacturer of carbide tipped circular
saw blades.

Timbercraft Homes, Inc.
85 Martin Road
Port Townsend, WA 98368
Tel: (360) 385-3051
Fax: (360) 385-7745
Since 1979, high quality timber frame
structures, components, and
architectural engineering.
E-mail: info@timbercraft.com
Web site: http://www.timbercraft.com
Fax: (802) 295-6444
Publisher of quality books, specializing
in alternative, natural & traditional
homes for the owner/builder.

Clay

Maine

Proclay
C/O Fox Maple
PO Box 249
Brownfield, ME 04010
Tel: (207) 935-3720
Fax: (207) 935-4575
Light-clay infill techniques, clay & lime
plasters, clay building materials,
workshops and consulting.
E-mail: foxmaple@nxi.com

Joiners' Quarterly
PO Box 249
Brownfield, ME 04010
Tel: (207) 935-3720
Fax: (207) 935-4575
E-mail: foxmaple@nxi.com
Web site: http://www.nxi.com/WWW/
joinersquarterly

Ohio

Superior Clay Corporation
PO Box 352, 6566 Superior Road SE
Uhrichsville, OH 44683
Tel: (614) 922-4122
Fax: (614) 922-6626
Clay flue lining, Rumford fireplace
components, clay chimney pots, ground
fired clay.
E-mail: mcclave@tusconet.com
Web site: rumford.com

Natural Homesteads
13182 N. Boone Road
Columbia Station, OH 44028
Tel: (440) 236-3344
Natural building design/consultation;
slide presentations; straw-bale and cob
workshops.

Quikspray, Inc.
PO Box 327
Port Clinton, OH 43452-9485
Tel: (419) 732-2611, (419) 732-2601
Fax: (419) 734-2628
Spray guns for clay & plaster.

Oregon

Cob Cottage Co.
PO Box 123
Cottage Grove, OR 97424
Tel: (541) 942-2005
Fax: (541) 942-3021
Information and workshops on building
with cob (sand, clay, straw).
Web site: http://www.deatech.com/
cobcottage

Germany

Uelzener Maschinenfabrik
Friedrich Maurer Gmbh
D-65843 Sulzbach/Ts.
Wiesenstrasse 18
Germany
Tel: 06196-05840
Fax: 06196-71273
Professional German-made clay
construction equipment.

Design Consultants

Arizona

The Canelo Project
HCL Box 324
Elgin, AZ 85611
Tel: (520) 455-5548
Fax: (520) 455-9360
Straw bale building/earthen floors and
plasters, workshops, resources,
consulting.
E-mail: absteen@dakotacom.net
Web site: http://www.deatech.com/
canelo

California

Eos Institute
580 Broadway, Suite 200
Laguna Beach, CA 92651
Tel: (714) 497-1896
Fax: (714) 497-7861
Educational nonprofit for the study of
sustainable living. Resources,
consulting, and programs on ecological
community design. Library, lectures,
workshops.
E-mail: eos@igpc.org

Florida

Freedom Builders
1013 Naples Drive
Orlando, FL 32804
Tel: (407) 647-5849
Fax: (407) 645-5652
Internet informational & advertising site–
log & t.f design–video productions.
E-mail: freedom@magicnet.net
Web site: www.magicnet.net/freedom

Georgia

Upper Loft Design, Inc.
Rt. 1 Box 2901
Lakemont, GA 30552
Tel: (706) 782-5246
Fax: (706) 782-6840
A timberframe design/build and turn-key
housewright company.
Web site: http://www.upperloft@stc.net

Indiana

Timbersmith, Inc.
4040 Farr Road
Bloomington, IN 47408
Tel: (812) 336-7424
Our frames exhibit traditional wooden
joinery and can be finely detailed to
produce one-of-a-kind creations.

Kansas

Elemental Resources
PO Box 21, 1320 E. 94th St. South
Haysville, KS 67060
Tel: (316) 788-3678
Fax: same
Renewable energy. Specializing in
design & installation of photovoltaic &
wind hybrid systems.
E-mail: cvdow@aol

Natural Habitat
PO Box 21, 1320 E. 94th St. South
Haysville, KS 67060
Tel: (316) 788-3676
Feng shui/bau-biologie consulting. New
and existing structures.

Kentucky

The Raven River Co., Inc.
125 Twin Creek–Connorsville Road
Sadieville, KY 40370
Tel: (606) 235-0368
Fax: same
Artisans of fine timber frames and other
things.
E-mail: ravenriver@kitt.net

Massachusetts

Greenspace Collaborative
PO Box 107
Ashfield, MA 01330
Tel: (413) 369-4905
Buildings of straw bales and other
natural materials detailed for the
northeastern climate.

Bamboo Fencer
31 Germania St.
Jamaica Plain, MA 02130-2314
Tel: (617) 524-6137
Fax: (617) 524-6100
Manufactures and imports fences,
gates, and other products.
E-mail: dave@bamboofencer.com
Web site: http://www.bamboofencer.com

Maine

Talmage Solar Engineering, Inc.
18 Stone Road
Kennebunkport, ME 04046
Tel: (207) 967-5945
Fax: (207) 967-5754
Design and sale of solar electric
components for off-grid or utility
interface.
E-mail: tse@talmagesolar.com
Web site: www.talmagesolar.com

Connolly & Co. Timber Frame Homes &
Barns
10 Atlantic Highway
Edgecomb, ME 04556
Tel: (207) 882-4224
Fax: (207) 882-4247
Custom timber frame homes & barns
built to last. Traditional oak-pegged
mortise and tenon joinery. Design
services. Project management. Frames
to complete projects. Visit our facility in
Maine and observe our commitment to
excellence.
E-mail: connolly@lincoln.midcoast.com

Fox Maple School Of Traditional
Building
PO Box 249
Brownfield, ME 04010
Tel: (207) 935-3720
Fax: (207) 935-4575
Workshops for introductory & advanced
timber framing. Other workshops
available in the areas of thatch, clay and
alternative building systems. Fox Maple
strives for quality craftsmanship, with a
view towards a sustainable future.
E-mail: foxmaple@nxi.com
Web site: http://www.nxi.com/WWW/
joinersquarterly

Minnesota

Carroll, Franck & Associates
1357 Highland Parkway
St. Paul, MN 55116
Tel: (612) 690-9162
Fax: (612) 690-9156
Engineering of architectural structures,
traditional joinery and concealed steel
connections.
E-mail: carrfran@gold.tc.umn.edu

Company Listings by Subject

Montana

Center For Resourceful Building
Technology
PO Box 100, 516 S. Orange
Missoula, MT 59806
Tel: (406) 549-7678
Fax: (406) 549-4100
Non-profit educating the public on
environmentally responsible
construction practices.

North Carolina

Goshen Timber Frames, Inc.
104 Wykle Road
Franklin, NC 28734
Tel: (704) 524-8662
Fax: same
Ongoing workshops and
apprenticeships in timber framing and
design; design services; frame sales.
E-mail: goshen@dnet.net
Web site: http://
www.timberframemag.com

New Hampshire

Day Pond Woodworking
PO Box 299, Rt. 114
Bradford, NH 03221
Tel: (603) 938-2375
Over 17 years experience building
custom timber frame homes, etc.

Specialty Timberworks
PO Box 261, Brownfield Road
Eaton, NH 03832
Tel: (603) 447-5625
Fax: same
Designers & fabricators of new, and
reconstruction of antique timber frames.
3-D CADD services.

Springpoint Design
2210 Pratt Road
Alstead, NH 03602
Tel: (603) 835-2433 Fax: (603) 835-7825
Architectural design/consulting: health,
sustainability, efficiency–timber frames,
alternative enclosures.

New York

Tea House Design, Inc.
PO Box 99, 11 Benedict Road
Waccabuc, NY 10597
Tel: (914) 763-3078
Fax: (914) 763-6165
27 years experience. 100 mile radius
NYC. Innovative and diligent.

Eastfield Village
PO Box 539, 104 Mud Pond Road
Nassau, NY 12062
Tel: (518) 766-2422
Fax: same
School of historic preservation and early
American trades.

Barkeater Design Build Company
35 Wellington Street
Malone, NY 12953
Tel: (518) 483-5282
Fax: same
Designer/builders specializing in stone
slipform construction. Workshops
available.
E-mail: barkeatr@slic.com

Ohio

Natural Homesteads
13182 N. Boone Road
Columbia Station, OH 44028
Tel: (440) 236-3344
Natural building design/consultation;
slide presentations; straw-bale and cob
workshops.

Oregon

Terry F. Johnson Building Design
1013 NW Taylor Ave.
Corvallis, OR 97330
Tel: (541) 757-8535
Fax: (541) 753-4916
Custom plans for timber framed homes,
barns and outbuildings.
E-mail: sarah@peak.org

Confluence Design & Construction
PO Box 1258, 1013 NW Taylor
Corvallis, OR 97339
Tel: (514) 757-0511
Fax: (541) 753-4916
"Where thinking and doing are still one."
Design, frames, consultation.

Rhode Island

South County Post & Beam
521 Liberty Lane
West Kingston, RI 02892
Tel: (401) 783-4415
Fax: (401) 783-4494
A full service timber frame company,
wide pine distributor.

Vermont

Memphremagog Heat Exchangers, Inc.
PO Box 490
Newport, VT 05855
Tel; (800) 660-5412
Fax: (802) 895-2666
Indoor air quality solutions for tightly
built homes since 1982.
E-mail: info@mhevt.com
Web site: www.mhevt.com

Vermont Sun Structures, Inc.
42 Walker Hill Road
Williston, VT 05495
Tel: (802) 879-6645
Glulam timber framed sunrooms &
greenhouses, fully "weeped" & water
tight!

Environmental Building News
RR 1, Box 161
Brattleboro, VT 05301
Tel: (802) 257-7300
Fax: (802) 257-7304
The leading publication on
environmentally responsible design and
construction.
E-mail: ebn@ebuild.com
Web site: http://www.ebuild.com

Washington

Ark II Inc.
HCR 73 Box 67
Twisp, WA 98856
Tel: (509) 997-2418
Fax: (509) 997-4434
Fine quality timber frame & log
buildings.

Greenfire Institute
PO Box 1040
Winthrop, WA 98862
Tel: (509) 996-3593
Fax: same
Straw bale construction training,
consultation and design.
E-mail: greenfire@igc.org
Web site: www.balewolf.com

Richard Berg, Architect
727 Taylor St.
Port Townsend, WA 98368
Tel: (360) 379-8090
Fax: (360) 379-8324
Architectural practice specializing in
comfortable, energy-efficient, quality
timber framed homes.
E-mail: rberg@olympus.net

West Virginia

Wind Bell Hollow/C.J. Jammer
HC 40 Box 36
Lewisburg, WV 24901
Tel: (304) 645-6466
Design/drafting of timber framed homes
and other natural house designs.

Manitoba

A & K Technical Services
PO Box 22
Anola, MB, Canada R0E 0A0
Tel: (204) 866-3262 Fax: (204) 866-3287
Structural engineering in wood.
"Stackwall" house construction design,
consulting, manual.
E-mail: krisdick@mb.sympatico.ca

Ontario

Alderaan Stone/Timber Homes
PO Box 313, 6-14845 Yonge Street
Aurora, Ontario, Canada L4G 6H8
Tel: (905) 713-0001
Fax: (905) 713-0134
Traditional materials and craftsmanship.
Comprehensive custom reproductions of
early Canadian homes.
Web site: www.craftsman-book.com

Northern Timberhouse, Ltd.
PO Box 71, Hwy. 35 South
Minden, Ontario, Canada K0M 2K0
Tel: (705) 286-3791
Fax: (705) 286-6168
Canadian timber frames and hand-
crafted log homes since 1984.
E-mail: nortim@halhinet.on.ca

Bear Timber Frame Homes
PO Box 124
Ajax, Ont, Canada L1S 3C2
Tel: (905) 428-6505
Designers of timber frame and energy-
efficient (R2000) homes.

Doors & Windows

California

Maxwell Pacific
PO Box 4127
Malibu, CA 90264
Tel: (310) 457-4533
Douglas fir, redwood, pine, cedar,
barnwood, used and new.

Urban Ore, Inc.
1333 Sixth St.
Berkeley, CA 94710
Tel: (510) 559-4460
Fax: (510) 528-1540
Buy, sell, trade good used lumber,
doors, windows, fixtures, hardware.

Connecticut

Shuttercraft, Inc.
282 Stepstone Hill
Guilford, CT 06437
Tel: (203) 453-1973
Fax: (203) 245-5969
Exterior and interior wood shutters for
authentic restoration, hinges, holdbacks.
E-mail: shutter@iconn.net
Web site: http://www.galaxymall.com/
shops/shuttercraft.html

Roto Frank Of America, Inc.
PO Box 599, Research Park
Chester, CT 06412-0599
Tel: (860) 243-0893
Fax: (860) 526-3785
World's best roof window: Roto designs
and manufactures innovative skylights.

Idaho

Alternative Timber Structures
1054 Rammel Mt. Rd.
Tetonia, ID 83452
Tel: (208) 456-2711
Fax: same
Custom door manufacturer, custom
sizes, interior & exterior–Davis Frame
rep—

Stein & Collett
PO Box 4065, 201 South Mission Street
McCall, ID 83638
Tel: (208) 634-5374
Fax: (208) 634-8228
Beams, flooring, doors, stair systems.
Both new and recycled woods custom
architectural millwork. Unique and
unusual species are our specialty.

Massachusetts

Architectural Detail In Wood
41 Parker Road
Shirley, MA 01404
Tel: (508) 425-9026
Reproduction windows, traditional
joinery, matched profiles, all heartwood,
any glazing.

Amherst Woodworking & Supply, Inc.
30 Industrial Drive
Northampton, MA 01061
Tel: (800) 532-9110 Fax: (413) 582-0164
Moldings–doors–stair parts–plank
flooring–20+species hardwood lumber.
E-mail: amwooco@copperbeech.com
Web site: www.copperbeech.com

Architectural Components, Inc.
26 North Leverett Road
Montague, MA 01351
Tel: (413) 367-9441 Fax: (413) 367-9461
Architectural components, Inc.
specializes in reproducing historic
doorways, doors & windows.
E-mail:
arch.components.inc@worldnet.att.net

Maine

Sun Architectural Woodworks, Inc.
RR 1 Box 8080
West Baldwin, ME 04091
Tel: (207) 625-7000
Custom design and fabrication of sash,
windows, window-walls, palladian
windows, and doors & entrances. 18th
century design and construction a
"specialty".

Montana

Specialty Woodworks Company
PO Box 1450
Hamilton, MT 59840
Tel: (406) 363-6353 Fax: (406) 363-6373
Established 1981. Manufactures custom
hand-crafted doors and cabinets.
Specializing in unique blue stain pine,
knotty pine, and other rustic hardwoods.
Catalog $7.

New Hampshire

Lamson-Taylor Custom Doors
Tucker Road
South Acworth, NH 03607
Tel: (603) 835-2992, Fax: same
Insulated wood doors, entrances:
arched work, art glass.

Pennsylvania

Kestrel Shutters
PO Box 12, 3250 St. Peters Road
St. Peters, PA 19470-0012
Tel: (800) 494-4321, (610) 409-6444
Fax: (610) 469-6881
Custom sized, pegged mortise & tenon
shutters available assembled and D.I.Y.
E-mail: kestrel@fast.net
Web site: http://www.diyshutters.com

Idaho

Alternative Timber Structures

Wisconsin

Hurd Millwork Company
575 S. Wheelen Ave.
Medford, WI 54451
Tel: (715) 748-2011
Fax: (715) 748-6043
Wood, aluminum-clad wood and vinyl
windows and patio doors.
Web site: http://www.hurd.com

Eco-Building Schools

Arizona

The Canelo Project
HCL Box 324
Elgin, AZ 85611
Tel: (520) 455-5548
Fax: (520) 455-9360
Straw bale building/earthen floors and
plasters, workshops, resources,
consulting.
E-mail: absteen@dakotacom.net
Web site: http://www.deatech.com/
canelo

Arcosanti
HC 74, Box 4136
Mayer, AZ 86333
Tel: (520) 632-7135
Fax: (520) 632-6229
E-mail: arcosanti@aol.com

California

Real Goods
555 Leslie St.
Ukiah, CA 95482
Tel: (707) 468-9292
Fax: (707) 462-9394
Solar, wind, hydro, efficient lighting,
water, catalogs, books and institute.

Cal-Earth Institute
10225 Baldy Lane
Hesperia, CA 92345
Tel: (619) 244-0614, (619) 956-7533
Fax: (619) 244-2201
E-mail: calearth@aol.com

Eos Institute
580 Broadway, Suite 200
Laguna Beach, CA 92651
Tel: (714) 497-1896
Fax: (714) 497-7861
Educational nonprofit for the study of
sustainable living. Resources,
consulting, and programs on ecological
community design. Library, lectures,
workshops.
E-mail: eos@igpc.org

Colorado

Solar Energy International
PO Box 715
Carbondale, CO 81623
Tel: (970) 963-8855
Fax: (970) 963-8866
Hands-on workshops in solar home
design, straw bale, rammed earth,
adobe, photovoltaics, wind, hydro, solar
cooking & consulting.
E-mail: sei@solarenergy.org

DC, Washington

Sandra Leibowitz
Eco-Building Schools
3220 N Street NW #218
Washington, DC 20007
$7 ($6 + $1 postage) for Eco-Building
Schools: A directory of alternative
educational resources in
environmentally sensitive design.
Detailed info on 35 eco-building schools
across the U.S.
Web site: http://www.ecodesign.org/edi/
eden

Florida

International Institute for Bau-Biologie
1401 A Cleveland St.
Clearwater, FL 34615
Tel: (813) 461-4371
Holistic education in the creation of
homes & offices that are harmonious
and healthy to the occupants and have
no adverse effect on the environment.
E-mail: baubiologie@earthlink.net
Web site: http://www.bau-
biologieusa.com

Massachusetts

The Heartwood School
Johnson Hill Road
Washington, MA 01235
Tel: (413) 623-6677
Fax: (413) 623-0277
Workshops in homebuilding, timber
framing, woodworking, and more.
E-mail: info@heartwoodschool.com
Web site: www.heartwoodschool.com

Maine

Fox Maple School Of Traditional
Building
PO Box 249
Brownfield, ME 04010
Tel: (207) 935-3720
Fax: (207) 935-4575
Workshops for introductory & advanced
timber framing. Other workshops
available in the areas of thatch, clay and
alternative building systems. Fox Maple
strives for quality craftsmanship, with a
view towards a sustainable future.
E-mail: foxmaple@nxi.com
Web site: http://www.nxi.com/WWW/
joinersquarterly

Minnesota

Energy Efficient Building Association
2950 Metro Drive #108
Minneapolis, MN 55425
Tel: (612) 851-9940
Fax: (612) 851-9507
EEBA produces & presents training
based on the "systems approach".
E-mail: EEBANews@aol.com
Web site: http://www.eeba.org

New Mexico

Natural Building Resources
Star Rt. 2, Box 119
Kingston, NM 88042
Tel: (505) 895-5652
Fax: (505) 895-3326
Books and videos on natural building.
Host–Natural Building Colloquium.
E-mail: blackrange@zianet.com
Web site: www.zianet.com/blackrange

Natural House Building Center
2300 West Alameda, A5
Santa Fe, NM 87501
Tel: (505) 471-5314
Fax: (505) 471-3714
Hands-on workshops: timber framing,
straw-clay construction, earth floors &
plastering.

Southwest Solaradobe School
PO Box 153
Bosque, NM 87006
Tel: (505) 861-1255
Fax: (505) 861-1304

New York

Eastfield Village
PO Box 539, 104 Mud Pond Road
Nassau, NY 12062
Tel: (518) 766-2422
Fax: same
School of historic preservation and early
American trades.

Barkeater Design Build Company
35 Wellington Street
Malone, NY 12953
Tel: (518) 483-5282
Fax: same
Designer/builders specializing in stone
slipform construction. Workshops
available.
E-mail: barkeatr@slic.com
Web site: www.xlic.com/~barkeatr/
home.html

Earthwood Building School
366 Murtagh Hill Road
West Chazy, NY 12992
Tel: (518) 493-7744
Fax: same, phone first
Teaches cordwood masonry and
underground housing. Books, videos
and workshops.
Web site: http://www.interlog.com/
newood

Oregon

Cob Cottage Co.
PO Box 123
Cottage Grove, OR 97424
Tel: (541) 942-2005
Fax: (541) 942-3021
Information and workshops on building
with cob (sand, clay, straw).
Web site: http://www.deatech.com/
cobcottage

Groundworks
PO Box 381
Murphy, OR 97533
Tel: (541) 471-3470
Workshops and handbook available on
cob (hand-sculpted earth) construction.
Web site: http://www.cpros.com/
~sequoia

Pennsylvania

Feng Shui Institute
160 Hopwood Road
Collegeville, PA 19426
Tel: (610) 489-2684
Education to develop the capacity to
heal environments and transform lives.
Geomancy, color, Medicine Wheel, land
healing & landscaping.

Texas

Owner Builder Center At Houston
Community College
PO Box 7849, 4141 Costa Rica
Houston, TX 77092
Tel: (713) 956-1178
Fax: (713) 956-7413
Non credit instructional program for
residential building–hands-on and
lecture classes.

Vermont

Yestermorrow Design/Build School
RR 1 Box 97-5
Warren, VT 05674
Tel: (802) 496-5545
Fax: (802) 496-5540
Offers hands-on courses in residential
design and "green" construction.
E-mail: ymschool@aol.com
Web site: www.yestermorrow.org

Washington

Greenfire Institute
PO Box 1040
Winthrop, WA 98862
Tel: (509) 996-3593
Fax: same
Straw bale construction training,
consultation and design.
E-mail: greenfire@igc.org
Web site: www.balewolf.com

Flooring

California

Hendricksen Naturlich Flooring-Interiors
PO Box 1677
Sebastopol, CA 95473
Tel: (707) 824-0914
Fax: (800) 329-9398
Flooring for your health and the planet's.
Wool carpet, jute, true linoleum. $10
introductory kit and catalog.

Connecticut

Chestnut Specialists, Inc.
PO Box 217, 365 Harwinton Ave
Plymouth, CT 06782
Tel: (860) 283-4209
Fax: same
Remanufactured flooring from reclaimed
antique lumber. Dimensional antique
lumber.

Kansas

Design Materials, Inc.
241 S 55th St.
Kansas City, KS 66106
Tel: (800) 654-6451
Fax: (913) 342-9826
"Carpets grown by nature." Jute, wool,
seagrass.

Massachusetts

Cataumet Sawmill
494 Thomas Landers Road
E. Falmouth, MA 02536
Tel: (508) 457-9239
Fax: (508) 540-3626
Antique heart pine flooring "for a home
of distinction".

Green River Lumber, Inc.
PO Box 329
Gt. Barrington, MA 01230
Tel: (413) 528-9000
Fax: (413) 528-2379
Manufacturer of certified and non-
certified plank hardwood flooring.

Maryland

Vintage Lumber Co., Inc.
PO Box 104, 1 Council
Woodsboro, MD 21798
Tel: (800) 499-7859
Fax: (301) 845-6475
Reclaimed, remilled and remarkable
tongue and groove antique wood
flooring.
E-mail: woodfloors@vintagelumber.com
Web site: www.vintagelumber.com

New Hampshire

Carlisle Restoration Lumber
HCR 32 Box 556C
Stoddard, NH 03464
Tel: (800) 595-9663
Fax: (603) 446-3540
Traditional wide plank flooring custom
milled up to 20" wide.
Web site: www.wideplankflooring.com

New Mexico

Plaza Hardwood, Inc.
5 Enebro Court
Santa Fe, NM 87505
Tel: (800) 662-6306
Fax: (505) 466-0456
Distributor of wood flooring and lumber
from certified sustainable forest
resources.

Rhode Island

South County Post & Beam
521 Liberty Lane
West Kingston, RI 02892
Tel: (401) 783-4415
Fax: (401) 783-4494
A full service timber frame company,
wide pine flooring distributor.

Virginia

Vintage Pine Co.
PO Box 85
Prospect, VA 23960
Tel: (804) 574-6531
Fax: (804) 574-2401
Antique heart pine flooring and stair
parts.

Mountain Lumber Co.
PO Box 289, 6812 Spring Hill Road
Ruckersville, VA 22968
Tel: (804) 985-3646
Fax: (804) 985-4105
Flooring, moldings, and stair parts milled
from reclaimed wood.
E-mail: sales@mountainlumber.com
Web site: http://
www.mountainlumber.com

Washington

Resource Woodworks
627 E. 60th Street
Tacoma, WA 98404 Tel: (206) 474-3757
Fax: (206) 474-1139
Custom milling & planing of reclaimed
Douglas fir timbers, also flooring & trim
package available. We ship anywhere.

Hardware

Colorado

Planetary Solutions
2030 17th Street
Boulder, CO 80302
Tel: (303) 442-6228, (303) 444-3730
Fax: (303) 442-6474
Natural hardware store.

Florida

The Healthy Home Center
1403 A Cleveland St.
Clearwater, FL 34615
Tel: (813) 447-4454
Fax: (813) 447-0140
Paints & stains, flooring, insulation, air
purification, cleaning supplies...

The Eco Store, Inc.
2441 Edgewater Drive
Orlando, FL 32804
Tel: (407) 426-9949
Energy savers, household products,
paints, varnishes, solar, cleaning
products.

Massachusetts

Old Sturbridge Village
One Old Sturbridge Village Road
Sturbridge, MA 01566
Tel: (508) 347-3362
Fax: (508) 347-0369
Hand-forged wrought iron hinges,
latches and more.

Tremont Nail Co.
PO Box 111, 8 Elm St.
Wareham, MA 02571
Tel: (508) 295-0038
Fax: (508) 295-1365
Manufacturer of restoration pattern steel
cut nails; colonial hardware distributor.
E-mail: cutnails@aol.com

Konceptual
Architectural Hardware
PO Box 99
North Quincy, MA 02171-0099

Minnesota

The Woodworkers' Store
4365 Willow Dr.
Medina, MN 55340
Tel: (800) 279-4441
Fax: (612) 478-8395
Woodworking hardware, wood, tools and
know-how.
E-mail: rocklerl@pclink.com
Web site: www.woodworkerstore.com

New Hampshire

Scott Northcott Woodturning
RR#1 Box 624
Walpole, NH 03608
Tel: (603) 756-4204
Hardwood pegs for timber framing.

Woodstock Soapstone Co., Inc.
66 Airpark Road
W. Lebanon, NH 03784
Tel: (603) 298-5955

New York

Lee Valley Tools Ltd.
PO Box 178012 East River St.
Ogdensburg, NY 13669-0490
Tel: (800) 871-8158 Fax: (800) 513-7885
Our 236-page full-color catalog has the
widest selection of woodworking hand
tools in the market.
Web site: http://www.leevalley.com

Historic Housefitters Co.
Dept. 6027 Farm to Market Road
Brewster, NY 10509
Tel: (914) 278-2427
Hand-wrought hardware and lighting.

Crosscut Saw Company
PO Box 7871
Seneca Falls, NY 13148
(315) 568-5755

Ohio

Lehman's
Box 41
Kidron, OH 44636
How the Amish live without electricity.
Over 2,500 items including stoves,
refrigerators, lights, appliances,
woodworking and garden tools.

Pennsylvania

Kestrel Shutters
PO Box 12, 3250 St. Peters Road
St. Peters, PA 19470-0012
Tel: (800) 494-4321, (610) 409-6444
Fax: (610) 469-6881
Custom sized, pegged mortise & tenon
shutters available assembled and D.I.Y.
E-mail: kestrel@fast.net
Web site: http://www.diyshutters.com

Simply Natural
RR#2, Box 136
Tamaqua, PA 18252
Tel: (503) 222-3881
Products that are natural, healthy, and
earth-friendly.

Tennessee

Cumberland General Store
#1 Highway 68
Crossville, TN 38555
One of a kind old time mercantile and
hardware company.

Company Listings by Subject

Vermont

Bethel Mills, Inc.
PO Box 61, 1 North Main
Bethel, VT 05032
Tel: (800) 234-9951 Fax: (802) 234-5631
Retail lumber, building materials, and
tools for the serious contractor.
E-mail: bml@sover.net
Web site: bethelmills.com

West Virginia

Woodcraft Supply
PO Box 1686, 210 Wood County
Industrial Park
Parkersburg, WV 26102
Tel: (800) 225-1153
Fax: (304) 428-8271
Quality woodworking tools, books,
hardware, hardwoods; plus tool
sharpening service.
E-mail: custserv@woodcraft.com
Web site: www.woodcraft.com

Log Homes

Florida

Freedom Builders
1013 Naples Drive
Orlando, FL 32804
Tel: (407) 647-5849
Fax: (407) 645-5652
Internet informational & advertising site–
log & t.f. design–video productions.
E-mail: freedom@magicnet.net
Web site: www.magicnet.net/freedom

Georgia

Hearthstone Log & Timberframe Homes
120 Carriage Drive
Macon, GA 31210
Tel: (800) 537-7931
Fax: (912) 477-6535
21 years experience, CADD design,
professional erection and dry-in
services.
E-mail:
hearthstonehomes@mindspring.com
Web site: www.mindspring.com/
~hearthstonehomes

Idaho

Woodhouse
PO Box 801
Ashton, ID 83420
Tel: (208) 652-3608
Fax: (208) 652-3628
Supplying all specialized tools and
materials for log-timber construction.
Providing owner and/or professional with
largest selection of quality products
available.

Jeff Pedersen–Logsmith
PO Box 788, Hwy. 93 North
Challis, ID 83226
Tel: (208) 879-4211
Fax: (208) 879-5574
Traditional broadaxe-hewn dovetail and
round log scribe-fit log homes.
Broadaxe-hewn and round log timber
frames.
E-mail: jplogs@cyberhighway.net

Maine

Timberstone Builders
RR 1 Box 3125
Freedom, ME 04941
Tel: (207) 589-4675
Fax: same
We specialize in chink-style log buildings
and Rumford fireplaces.

Michigan

Northern Land & Lumber Co.
7000 P Rd.
Gladstone, MI 49837
Tel: (906) 786-2994
Fax: (906) 786-2926
Primary manufacturer of log home kits &
components.
E-mail: nlandl@up.net
Web site: www.deltami.org/nlandl

Missouri

Timberland Design/Hearthstone
15444 Clayton Road, Ste. 325-6
St. Louis, MO 63011
Tel: (800) 680-8833, (314) 341-8833
Fax: (314) 341-8833
Architect, Hearthstone distributor,
specializing in timber frame/log designs
& packages.

North Carolina

Mountain Construction Enterprises
PO Box 1177, 353 Devonwood Drive
Boone, NC 28607
Tel: (704) 264-1231
Fax: (704) 264-4863
Custom traditionally mortised oak timber
frames with stress skin panels.
E-mail: Mtnconst@skybest.com
Web site: http://blowingrock.com/nc/
timberframe

Enertia Building Systems, Inc.
13312 Garffe Sherron Road
Wake Forest, NC 27587
Tel: (919) 556-0177
Fax: (919) 556-1135
Design/prefabrication of solid wood
solar/geothermal environmental homes.

Timberfab, Inc.
PO Box 399, 200 W. Hope Lodge St.
Tarboro, NC 27886
Tel: (800) 968-8322
Fax: (919) 641-4142
Log and timber frame structures,
components and supplies.
E-mail: tfab@coastalnet.com
Web site: http://www4.coastalnet.com/
timberfab

New Hampshire

Dan Dustin–Custom Hand-Hewing
1107 Penacook Road
Contoocook, NH 03229
Tel: (603) 746-5683
Expert adze and broadaxe work–your
material–my yard.

New York

Alternate Energy Systems
PO Box 344
Peru, NY 12972
Tel: (518) 643-0805
Fax: (518) 643-2012
Masonry heaters–timber frame and log
homes–a natural blend–call.

Lok-N-Logs, Inc.
PO Box 677, Route 12
Sherburne, NY 13460
Tel: (800) 343-8928, (607) 674-4447
Fax: (607) 674-6433
Producer of top quality, pre-cut log home
packages–lifetime limited warranty!
E-mail: lnlinfo@loknlogs.com
Web site: http://www.loknlogs.com
Catalog: $12.95

Ohio

Hochstetler Milling
552 St. Rt. 95
Loudonville, OH 44842
Tel: (419) 281-3553, (419) 368-0004
Oak timber 4-sided planing. Pine log
home logs 10 profiles.

Hearthstone Log & Timberframe Homes
4974 Wortman Road
Zanesville, OH 43701
Tel: (614) 453-6542
Fax: same
Oak or pine timber frames, and square,
hand-hewn log homes.

Tennessee

Hearthstone, Inc.
1630 E. Hwy. 25-70
Dandridge, TN 37725
Tel: (800) 247-4442 Fax: (423) 397-9262
Traditionally joined timber frames and
finely crafted dovetailed log homes.
E-mail: sales@hearthstonehomes.com
Web site: www.hearthstonehomes.com

Vermont

Real Log Homes
PO Box 202, National Information
Center
Hartland, VT 05048
Tel: (800) 732-5564 Fax: (802) 436-2150
Pre-cut log home packages over 19,000
worldwide since 1963. Catalog $10.
Web site: http://www.realloghomes.com

Washington

Ark II Inc.
HCR 73 Box 67
Twisp, WA 98856
Tel: (509) 997-2418 Fax: (509) 997-4434
Fine quality timber frame & log
buildings.

Timbercraft Homes, Inc.
85 Martin Road
Port Townsend, WA 98368
Tel: (360) 385-3051
Fax: (360) 385-7745
Since 1979, high quality timber frame
structures, components, and
architectural engineering.
E-mail: info@timbercraft.com
Web site: http://www.timbercraft.com

Wisconsin

Standard Tar Products Co., Inc.
2456 West Cornell St.
Milwaukee, WI 53209-6294
Tel: (800) 825-7650
Fax: (414) 873-7737
"Organiclear" protective wood coatings
& finishes for log homes & restoration.

Alberta

Goldec International Equipment, Inc.
6760 65 Ave.
Red Deer, Alberta, Canada T4R 1G5
Tel: (403) 343-6607
Fax: (403) 340-0640
De-bark logs with our chainsaw
attachment. The amazing Log Wizard!
E-mail: goldec@telusplanet.net
Web site: goldec.com

Ontario

The Timbersmith Log Construction,
Limited
General Delivery
Hillsdale, Ontario, Canada L0L 1V0
Tel: (705) 725-2585
Fax: (705) 725-2590
Log and timber frame custom hand-
crafted homes.

Northern Timberhouse, Ltd.
PO Box 71, Hwy. 35 South
Minden, Ontario, Canada K0M 2K0
Tel: (705) 286-3791
Fax: (705) 286-6168
Canadian timber frames and hand-
crafted log homes since 1980.
E-mail: nortim@halhinet.on.ca

Canadian Log Home Supply
RR 2
Eganville, Ontario, Canada K0J 1T0
Tel: (800) 746-7773, (613) 628-2372
Fax: same
Sealants, finishes, preservatives,
cleaners and restoration products. Retail
and wholesale. Authorized Perma-Chink
distributor.

Masonry

Illinois

S. Patzer & Co.
3N743 Rt. 31
St. Charles, IL 60174
Tel: (630) 584-1081
Mason contractor specializing in unusual
fireplaces, masonry heaters, and ovens.

Maine

Brick Stove Works
15 Nelson Ridge South
Washington, ME 04574
Tel: (207) 845-2440
Fax: same
20 years experience designing and
building masonry heaters. Will travel.
E-mail: jpmanly@midcoast.com

Minnesota

D. Larsen Masonry Construction
10801 Jackpine Road NW
Bemidji, MN 56661
Tel: (218) 751-0523
Specialize in masonry heaters,
fireplaces and chimney relining.

New Hampshire

Wolf's Rock Farm
PO Box 298
Bradford, NH 03221
Tel: (603) 938-5344
Building stone delivered, wholesale
prices. Complete period reproduction,
restoration services. Rumford fireplaces.

New York

Barkeater Design Build Company
35 Wellington Street
Malone, NY 12953
Tel: (518) 483-5282
Fax: same
Designer/builders specializing in stone
slipform construction. Workshops
available
E-mail: barkeatr@slic.com

Ontario

Alderaan Stone/Timber Homes
PO Box 313, 6-14845 Yonge Street
Aurora, Ontario, Canada L4G 6H8
Tel: (905) 713-0001 Fax: (905) 713-0134
Traditional materials and craftsmanship.
Comprehensive custom reproductions of
early Canadian homes.
Web site: www.craftsman-book.com

Masonry Heaters

Connecticut

New England Hearth And Soapstone
127 North Street
Goshen, CT 06756
Tel: (860) 491-3091 Fax: same
Hand-crafted masonry heaters,
fireplaces, countertops and more in
soapstone and other materials, also
parts.
E-mail: nehearth@bigfoot.com
Web site: http://mha-net.org/users/nehs/

Illinois

S. Patzer & Co.
3N743 Rt. 31
St. Charles, IL 60174
Tel: (630) 584-1081
Mason contractor specializing in unusual
fireplaces, masonry heaters, and ovens.

Maine

Maine Wood Heat Co, Inc
RFD 1, Box 640
Norridgewock, ME 04957
Tel: (207) 696-5442
Fax: (207) 696-5856
Masonry heaters, cookstoves and
ovens. Construction, hardware, books,
plans, design. Hands-on workshops.

Timberstone Builders
RR 1 Box 3125
Freedom, ME 04941
Tel: (207) 589-4675
Fax: same
We specialize in chink-style log buildings
and Rumford fireplaces.

Brick Stove Works
15 Nelson Ridge South
Washington, ME 04574
Tel: (207) 845-2440
Fax: same
20 years experience designing and
building masonry heaters. Will travel.
E-mail: jpmanly@midcoast.com

Michigan

Sackett Brick Company
1303 Fulford St.
Kalamazoo, MI 49001
Tel: (800) 848-9440, (616) 381-4757
Fax: (616) 381-2684
Masonry heaters: sales, design, consult,
build. Importers of Tulikivi and dealers
for most Heater Core kits.

Minnesota

D. Larsen Masonry Construction
10801 Jackpine Road NW
Bemidji, MN 56661
Tel: (218) 751-0523
Specialize in masonry heaters,
fireplaces and chimney relining.

Montana

Cornerstone Masonry Distributing, Inc.
PO Box 83
Pray, MT 59065
Tel: (406) 333-4383
Fax: same
Specializing in Tulikivi soapstone
masonry heaters, bakeovens, and
cookstoves.
E-mail: radiant@alpinet.com
Web site: http://www.tulikivi.com

New York

Alternate Energy Systems
PO Box 344
Peru, NY 12972
Tel: (518) 643-0805
Fax: (518) 643-2012
Masonry heaters–timber frame and log
homes–a natural blend–call.

North Carolina

Vesta Masonry Stove, Inc.
373 Old 7 Mile Ridge Road
Burnsville, NC 28714
Tel: (704) 675-5666, (800) 473-5240
Fireplace masons specializing in
masonry heater sales, construction and
design. Saunas, cooker & bake ovens.

Ohio

Superior Clay Corporation
PO Box 352, 6566 Superior Road SE
Uhrichsville, OH 44683
Tel: (614) 922-4122
Fax:(614) 922-6626
Clay flue lining, Rumford fireplace
components, clay chimney pots, ground
fired clay.
E-mail: mcclave@tusconet.com
Web site: rumford.com

Top Hat Chimney Sweeps D.B.A. TNT
Masonry Heaters
12380 Tinker's Creek Road
Cleveland, OH 44125
Tel: (216) 524-5431
Wood-fired masonry heaters, bake
ovens, and cookstoves.
Web site: http://rnha-net.org/users/tnt/
index.htm

Heartwood Timber Frames
6660 Heartwood Place
Swanton, OH 43558
Tel: (419) 875-5500
Fax: same
Crafting beautiful timber frames, panel
homes, and masonry heaters.

Oregon

Kachelofen Unlimited
1407 Caves Camp Road
Williams, OR 97544
Tel: (503) 846-6196
Hand-crafted ceramic tile stoves, a
source of healthy, radiant heat. Creates
a healthy room climate.

Pennsylvania

Mid-Atlantic Masonry Heat, Inc.
PO Box 277
Emigsville, PA 17318-0277
Tel: (800) 213-0903
Fax: (717) 854-1373
Mid-Atlantic and southeastern regional
distributor Tulikivi natural soapstone
fireplaces, bake ovens, cookstoves,
heater benches, floor and wall tile.

Utah

Blofire, Inc.
3220 Melbourne
Salt Lake City, UT 84106
Tel: (801) 486-0266
Fax: (801) 486-8100
Increased quality of life through efficient,
wonderful, natural heating.

Virginia

Masonry Heater Association Of North
America
11490 Commerce Pk. Dr., Suite 300
Reston, VA 20191
Tel: (703) 620-3171
Fax: (703) 620-3928
Association of builders, designers &
researchers of masonry heaters.
Web site: http://mha-net.org/

Tulikivi U.S.
PO Box 7825
Charlottesville, VA 22906-7825
Tel: (804) 977-5500
Fax: (804) 977-5164
Tulikivi (two-lee-kee-vee) soapstone
fireplaces, bake ovens, cookstoves—
efficient radiant heat.

Washington

Dietmeyer, Ward & Stroud, Inc.
PO Box 323, 12027 SW Wesleyan Way
Vashon, WA 98070
Tel: (206) 463-3722
Fax: (206) 463-6335
Manufacturer of modular masonry
heater kits, the Envirotech radiant
fireplace.

Ontario

Temp-Cast Enviroheat Ltd.
PO Box 94059, 3332 Yonge St.
Toronto, Ontario, Canada M4N 3R1
Tel: (416) 322-6084
Fax: (416) 486-3624
Fully modular masonry heaters–quick
and easy assembly–wood or gas.
E-mail: staywarm@tempcast.com
Web site: http://www.tempcast.com

Materials

Arizona

Sirocco Trading Company
110 East Wing Drive
Sedona, AZ 86336
Tel: (520) 204-2516
Fax: (520) 282-3716
Recycled wood products, solid timbers,
boards; Douglas fir, redwood, more.
E-mail: eeh3@sedona.net

California

Bamboo-Smiths
PO Box 1801
Nevada City, CA 95959
Tel: (916) 292-9449
Fax: (916) 292-9460
Bamboo items in traditional Japanese or
adapted styles. Specialty tools and
classes available.

Colorado

Planetary Solutions
2030 17th Street
Boulder, CO 80302
Tel: (303) 442-6228, (303) 444-3730
Fax: (303) 442-6474
Natural hardware store.

Building for Health Materials Center
PO Box 113
Carbondale, CO 81623
Tel: (970) 963-0437
Fax: (970) 963-3318
Created to provide a central supplier for
healthy, environmentally sound building
products to meet your building material
needs and requirements.
E-mail: crose@rof.net

Connecticut

New England Hearth And Soapstone
127 North Street
Goshen, CT 06756
Tel: (860) 491-3091
Fax: same
Hand-crafted masonry heaters,
fireplaces, countertops and more in
soapstone and other materials, also
parts.
E-mail: nehearth@bigfoot.com
Web site: http://mha-net.org/users/nehs/

Florida

Tropical American Tree Farms
C/O AAA Express Mail, 1641 NW 79th
Avenue
Miami, FL 33126
Tel: (800) 788-4918, 011 (506) 787-0020
Fax: 011 (506) 787-0051
Growing precious tropical hardwoods on
tree farms in Costa Rica.
E-mail: tatfsa.sol.racsa.co.cr

The Healthy Home Center
1403 A Cleveland St.
Clearwater, FL 34615
Tel: (813) 447-4454
Fax: (813) 447-0140
Paints & stains, flooring, insulation, air
purification, cleaning supplies...

The Eco Store, Inc.
2441 Edgewater Drive
Orlando, FL 32804
Tel: (407) 426-9949
Energy savers, household products,
paints, varnishes, solar, cleaning
products.

Georgia

Upper Loft Design, Inc.
Rt. 1 Box 2901
Lakemont, GA 30552
Tel: (706) 782-5246
Fax: (706) 782-6840
A timberframe design/build and turn-key
housewright company.
Web site: http://www.upperloft@stc.net

Tenneco Building Products
2907 Log Cabin Drive
Smyrna, GA 30080
Tel: (404) 350-1323
Fax: (404) 350-1489
Extruded polystyrene rigid foam
insulation, underlayments and
housewrap.

Iowa

Agriboard Industries
PO Box 645
Fairfield, IA 52556
Tel: (515) 472-0363
Complete, OSB laminated, compressed
wheat straw panel building systems.
E-mail: agriboard@lisco.com

Maryland

Slate International
15106 Marlboro Pike
Upper Marlboro, MD 20772
Tel: (800) 343-9785, (301) 952-0120
Fax: (301) 952-0295
Slate International is a nationwide
supplier of high grade roofing slate and
slate ridge vents.

Massachusetts

The Old Fashioned Milk Paint Co.
436 Main St.
Groton, MA 01450-0222
Tel: (508) 448-6336
Fax: (508) 448-2754

Amherst Woodworking & Supply, Inc.
30 Industrial Drive
Northampton, MA 01061
Tel: (800) 532-9110
Fax: (413) 582-0164
Moldings-doors-stair parts-plank
flooring-20+species hardwood lumber
E-mail: amwooco@copperbeech.com
Web site: www.copperbeech.com

W.D. Cowls, Inc.
PO Box 9677, 134 Montague Road
North Amherst, MA 01059-9677
Tel: (413) 549-1403
Fax: (413) 549-0000
Timbers to 26', NELMA certified to
grade boards, structural lumber and
timbers.

Cataumet Sawmill
494 Thomas Landers Road
E. Falmouth, MA 02536
Tel: (508) 457-9239
Fax: (508) 540-3626
Antique heart pine flooring "for a home
of distinction".

Karp Woodworks
136 Fountain Street
Ashland, MA 01721
Tel: (508) 881-7000
Fax: (508) 881-7684
Sustainably harvested certified tropical
& domestic woods. "Furnature", an
organic, sustainable and chemical-free
line of upholstered furniture. "Certified

Serenity", a line of comfortable and
colorful sunroom/patio furniture from
certified sustainable sources.

Green River Lumber, Inc.
PO Box 329
Gt. Barrington, MA 01230
Tel: (413) 528-9000
Fax: (413) 528-2379
Manufacturer of certified and non-
certified plank hardwood flooring.

Forester Moulding & Lumber
152 Hamilton St.
Leominster, MA 01453
Tel: (978) 840-3100
Fax: (978) 534-8356
Manufacturer of 1800 hardwood
mouldings in 22+ wood species.
Web site: www.forestermoulding.com

Johnson Clapboard Mill
134 Wendell Road
Shutesbury, MA 01072
Tel: (413) 259-1271
Fax: same
Manufacturer of restoration quality
clapboard siding.

Minnesota

AFM Corporation
PO Box 246, 24000 W. Hwy. 7, Ste. 201
Excelsior, MN 55331
Tel: (612) 474-0809
Fax: (612) 474-2074
Manufacturers of insulated structural
building panels.
E-mail: afmcorp@worldnet.att.net
Web site: www.afmcorp-spsfoam.com

Midwest Hardwood Corp.
9540 83rd Ave. N.
Maple Grove, MN 55369
Tel: (612) 425-8700
Fax: (612) 391-6740
Northern hardwood lumber
manufacturer.
E-mail: MWHWD@ix.netcom.com

Missouri

Woodmaster Tools
1431 N. Topping Ave.
Kansas City, MO 64120
Tel: (816) 483-7203
Make mirror-smooth custom molding
with the Woodmaster planer/molder.

Industrial AG Innovations
2725 N. Westwood Blvd, Suite 7
Poplar Bluff, MO 63901
Tel: (573) 785-3355
Fax: (573) 785-3059
Hemp fiberboard products. 100% hemp
particles and a typical UF resin.

North Carolina

Timberfab, Inc.
PO Box 399, 200 W. Hope Lodge St.
Tarboro, NC 27886
Tel: (800) 968-8322
Fax: (919) 641-4142
Log and timber frame structures,
components and supplies.
E-mail: tfab@coastalnet.com
Web site: http://www4.coastalnet.com/
timberfab

New Hampshire

Scott Northcott Woodturning
RR#1 Box 624
Walpole, NH 03608
Tel: (603) 756-4204
Hardwood pegs for timber framing.

Woodstock Soapstone Co., Inc.
66 Airpark Road
W. Lebanon, NH 03784
Tel: (603) 298-5955

James Derby Construction
PO Box 157
Gilmanton, NH 03237
Tel: (603) 267-7361
Fax: Same
Antique buildings and materials for sale.
Hard pine flooring and more.

New York

Historic Paints Ltd.
RR1 Box 474
East Meredith, NY 13757-9740
Tel: (800) 664-6293

UC Coatings Corporation
PO Box 1066j
Buffalo, NY 14215
Tel: (706) 833-9366
Producer of Anchorseal end-sealer. For
logs and timbers. Eliminates up to 90%
or more of end-checking.

Rector Cork Insulation
9 West Prospect Ave.
Mount Vernon, NY 10550
Tel: (914) 699-5755,6,7
Fax: (914) 699-5759
Architects and engineers specify cork
because of its superior insulation values,
long life, structural strength & decorative
values.

Hilltop Slate, Inc.
PO Box 201
Middle Granville, NY 12849
Tel: (518) 642-2270
Fax: (518) 642-1220
Hilltop Slate has been a leading supplier
of roofing and structural slate since
1948.

Ohio

Custom Roof Thatching & Supplies
PO Box 62054
Cincinnati, OH 45262
Tel: (513) 772-4979
Fax: (513) 772-6313
Has thatched in U.S. since 1986. A
guide to roof thatching in the U.S. $6.00
Web site: http://www.roofthatch.com

Oregon

Environmental Building Supplies
1314 NW Northrup St.
Portland, OR 97209
Tel: (503) 222-3881
Low-toxic, renewable and recycled
materials. Hardwood floors, carpet,
linoleum, tile, paint, finishes.

Rhode Island

Liberty Cedar
535 Liberty Lane
W. Kingston, RI 02892
Tel: (800) 882-3327, (401) 789-6626
Fax: (401) 789-0320
Naturally decay-resistant exterior wood
products specializing in wood roofing.

Tennessee

Perma "R" Products, Inc.
106 Perma R Road
Johnson City, TN 37603
Tel: (800) 251-7532
Fax: (423) 929-7271
Panel supplier to the southeast, midwest
& mid-Atlantic.
E-mail: sip@washington.xtn.net
Web site: http://www.sipsproducts.com

Vermont

Vermont Stresskin Panels
RR 2 Box 2794
Cambridge, VT 05444
Tel: (802) 644-8885
Fax: (802) 644-8797
Stresskin panel enclosure systems for
timber frame structures.

Company Listings by Subject _____

Foard Panel, Inc.
8 Marlboro Avenue
Brattleboro, VT 05301
Tel: (802) 254-3972
Fax: same
Manufacturers and professional
installers of high-quality urethane and
EPS panels.
E-mail: shippees@sover.net

Second Harvest Salvage & Demo
PO Box 194-E, RR1
Jeffersonville, VT 05464
Tel: (802) 644-8169
Specializing in hand hewn frames and
antique flooring and lumbers.

Organic Oat Straw
RR#1 Box 520
Orleans, VT 05860
Tel: (802) 754-2028
Straw bales for building.

Bethel Mills, Inc.
PO Box 61, 1 North Main
Bethel, VT 05032
Tel: (800) 234-9951
Fax: (802) 234-5631
Retail lumber, building materials, and
tools for the serious contractor.
E-mail: bml@sover.net
Web site: bethelmills.com

Foam Laminates Of Vermont
PO Box 102, Rte. 116, Varney Hill Rd.
Hinesburg, VT 05461
Tel: (802) 453-4438
Fax: (802) 453-2338
F.L.V. manufactures stresskin panels for
the timber frame industry.
E-mail: foamlam@sover.net
Web site: www.sover.net/~foamlam

Belgian Woodworks
1068 Ireland Road
Starksboro, VT 05487
Tel: (802) 453-4787
Custom mouldings, banisters and
newels in sustainably harvested
northern hardwoods.

The New England Slate Company
RD 1, Box 1181, Burr Pond Road
Sudbury, VT 05733
Tel: (802) 247-8809
Fax: (802) 247-0089
Quality roofing slate for repair work,
restorations, and new construction.

Washington

Bear Creek Lumber
PO Box 669, 495 Eastside County
Road
Winthrop, WA 98862
Tel: (800) 571-7191
Fax: (509) 997-2040
Western cedar, fir, redwood. Traditional
patterns, decking, timbers and beams.
Delivery available nationwide.

Environmental Home Center
1724 4th Ave. S
Seattle, WA 98134
Tel :(800) 281-9785
Paints, finishes & adhesives, low toxic
flooring & carpets, sustainably harvested
woods.

Wisconsin

Abatron Inc.
5501-95th Ave
Kenosha, WI 53144
Tel: (414) 653-2000
Fax: (414) 653-2019
Wood, concrete, metal restoration
products; adhesives; moldmaking
compounds.
E-mail: info@abatron.com
Web site: http://www.abatron.com

Standard Tar Products Co., Inc.
2456 West Cornell St.
Milwaukee, WI 53209-6294
Tel: (800) 825-7650
Fax: (414) 873-7737
"Organiclear" protective wood coatings
& finishes for log homes & restoration.

Ontario

Canadian Log Home Supply
RR 2
Eganville, Ontario, Canada K0J 1T0
Tel: (800) 746-7773, (613) 628-2372
Fax: same
Sealants, finishes, preservatives,
cleaners and restoration products. Retail
and wholesale. Authorized Perma-Chink
distributor.

Miscellaneous

American Formulating & Manufacturing
350 W Ash St., Suite 700
San Diego, CA 92101
Tel: (619) 239-0321
Fax: (619) 239-0565
Quality paints, stains, cleaners and
sealers formulated without the toxic
chemicals commonly used. Designed to
prevent or alleviate indoor air pollution.

Acorn Timber Frames, Ltd.
RR 1
Hantsport, Kings County, NS, Canada
B0P 1P0
Tel: (902) 684-9708
Fax: same
Traditional joinery: homes, churches,
farm/garden/tourism/vacation structures,
great rooms, restorations. Serving
Canada and alluring locations with your
requirements since 1978.

Lite-Form International
PO Box 774, 1210 Steuben St.
Sioux City, IA 51102
Tel: (712) 252-3704
Fax: (712) 252-3259
Insulating forms for cast in place
foundations & walls.
E-mail: liteform@pionet.net
Web site: http://www.pionet.net/
~liteform/index.html

Midway Village & Museum Center
6799 Guilford Road
Rockford, IL 61107
Tel: (815) 397-9112
Fax: (815) 397-9156
Turn-of-the-century village and Rockford
area history center.

The Raven River Co., Inc.
125 Twin Creek–Connorsville Road
Sadieville, KY 40370
Tel: (606) 235-0368
Fax: same
Artisans of fine timber frames and other
things.
E-mail: ravenriver@kitt.net

Slate International
15106 Marlboro Pike
Upper Marlboro, MD 20772
Tel: (800) 343-9785, (301) 952-0120
Fax: (301) 952-0295
Slate International is a nationwide
supplier of high grade roofing slate and
slate ridge vents.

Hancock Shaker Village
PO Box 927, Rtes. 20 & 41
Pittsfield, MA 01202
Tel: (413) 443-0188
Fax: (413) 447-9357
200 year-old original Shaker site, crafts
demonstrations, working farm.
E-mail: info@hancockshakervillage
Web site: http://
www.hancockshakervillage.org

Earthstar Energy Systems
PO Box 626
Waldoboro, ME 04572
Tel: (800) 323-6749, (800) 660-6749 (in
Maine)
Complete energy system design &
product sales.

Midwest Hardwood Corp.
9540 83rd Ave. N.
Maple Grove, MN 55369
Tel: (612) 425-8700
Fax: (612) 391-6740
Northern hardwood lumber
manufacturer.
E-mail: MWHWD@ix.netcom.com

Industrial AG Innovations
2725 N. Westwood Blvd, Suite 7
Poplar Bluff, MO 63901
Tel: (573) 785-3355
Fax: (573) 785-3059
Hemp fiberboard products. 100% hemp
particles and a typical UF resin.

Specialty Woodworks Company
PO Box 1450
Hamilton, MT 59840
Tel: (406) 363-6353
Fax: (406) 363-6373
Established 1981. Manufactures custom
hand-crafted doors and cabinets.
Specializing in unique blue stain pine,
knotty pine, and other rustic hardwoods.
Catalog $7.

Dan Dustin–Custom Hand-Hewing
1107 Penacook Road
Contoocook, NH 03229
Tel: (603) 746-5683
Expert adze and broadaxe work–your
material–my yard.

Scott Northcott Woodturning
RR#1 Box 624
Walpole, NH 03608
Tel: (603) 756-4204
Hardwood pegs for timber framing.

Wolf's Rock Farm
PO Box 298
Bradford, NH 03221
Tel: (603) 938-5344
Building stone delivered, wholesale
prices. Complete period reproduction,
restoration services. Rumford fireplaces.

Cepco Tool Co.
PO Box 153, 295 Van Etten Road
Spencer, NY 14883
Tel: (607) 589-4313
Fax: same
Board straightening/joining tools,
Bowrench deck tool, Quick-Jack
construction jack.

UC Coatings Corporation
PO Box 1066j
Buffalo, NY 14215
Tel: (706) 833-9366
Producer of Anchorseal end-sealer. For
logs and timbers. Eliminates up to 90%
or more of end-checking.

Construction Business & Technology
Conference
PO Box 2010, West Main St.
Richmond, VT 05477
Tel: (800) 375-5981
Fax: (802) 434-4467
Unique conference and expo featuring
practical information and hands-on
learning opportunities.
E-mail: cbtc@bginet.com
Web site: www.bginet.com

Acorn Crane Service
PO Box 68, Main Road
Huntington, VT 05462
Tel: (800) 990-1953
14 ton National crane, 76' tip height,
Ford 9000 flatbed

The New England Slate Company
RD 1, Box 1181, Burr Pond Road
Sudbury, VT 05733
Tel: (802) 247-8809
Fax: (802) 247-0089
Quality roofing slate for repair work,
restorations, and new construction.

Snorkel Stove Company
4216 6th Avenue S.
Seattle, WA 98108
Tel: (206) 340-0981
Fax: (206) 340-0982
Cedar, wooden hot tubs heated with
underwater stoves—available in kits.
E-mail: hottubs@snorkel.com
Web site: www.snorkel.com

Woodmaster Foundations, Inc.
PO Box 66, 845 Dexter St.
Prescott, WI 54021
Tel: (715) 262-3655
Fax: (715) 262-5079
Permanent wood foundations, earth
sheltered structures and wall building
panels.
E-mail: woodmstr@pressenter.com
Web site: www.pressenter.com/
~woodmstr/

Misc.

Architectural Applications

Tulikivi U.S.
PO Box 7825
Charlottesville, VA 22906-7825
Tel: (804) 977-5500
Fax: (804) 977-5164
Tulikivi (two-lee-kee-vee) soapstone
fireplaces, bake ovens, cookstoves—
efficient radiant heat.

Architectural Drafting

Day Pond Woodworking
PO Box 299, Rt. 114
Bradford, NH 03221
Tel: (603) 938-2375
Over 17 years experience building
custom timber frame homes, etc.

Bamboo

Bamboo-Smiths
PO Box 1801
Nevada City, CA 95959
Tel: (916) 292-9449
Fax: (916) 292-9460
Bamboo items in traditional Japanese or
adapted styles. Specialty tools and
classes available.

Bamboo Fencer
31 Germania St.
Jamaica Plain, MA 02130-2314
Tel: (617) 524-6137
Fax: (617) 524-6100
Manufactures and imports fences,
gates, and other products.
E-mail: Dave@bamboofencer.com
Web site: http://www.bamboofencer.com

Bau-Biologie

International Institute for Bau-Biologie
1401 A Cleveland St.
Clearwater, FL 34615
Tel: (813) 461-4371
Holistic education in the creation of
homes & offices that are harmonious
and healthy to the occupants and have
no adverse effect on the environment.
E-mail: baubiologie@earthlink.net
Web site: http://www.bau-
biologieusa.com

Natural Habitat
PO Box 21, 1320 E. 94th St. South
Haysville, KS 67060
Tel: (316) 788-3676
Feng Shui/bau-biologie consulting. New
and existing structures.

Building Systems

Pumice-Crete Building Systems
PO Box 539
El Prado, NM 87529
Tel: (505) 776-5879
Fax: (505) 758-6954
E-mail: machardy@newmex.com
Web site: www.taosnet.com/pumice-
crete/index.html

Advanced Earthen Construction
Technologies, Inc.
Tel: (210) 349-6960
Fax: (210) 349-2561, or 492-0222
Compressed Soil Block machine
produces an inexpensive, durable,
attractive , and energy efficient building
material from locally available soils.
Produces 960 blocks per hour.
E-mail: vwehman@connecti.com

A & K Technical Services
PO Box 22
Anola, MB, Canada R0E 0A0
Tel: (204) 866-3262
Fax: (204) 866-3287
Structural engineering in wood.
"Stackwall" house construction design,
consulting, manual.
E-mail: krisdick@mb.sympatico.ca

Davis Caves Construction, Inc.
PO Box 69
Armington, IL 61721
Tel: (309) 392-2574
Fax: (309) 392-2578
We will design and build to your specific
floorplan, or choose from our 80 page
planbook.
E-mail: earthome@daviscaves.com
Web site: www.daviscaves.com/
builder.htm

Carpet

Hendricksen Naturlich Flooring-Interiors
PO Box 1677
Sebastopol, CA 95473
Tel: (707) 824-0914
Fax: (800) 329-9398
Flooring for your health and the planet's.
Wool carpet, jute, true linoleum. $10
introductory kit and catalog.

Design Materials, Inc.
241 S 55th St.
Kansas City, KS 66106
Tel: (800) 654-6451
Fax: (913) 342-9826
"Carpets grown by nature." Jute, wool,
seagrass.

Building for Health Materials Center
PO Box 113
Carbondale, CO 81623
Tel: (970) 963-0437
Fax: (970) 963-3318
Created to provide a central supplier for
healthy, environmentally sound building
products to meet your building material
needs and requirements.
E-mail: crose@rof.net

Certified Erection Crews

Hearthstone Log & Timberframe Homes
120 Carriage Drive
Macon, GA 31210
Tel: (800) 537-7931
Fax: (912) 477-6535
21 years experience, CADD design,
professional erection and dry-in
services.E-mail:
hearthstonehomes@mindspring.com
Web site: www.mindspring.com/
~hearthstonehomes

Crane Service

Acorn Crane Service
PO Box 68, Main Road
Huntington, VT 05462
Tel: (800) 990-1953
14 ton national crane, 76' tip height,
Ford 9000 flatbed.

Cupolas

Allen Woodworking And Cupolas
2242 Bethel Road
Lansdale, PA 19446
Tel: (215) 699-8100
Fax: same
Custom redwood, cedar, poplar cupolas;
portable sawmill with backhoe services.

Custom Sawing

Timber Frame Systems, Inc.
PO Box 458, 28 Main St.
Frankford, DE 19945
Tel: (302) 732-9428
Fax: (302) 537-4971
Manufacturer of custom post & beam
frame kits.

Directory

Sandra Leibowitz
Eco-Building Schools
3220 N Street NW #218
Washington, DC 20007
$7 ($6 + $1 postage) for Eco-Building
Schools: A directory of alternative
educational resources in
environmentally sensitive design.
Detailed info on 35 eco-building schools
across the U.S.
Web site: http://www.ecodesign.org/edi/
eden

Dust Control

Dust Door & Wall System
524 Green St.
Boylston, MA 01505
Modular zipper doors & wall panels
which attach with no damage.

Education, Conference

Construction Business & Technology
Conference
PO Box 2010, West Main St.
Richmond, VT 05477
Tel: (800) 375-5981
Fax: (802) 434-4467
Unique conference and expo featuring
practical information and hands-on
learning opportunities.
E-mail: cbtc@bginet.com
Web site: www.bginet.com

Framing Connectors

TIBVITSS Unlimited, LLC
PO Box 267, 35500 East Colfax Avenue
Watkins, CO 80137
Tel: (303) 261-7775
Fax: (303) 261-7778
Innovative metal connectors for simple
yet strong continuous load paths.

General Contractors

Legacy Timber Frames, Inc.
691 County Rd. 70
Stillwater, NY 12170
Tel: (518) 279-9108
Fax: (518) 581-9219
Custom designed, traditional timber
frame construction.

Millcreek Classic Homes
1009 Parchment Drive SE
Grand Rapids, MI 49546
Tel: (616) 949-3012
Fax: (616) 949-4477
Design and build Riverbend timber
frame custom homes.

R.G. White Construction
PO Box 14734, 5800 Firestone Road
Jacksonville, FL 32238
Tel: (904) 778-8352
Fax: same
Building fine quality cracker style and
craftsman style homes.

Healthy Homes, Bau-Biologie

Institute For Bau-Biologie (IBE)
PO Box 387, 1401A Cleveland St.
Clearwater, FL 33757
Tel: (813) 461-4371
Fax: (813) 441-4373
Home study courses, seminars,
consulting on "healthy homes and
offices"

Renaissance Developments
10704 Oviatt Road
Honor, MI 49640
Tel: (616) 326-4009
Sustainable building, healthy creative
dreamspaces, bau-biologie, owner-
builder involvement welcome.

Hemp

Industrial AG Innovations
2725 N. Westwood Blvd, Suite 7
Poplar Bluff, MO 63901
Tel: (573) 785-3355
Fax: (573) 785-3059
Hemp fiberboard products. 100% hemp
particles and a typical UF resin.

The Ohio Hempery, Inc.
7002 State Route 329
Guysville, OH 45735
Tel: (614) 662-4367
Fabric, paper, oil, clothes, shoes, skin &
body care, twine, seeds, stalks, sliver,
yarn and hurds manufactured from
hemp. Free catalog.

Hot Tubs

Snorkel Stove Company
4216 6th Avenue S.
Seattle, WA 98108
Tel: (206) 340-0981
Fax: (206) 340-0982
Cedar, wooden hot tubs heated with
underwater stoves–available in kits.
E-mail: hottub@snorkel.com
Web site: www.snorkel.com

Humidors, Wine Cellars

Ellison Timberframes
20 Six Penny Lane
Harwichport, MA 02646
Tel: (508) 430-0407
Award-winning design/build company.
No steel connections used. Humidors,
wine cellars

Insulating Concrete Forms

Lite-Form International
PO Box 774, 1210 Steuben St.
Sioux City, IA 51102
Tel: (712) 252-3704
Fax: (712) 252-3259
Insulating forms for cast in place
foundations & walls.
E-mail: liteform@pionet.com
Web site: http://www.pionet.net/
~liteform/index.html

Insulation

Tenneco Building Products
2907 Log Cabin Drive
Smyrna, GA 30080
Tel: (404) 350-1323
Fax: (404) 350-1489
Extruded polystyrene rigid foam
insulation, underlayments and
housewrap.

Rector Cork Insulation
9 West Prospect Ave.
Mount Vernon, NY 10550
Tel: (914) 699-5755,6,7
Fax: (914) 699-5759
Architects and engineers specify cork
because of its superior insulation values,
long life, structural strength & decorative
values.

Building for Health Materials Center
PO Box 113
Carbondale, CO 81623
Tel: (970) 963-0437
Fax: (970) 963-3318
Created to provide a central supplier for
healthy, environmentally sound building
products to meet your building material
needs and requirements.
E-mail: crose@rof.net

Low Toxic Paints & Finishes

Environmental Home Center
1724 4th Ave. South
Seattle, WA 98134
Tel: (800) 281-8275, (206) 682-8275
Retail/wholesale—environmentally
responsible building materials and
decorating supplies.
E-mail: info@enviresource.com
Web site: www.enviresource.com

The Healthy Home Center
1403 A Cleveland St.
Clearwater, FL 34615
Tel: (813) 447-4454
Fax: (813) 447-0140
Paints & stains, flooring, insulation, air
purification, cleaning supplies...

The Eco Store, Inc.
2441 Edgewater Drive
Orlando, FL 32804
Tel: (407) 426-9949
Energy savers, household products,
paints, varnishes, solar, cleaning
products.

American Formulating & Manufacturing
350 W Ash St., Suite 700
San Diego, CA 92101
Tel: (619) 239-0321
Fax: (619) 239-0565
Quality paints, stains, cleaners and
sealers formulated without the toxic
chemicals commonly used. Designed to
prevent or alleviate indoor air pollution.

Earth Studio
6761 Sebastopol Ave., Suite 8
Sebastopol, CA 95472
Tel: (707) 823-2569
Petroleum-free & biodegradable natural
paints and finishes. Free Catalog.

Building for Health Materials Center
PO Box 113
Carbondale, CO 81623
Tel: (970) 963-0437 Fax: (970) 963-3318
Created to provide a central supplier for
healthy, environmentally sound building
products to meet your building material
needs and requirements.
E-mail: crose@rof.net

Eco Design Co.
1365 Rufina Circle
Santa Fe, NM 87505
Tel: (800) 621-2591, (505) 438-3448
Fax: (505) 438-0199
The natural choice. Natural paints,
stains & healthy home products catalog.

Machinery

Wilke Machinery Co.
3230 Susquehanna Trail
York, PA 17402
Tel: (717) 764-5000
Fax: (717) 764-3778
Distributors of quality woodworking
machinery and home of Bridgewood
Brand machinery.
Web site: www.wilkemach.com

Manufacturer

J-Deck Building Systems
2587 Harrison Road
Columbus, OH 43204
Tel: (614) 274-7755
Fax: (614) 274-7797
Insulated composite panels: crawl,
basement, floor, wall and roof panels,
residential and commercial.

Museum

Hancock Shaker Village
PO Box 927, Rtes. 20 & 41
Pittsfield, MA 01202
Tel: (413) 443-0188
Fax: (413) 447-9357
200 year-old original Shaker site, crafts
demonstrations, working farm.
E-mail: info@hancockshakervillage
Web site: http://
www.hancockshakervilLage.org

Paint

Historic Paints Ltd.
RR1 Box 474
East Meredith, NY 13757-9740
Tel: (800) 664-6293

The Old Fashioned Milk Paint Co.
436 Main St.
Groton, MA 01450-0222
Tel: (508) 448-6336
Fax: (508) 448-2754

Pegs

Scott Northcott Woodturning
RR#1 Box 624
Walpole, NH 03608
Tel: (603) 756-4204
Hardwood pegs for timber framing.

Pipe Tracing

Easy Heat, Inc.
31977 US 20 E.
New Carlisle, IN 46552
Tel: (219) 654-3144
Fax: (219) 654-7739
Electrical radiant heating cable
solutions.
E-mail: mgb~1@msn.com
Web site: www.easyheat.com

Shutters

Kestrel Shutters
PO Box 12, 3250 St. Peters Road
St. Peters, PA 19470-0012
Tel: (800) 494-4321, (610) 409-6444
Fax: (610) 469-6881
Custom sized, pegged mortise & tenon
shutters available assembled and D.I.Y.
E-mail: kestrel@fast.net
Web site: http://www.diyshutters.com

Shuttercraft, Inc.
282 Stepstone Hill
Guilford, CT 06437
Tel: (203) 453-1973
Fax: (203) 245-5969
Exterior and interior wood shutters for
authentic restoration, hinges, holdbacks.
E-mail: shutter@iconn.net
Web site: http://www.galaxymall.com/
shops/shuttercraft.html

Skylights

Roto Frank Of America, Inc.
PO Box 599, Research Park
Chester, CT 06412-0599
Tel: (860) 243-0893 Fax: (860) 526-3785
World's best roof window: Roto designs
and manufactures innovative skylights.

Slate

The New England Slate Company
RD 1, Box 1181, Burr Pond Road
Sudbury, VT 05733
Tel: (802) 247-8809 Fax: (802) 247-0089
Quality roofing slate for repair work,
restorations, and new construction.

Hilltop Slate, Inc.
PO Box 201
Middle Granville, NY 12849
Tel: (518) 642-2270 Fax: (518) 642-1220
Hilltop Slate has been a leading supplier
of roofing and structural slate since
1948.

Slate International
15106 Marlboro Pike
Upper Marlboro, MD 20772
Tel: (800) 343-9785, (301) 952-0120
Fax: (301) 952-0295
Slate International is a nationwide
supplier of high grade roofing slate and
slate ridge vents.

Soapstone

Woodstock Soapstone Co., Inc.
66 Airpark Road
W. Lebanon, NH 03784
Tel: (603) 298-5955

Software

Tree Talk
PO Box 426, 431 Pine Street
Burlington, VT 05402
Tel: (802) 865-1111
Fax: (802) 863-4344
Multimedia CD-ROM on wood. 900
species. Database. Video. Pictures.
Maps.
E-mail: wow@together.net
Web site: http://www.woodweb.com/~treetalk/
home.html

Passive Solar Industries Council
1511 K Street, Suite 600
Washington, DC 20005
Tel: (202) 628-7400 Fax: (202) 393-5043
PSIC independent nonprofit advancing
climate responsive buildings.
E-mail: PSICouncil@aol.com
Web site: http://www.psic.org

Stairbuilding

Sun Architectural Woodworks, Inc.
RR 1 Box 8080
West Baldwin, ME 04091
Tel: (207) 625-7000
Custom stairs & design a specialty.
Exceptional quality with large circular
stairs. All components & millwork are
fabricated in "our" own shop.

Southern Breeze Timberworks
PO Box 635
Travelers Rest, SC 29690
Tel: (864) 834-3706
Quality hand-wrought joinery.

Structural Engineer

Carroll, Franck & Associates
1357 Highland Parkway
St. Paul, MN 55116
Tel: (612) 690-9162
Fax: (612) 690-9156
Engineering of architectural structures,
traditional joinery and concealed steel
connections.
E-mail: carrfran@gold.tc.umn.edu

Company Listings by Subject

Tool Sharpening

Miller's Sharpening Service
11301 N. Webb
Alliance, OH 44601
Tel: (330) 821-6240

Trusses

Pacific Post & Beam
PO Box 13708
San Luis Obispo, CA 93406
Tel: (805) 543-7565
Fax: (805) 543-1287
Full service timber frame and truss
design and build.

Ventilation, HVAC

Venmar Ces
2525 Wentz Avenue
Saskatoon, SK, Canada S7K 2K9
Tel: (306) 242-3663
Fax: (306) 242-3484
Commercial HRV's (heat recovery
ventilators) and ERV's (energy recovery
ventilators).

Wheat Straw Panels

Agriboard Industries
PO Box 645
Fairfield, IA 52556
Tel: (515) 472-0363
Complete, OSB laminated, compressed
wheat straw panel building systems.
E-mail: agriboard@lisco.com

Wood Foundations

Woodmaster Foundations, Inc.
PO Box 66, 845 Dexter St.
Prescott, WI 54021
Tel: (715) 262-3655
Fax: (715) 262-5079
Permanent wood foundations, earth
sheltered structures and wall building
panels.
E-mail: woodmstr@pressenter.com
Web site: www.pressenter.com/
~woodmstr/

Wood Siding

Johnson Clapboard Mill
134 Wendell Road
Shutesbury, MA 01072
Tel: (413) 259-1271
Fax: same
Manufacturer of restoration quality
clapboard siding.

Workshops

Country Workshops
90 Mill Creek Road
Marshall, NC 28753
Tel: (704) 656-2280
Tools, books and instruction in traditional
woodworking with hand tools
E-mail: langsner@countryworkshops.org
Web site: countryworkshops.org

Alaska Craftsman Home Program, Inc.
PO Box 241647
Anchorage, AK 99524-1647
Tel: (907) 258-2247 (ACHP)
Fax: (907) 258-5352
Education and research advanced cold
climate home building techniques
E-mail: achp@alaska.net
Web site: http://www.alaska.net/~achp

Portable Sawmills

Alabama

Sawmill Exchange
PO Box 131267
Birmingham, AL 35213
Tel: (205) 969-3963
Fax: (205) 967-4620
Buy/sell service for used portable
sawmills.
E-mail: nml@mindspring.com
(Note: letter preceding @ is an "L")
Web site: http://www.sawmill-
exchange.com/

California

Crossroads Recycled Lumber
PO Box 184
O'Neals, CA 93645
Tel: (209) 868- 3646
Fax: same
Demolition salvage, portable sawmills,
dead & dying trees, timbers, flooring.
Natural buildings.

Granberg International
PO Box 70425, 200 South Garraro
Blvd.
Richmond, CA 94807-0425
Tel: (510) 237-2099 Fax: (510) 237-1667
Manufacturer of the Alaskan sawmill.
Attachments and accessories for
sharpening chainsaws.
E-mail: granberg@aol.com
Web site: www.granberg.com

Illinois

The Edge Woodworks
Rt. 1 Box 179
Grafton, IL 62037
Tel: (618) 786-2442
Traditional hand-crafted joinery, portable
sawmill, owner-builder friendly.
E-mail: edgewrks@gtec.com

Indiana

Wood-Mizer Products, Inc.
8180 W. 10th Street
Indianapolis, IN 46214
Tel: (317) 271-1542 Fax: (317) 273-1011
Transportable sawmills and accessories:
lowers lumber costs and improves
quality.
E-mail: adindy@woodmizer.com
Web site: http://www.woodmizer.com

Missouri

TimberKing
1431 N. Topping Ave.
Kansas City, MO 64120
Tel: (800) 942-4400 Fax: (816) 483-7203
Cut 45 foot beams with TimberKing's
bandmill.

Woodland Manufacturing; Vertical Band
Sawmills
PO Box 1540, 1409 Black River
Industrial Road
Poplar Bluff, MO 63902-7720
Tel: (573) 785-3810 Fax: (573) 785-0962
Advanced design, high production one-
man sawmills, built-in edger.

New York

Norwood Industries Inc.
90 Curtwright Dr., Unit 3
Amherst, NY 14221
Tel: (800) 567-0404
Portable sawmills.
E-mail:
norwood@norwoodindustries.com
Web site: www.norwoodindustries.com

Pennsylvania

Pocono Mt. Timber Frames
PO Box 644, Rt. 115
Brodheadsville, PA 18322
Tel: (717) 992-7515
Fax: (717) 992-9064
Design, fabrication, and erection of
timber frame barns and houses.
E-mail: etreible@ptd.net
Web site: www.pmtf.com

Allen Woodworking And Cupolas
2242 Bethel Road
Lansdale, PA 19446
Tel: (215) 699-8100
Fax: same
Custom redwood, cedar, poplar cupolas;
portable sawmill with backhoe services.

Alberta

Goldec International Equipment, Inc.
6760 65 Ave.
Red Deer, Alberta, Canada T4R 1G5
Tel: (403) 343-6607
Fax: (403) 340-0640
De-bark logs with our chainsaw
attachment. The amazing Log Wizard!
E-mail: goldec@TelusPlanet.net
Web site: goldec.com

Publishers

Cappers
Ogden Publications
1503 SW 42nd Street
Topeka, KS 66609-1265
Tel: (785) 274-4330
Fax: (785) 274-4305
A family-oriented publication providing
readers with "good news".
E-mail: cappers@kspress.com
Web site: www.cappers.com

Chelsea Green Publishing Company
PO Box 428
White River Junction, VT 05001
Tel: (802) 295-6300
Fax: (802) 295-6444
Publisher of quality books, specializing
in alternative, natural & traditional
homes for the owner/builder.

Construction Business & Computing
PO Box 2050, West Main St.
Richmond, VT 05477
Tel: (800) 375-5981
Fax: (802) 434-4467
Monthly newsletter on computer
applications and business techniques for
construction professionals.
E-mail: cbc@bginet.com
Web site: www.bginet.com

Craftsman Book Company
6058 Corte Del Cedro
Carlsbad, CA 92009
Tel: (800) 829-8123
Fax: (760) 438-0398
Professional construction books that
solve actual problems in the builder's
office and in the field.

Fine Homebuilding Magazine
PO Box 5506, 63 S. Main Street
Newtown, CT 06470-5506
Tel: (203) 426-8171
Fax: (203) 270-6751
Homebuilders share tips, techniques
and reviews of tools and materials.
E-mail: fh@taunton.com
Web site: http://www.taunton.com

GCR Publishing Group, Inc.
1700 Broadway
New York, NY 10019
Tel: (212) 541-7100
Fax: (212) 245-1241
Publisher of timber homes illustrated
magazine.

Iris Communications, Inc.
PO Box 5920
Eugene, OR 97405
Tel: (541) 484-9353
Fax: (541) 484-1645
Carefully selected books, videos and
software for green construction.
E-mail: iris@oikos.com
Web site: www.oikos.com

JLC Bookstore
PO Box 2050, West Main St.
Richmond, VT 05477
Tel: (800) 859-3669
Fax: (802) 434-4467
Hard to find books for construction
professionals.
Web site: bgibooks@aol.com

Joiners' Quarterly
PO Box 249
Brownfield, ME 04010
Tel: (207) 935-3720
Fax: (207) 935-4575
The timber framer's choice for hard core
information. JQ is also a leader in
blending modern technology and
traditional craftsmanship, bringing
innovative ideas for a sustainable future
to the forefront.
E-mail: foxmaple@nxi.com
Web site: http://www.nxi.com/WWW/
joinersquarterly

Journal Of Light Construction
RR 2 Box 146, West Main St.
Richmond, VT 05477
Tel: (800) 375-5981
Fax: (802) 434-4467
Leading monthly magazine written by
builders for builders.
Web site: www.bginet.com

Tools Of The Trade
PO Box 2001, West Main St.
Richmond, VT 05477
Tel: (800) 375-5981
Fax: (802) 434-4467
The only magazine devoted exclusively
to tools for construction professionals.
Web site: www.bginet.com

Arizona

Sirocco Trading Company
110 East Wing Drive
Sedona, AZ 86336
Tel: (520) 204-2516
Fax: (520) 282-3716
Recycled wood products, solid timbers,
boards; Douglas fir, redwood, more.
E-mail: eeh3@sedona.net

California

Crossroads Recycled Lumber
PO Box 184
O'Neals, CA 93645
Tel: (209) 868-3646
Fax: same
Demolition salvage, portable sawmills,
dead & dying trees, timbers, flooring.
Natural buildings.

Maxwell Pacific
PO Box 4127
Malibu, CA 90264
Tel: (310) 457-4533
Douglas fir, redwood, pine, cedar,
barnwood, used and new.

Michael Evenson Natural Resources
PO Box 157
Petrolia, CA 95558
Tel: (707) 629-3679
Fax: same
Recycled old growth redwood, Douglas-
fir, custom remilling.
E-mail: evenson@igc.apc.org

Urban Ore, Inc.
1333 Sixth St.
Berkeley, CA 94710
Tel: (510) 559-4460
Fax: (510) 528-1540
Buy, sell, trade good used lumber,
doors, windows, fixtures, hardware.

Jefferson Recycled Woodworks
PO Box 696, 1104 Firenze Ave.
McCloud, CA 96057
Tel: (916) 964-2740
Fax: (916) 964-2745
Reclaimed timbers, lumber and millwork.
Milled to your specifications.
E-mail: goodwood@telis.org
Web site: http://www.ecowood.com

Recycled Lumberworks
596 Park Blvd.
Ukiah, CA 95482
Tel: (707) 462-2567
Fax: (707) 462-8607
Quality recycled old growth timber, clear
heart redwood lumber from 100 year old
vat staves and Douglas fir flooring is our
specialty.

Connecticut

Chestnut Specialists, Inc.
PO Box 217, 365 Harwinton Ave.
Plymouth, CT 06782
Tel: (860) 283-4209
Fax: same
Remanufactured flooring from reclaimed
antique lumber. Dimensional antique
lumber.

Post & Beam Homes, Inc.
4 Sexton Hill Road South
East Hampton, CT 06424
Tel: (860) 267-2060, (800) 821-8456
(Connecticut only)
Fax: (860) 267-9515
Pine, oak, Doug fir or recycled lumber.
Frames hand-crafted in our workshop.
Our expert timber framers will construct
anywhere.

Idaho

Alternative Timber Structures
1054 Rammel Mt. Rd.
Tetonia, ID 83452
Tel: (208) 456-2711
Fax: same
Custom door manufacturer, custom
sizes, interior & exterior—Davis Frame
rep—

Stein & Collett
PO Box 4065, 201 South Mission
Street
McCall, ID 83638
Tel: (208) 634-5374
Fax: (208) 634-8228
Beams, flooring, doors, stair
systems. Both new and recycled
woods custom architectural
millwork. Unique and unusual
species are our specialty.

Illinois

Windlass Timber Framing, Inc.
137 N. Center St.
Naperville, IL 60540
Tel: (630) 355-1788
Fax: same
Timber frame barn removal, repair,
erection and sales.

Massachusetts

Cataumet Sawmill
494 Thomas Landers Road
E. Falmouth, MA 02536
Tel: (508) 457-9239
Fax: (508) 540-3626
Antique heart pine flooring "for a home
of distinction".

Maryland

Vintage Lumber Co., Inc.
PO Box 104, 1 Council
Woodsboro, MD 21798
Tel: (800) 499-7859
Fax: (301) 845-6475
Reclaimed, remilled and remarkable
tongue and groove antique wood
flooring.
E-mail: woodfloors@vintagelumber.com
Web site: www.vintagelumber.com

Craftwright-Timber Frame Company
100 Railroad Ave., #105
Westminster, MD 21157
Tel: (410) 876-0999
Custom hand-crafted timber frames,
antique frames and timbers available.

Maine
Barnstormers
RR 1 Box 566, North Rochester Road
East Lebanon, ME 04027-9730
Tel: (207) 658-9000
The barn recycling specialists. Antique
barns resourced, restored, shipped &
reassembled nationwide. Authentic
timber framing. Vintage lumber.

Michigan
Renaissance Developments
10704 Oviatt Road
Honor, MI 49640
Tel: (616) 326-4009
Sustainable building, healthy creative
dreamspaces, bau-biologie, owner-
builder involvement welcome.

Minnesota
Duluth Timber Company
PO Box 16717
Duluth, MN 55816
Tel: (218) 727-2145
Recycled timbers and planks from U.S.
and Canada. Doug fir, redwood and
pine. Resawn beams, flooring; "as is"
wholesale timbers.

North Carolina
Woodhouse, Inc.
PO Box 7336, 105 Creek Street
Rocky Mount, NC 27804
Tel: (919) 977-7336
Fax: (919) 641-4477
French oak, chestnut, antique heart pine
solid or laminate flooring.

The Joinery Co.
PO Box 518, 1600 Western Blvd.
Tarboro, NC 27886
Tel: (919) 823-3306
Fax: (919) 823-0818
Antique heart pine, engineered solid
wood flooring, stair parts, mouldings,
beams.

Harmony Exchange
Route 2, Box 843-A
Boone, NC 28607
Tel: (800) 968-9663
Antique, reclaimed & new growth.
Flooring, timber trusses, decking,
exposed beam systems, siding & more.
Catalog.

New Hampshire

Carlisle Restoration Lumber
HCR 32 Box 556C
Stoddard, NH 03464
Tel: (800) 595-9663
Fax: (603) 446-3540
Traditional wide plank flooring custom
milled up to 20" wide.
Web site: www.wideplankflooring.com

New Mexico

Plaza Hardwood, Inc.
5 Enebro Court
Santa Fe, NM 87505
Tel: (800) 662-6306
Fax: (505) 466-0456
Distributor of wood flooring and lumber
from certified sustainable forest
resources.

New York

New Energy Works Of Rochester, Inc.
1755 Pioneer Road
Shortsville, NY 14548
Tel: (716) 289-3220
Fax: (716) 289-3221
Timber frame production, reclaimed
wood milling; interior woodworks and
design.
E-mail: jononewt@aol.com

M. Fine Lumber Co., Inc.
175 Varick Ave.
Brooklyn, NY 11231
Tel: (718) 381-5200
Fax: (718) 366-8907
Buyer & seller of reusable lumber,
timber & flooring available.
E-mail: MerritF@Fine-Lumber.com
Web site: www.Fine-Lumber.com/
Lumber.html

Pioneer Millworks
1755 Pioneer Road
Shortsville, NY 14548
Tel: (716) 289-3220
Fax: (716) 289-3221
Reclaimed timbers from turn-of-the-
century buildings, S4S or rough sawn.
Hand-hewn barn timbers. Antique pine
and fir flooring. Custom millwork.

Pennsylvania

Conklin's Authentic Barnwood
RR 1, Box 70, Butterfield Road
Susquehanna, PA 18847
Tel: (717) 465-3832
Fax: same
Supplier antique barnwood, hand-hewn
beams, flooring and rustic materials.
E-mail: conklins@epix.net
Web site: conklins barnwood.com

Texas

What Its Worth, Inc.
PO Box 162135
Austin, TX 78716
Tel: (512) 328-8837
Fax: same
Recycled heart pine. Timbers, planks,
custom flooring, cabinet, door and
moulding stock. Sold by piece or truck
load. Virgin tidewater cypress mined
from south Louisiana waterway, cut wet
to spec. Or sold in log form.

Precision Woodworks
507 E. Jackson St.
Burnet, TX 78611
Tel: (512) 756-6950
Fax: same
New products from antique longleaf pine
and other used timbers.

Utah

Trestlewood (A Division Of Cannon
Structures, Inc.)
PO Box 1728, 241 W 500 N, Suite A
Provo, UT 84603-1728
Tel: (801) 375-2779
Fax: (801) 375-2757
Wholesaler of recycled Douglas fir,
redwood, SYD, etc. Timbers & products.
E-mail: bradnate@burgoyne.com

Virginia

Blue Ridge Timberwrights
2030 Redwood Drive
Christiansburg, VA 24073
Tel: (540) 382-1102
Fax: (540) 382-8039
Designers and manufacturers of hand-
crafted timber frame structures.

Vintage Pine Co.
PO Box 85
Prospect, VA 23960
Tel: (804) 574-6531
Fax: (804) 574-2401
Antique heart pine flooring and stair
parts.

Mountain Lumber Co.
PO Box 289, 6812 Spring Hill Road
Ruckersville, VA 22968
Tel: (804) 985-3646
Fax: (804) 985-4105
Flooring, moldings, and stair parts milled
from reclaimed wood.
E-mail: sales@mountainlumber.com
Web site: http://
www.mountainlumber.com

Washington

R.W. Rhine, Inc.
1124 112th St. E
Tacoma WA 98445
Tel: (253) 531-7223
Fax: (253) 531-9548
Salvage timbers, piling and wood
products.

The G.R. Plume Company
1373 West Smith Road, Suite A-1
Ferndale, WA 98248
Tel: (360) 384-2800
Fax: (360) 384-0335
Architectural timber millwork fabricated
from reclaimed Douglas fir.

Resource Woodworks
627 E. 60th Street
Tacoma, WA 98404
Tel: (206) 474-3757
Fax: (206) 474-1139
Custom milling & planing of reclaimed
Douglas fir timbers, also flooring & trim
package available. We ship anywhere.

British Columbia

Evergreen Specialties
1619 Evelyn
North Vancouver, BC, Canada V7K 1T9
Tel: (604) 988-8574
Fax: (604) 988-8576
Dry fir, cedar. Architectural beams,
poles, lumber, decking, masts &
planking.

Steward Management Ltd.
11110-284th Street
Maple Ridge, BC, Canada V2W 1T9
Tel: (604) 462-7712
Fax: (604) 462-8311
Recyclers of old growth timbers--will cut
& plane to size

Renewable Energy

Real Goods
555 Leslie St.
Ukiah, CA 95482
Tel: (707) 468-9292
Fax: (707) 462-9394
Solar, wind, hydro, efficient lighting,
water, catalogs, books and institute.

Solar Energy International
PO Box 715
Carbondale, CO 81623
Tel: (970) 963-8855
Fax: (970) 963-8866
Hands-on workshops on renewable
energy and environmental building
technologies.
E-mail: sei@solarenergy.org
Web site: http://www.solarenergy.org

Elemental Resources
PO Box 21, 1320 E. 94th St. South
Haysville, KS 67060
Tel: (316) 788-3678
Fax: same
Renewable energy. Specializing in
design & installation of photovoltaic &
wind hybrid systems.
E-mail: cvdow@aol

Research

A & K Technical Services
PO Box 22
Anola, MB, Canada R0E 0A0
Tel: (204) 866-3262
Fax: (204) 866-3287
Structural engineering in wood.
"Stackwall" house construction design,
consulting, manual.
E-mail: krisdick@mb.sympatico.ca

Alaska Craftsman Home Program, Inc.
PO Box 241647
Anchorage, AK 99524-1647
Tel: (907) 258-2247 (ACHP)
Fax: (907) 258-5352
Education and research advanced cold
climate home building techniques.
E-mail: achp@alaska.net
Web site: http://www.alaska.net/~achp

Aprovecho Research Center
80574 Hazelton Road
Cottage Grove, OR 97424
Tel: (541) 942-8198
Fax: (541) 942-0302
Demonstration research and education
center for sustainable living.
E-mail: apro@efn.org/~apro
Web site: http://www.efn.org/~apro

Berkshire House Publishers
480 Pleasant Street, Suite 5
Lee, MA 01238
Tel: (800) 321-8526
Fax: (413) 243-0303
Explore colonial barn lore with master
restorer Richard Babcock.

Carroll, Franck & Associates
1357 Highland Parkway
St. Paul, MN 55116
Tel: (612) 690-9162
Fax: (612) 690-9156
Engineering of architectural structures,
traditional joinery and concealed steel
connections.
E-mail: carrfran@gold.tc.umn.edu

Community Eco-Design Network
PO Box 6241, 3151-29th Ave. S, #103
Minneapolis, MN 55406
Tel: (612) 306-2326
Super-insulated construction planbook,
design services, northern climate
strawbale building system.
E-mail: erichart@mtn.org
Web site: http://www.umn.edu/n/home/
m037/kurtdand/cen

Energy Efficient Building Association
2950 Metro Drive #108
Minneapolis, MN 55425
Tel: (612) 851-9940
Fax: (612) 851-9507
EEBA produces & presents training
based on the "systems approach".
E-mail: EEBANews@aol.com
Web site: http://www.eeba.org

Fox Maple School Of Traditional
Building
PO Box 249
Brownfield, ME 04010
Tel: (207) 935-3720 Fax: (207) 935-4575
Workshops for introductory & advanced
timber framing. Other workshops
available in the areas of thatch, clay and
alternative building systems. Fox Maple
strives for quality craftsmanship, with a
view towards a sustainable future.
E-mail: foxmaple@nxi.com
Web site: http://www.nxi.com/WWW/
joinersquarterly

Journal Of Light Construction
RR 2 Box 146, West Main St.
Richmond, VT 05477
Tel: (800) 375-5981
Fax: (802) 434-4467
Leading monthly magazine written by
builders for builders.
Web site: www.bginet.com

Midway Village & Museum Center
6799 Guilford Road
Rockford, IL 61107
Tel: (815) 397-9112
Fax: (815) 397-9156
Turn-of-the-century village and Rockford
area history center.

NAHB Research Center
400 Prince George's Blvd.
Upper Marlboro, MD 20774-8731
Residential building research including
innovative/alternative materials and
systems.
E-mail: pyost@nahbrc.org
Web site: http://www.nahbrc.com

ORNL Buildings Technology Center
PO Box 2008, 1 Bethel Valley Road
Oak Ridge, TN 37831
Tel: (423) 574-4345
Fax: (423) 574-9338
Whole wall and roof R-value
measurements.
E-mail: jef@ornl.gov
Web site: www.ornl.gov/roofs+walls

Restoration

California

Urban Ore, Inc.
1333 Sixth St.
Berkeley, CA 94710
Tel: (510) 559-4460
Fax: (510) 528-1540
Buy, sell, trade good used lumber,
doors, windows, fixtures, hardware.

Idaho

Jeff Pedersen—Logsmith
PO Box 788, Hwy. 93 North
Challis, ID 83226
Tel: (208) 879-4211
Fax: (208) 879-5574
Traditional broadax-hewn dovetail and
round log scribe-fit log homes. Broadax-
hewn and round log timber frames.
E-mail: jplogs@cyberhighway.net

Illinois

Windlass Timber Framing, Inc.
137 N. Center St.
Naperville, IL 60540
Tel: (630) 355-1788
Fax: same
Timber frame barn removal, repair,
erection and sales.

Midway Village & Museum Center
6799 Guilford Road
Rockford, IL 61107
Tel: (815) 397-9112
Fax: (815) 397-9156
Turn-of-the-century village and Rockford
area history center.

Company Listings by Subject

Massachusetts

New England Preservation Services
95 West Squantum Street, Suite 705
Quincy, MA 02171
Tel: (617) 472-8934
Fax: (617) 770-8934
Restoration of 18th & 19th century homes and barns.
E-mail: 74131.1254@Compuserve.com

Berkshire House Publishers
480 Pleasant Street, Suite 5
Lee, MA 01238
Tel: (800) 321-8526
Fax: (413) 243-0303
Explore colonial barn lore with master restorer Richard Babcock.

Architectural Components, Inc.
26 North Leverett Road
Montague, MA 01351
Tel: (413) 367-9441
Fax: (413) 367-9461
Architectural Components, Inc. specializes in reproducing historic doorways, doors & windows.
E-mail: arch.components.inc@worldnet.att.net

Colonial Restorations
26 Main St.
Brookfield, MA 01506
Tel: (508) 867-4400
Structural restoration/repair of post & beam homes or barns.

Tremont Nail Co.
PO Box 111, 8 Elm St.
Wareham, MA 02571
Tel: (508) 295-0038
Fax: (508) 295-1365
Manufacturer of restoration pattern steel cut nails; colonial hardware distributor.
E-mail: cutnails@aol.com

Forester Moulding & Lumber
152 Hamilton St.
Leominster, MA 01453
Tel: (978) 840-3100
Fax: (978) 534-8356
Manufacturer of 1800 hardwood mouldings in 22+ wood species.
Web site: www.forestermoulding.com

Old-House Journal (Dovetail Publishers)
2 Main St.
Gloucester, MA 01930
Tel: (508) 283-3200
Fax: (508) 283-4629
Bimonthly magazine about restoring, maintaining, and decorating pre-1940's houses.

Old-House Journal Directory (Dovetail Publishers)
2 Main St.
Gloucester, MA 01930
Tel: (508) 283-3200
Fax: (508) 283-4629
Annual sourcebook for suppliers of reproduction hardware, lighting, building materials.

Maine

Connolly & Co. Timber Frame Homes & Barns
10 Atlantic Highway
Edgecomb, ME 04556
Tel: (207) 882-4224
Fax: (207) 882-4247
Custom timber frame homes & barns built to last. Traditional oak pegged mortise and tenon joinery. Design services. Project management. Frames to complete projects. Visit our facility in Maine and observe our commitment to excellence.
E-mail: connolly@lincoln.midcoast.com

Authentic Timberframes
Route 302, RR 2 Box 698
Bridgton, ME 04009
Tel: (207) 647-5720
Timber frame homes, barns, cottages, camps and signs. Traditional joinery, hand-crafted frames.
E-mail: tenon@maine.com
Web site: http://timberframe.maine.com

Barnstormers
RR1 Box 566, North Rochester Road
East Lebanon, ME 04027-9730
Tel: (207) 658-9000
The barn recycling specialists. Antique barns resourced, restored, shipped & reassembled nationwide. Authentic timber framing. Vintage lumber.

North Carolina

Woodhouse, Inc.
PO Box 7336, 105 Creek Street
Rocky Mount, NC 27804
Tel: (919) 977-7336
Fax: (919) 641-4477
French oak, chestnut, antique heart pine solid or laminate flooring.

The Joinery Co.
PO Box 518, 1600 Western Blvd.
Tarboro, NC 27886
Tel: (919) 823-3306
Fax: (919) 823-0818
Antique heart pine, engineered solid wood flooring, stair parts, mouldings, beams.

New Hampshire

Great Northern Barns
PO Box 912E, RFD2
Canaan, NH 03741
Tel: (603) 523-7134
Fax: (603) 523-7134 *51
Great northern barns dismantles and erects antique barn frames.
E-mail: ejl@endor.com
Web site: www.greatnorthernbarns.com

Specialty Timberworks
PO Box 261, Brownfield Road
Eaton, NH 03832
Tel: (603) 447-5625
Fax: same
Designers & fabricators of new and reconstruction of antique timber frames.
3-D CAD services.

New York

Tea House Design, Inc.
PO Box 99, 11 Benedict Road
Waccabuc, NY 10597
Tel: (914) 763-3078 Fax: (914) 763-6165
27 years experience. 100 mile radius NYC. Innovative and diligent.

Eastfield Village
PO Box 539, 104 Mud Pond Road
Nassau, NY 12062
Tel: (518) 766-2422 Fax: same
School of historic preservation and early American trades.

M. Fine Lumber Co., Inc.
175 Varick Ave.
Brooklyn, NY 11231
Tel: (718) 381-5200 Fax: (718) 366-8907
Buyer & seller of reusable lumber, timber & flooring available.
E-mail: MerrittF@Fine-Lumber.com
Web site: www.Fine-Lumber.com/Lumber.html

Rondout Woodworking, Inc.
29 Terra Road
Saugerties, NY 12477
Tel: (914) 246-5879
Fax: (914) 246-5845
Restoration specialist. Agricultural–industrial, waterwheels, windmills, barns, timber frames.

Texas

What Its Worth, Inc.
PO Box 162135
Austin, TX 78716
Tel: (512) 328-8837
Fax: same
Recycled heart pine. Timbers, planks, custom flooring, cabinet, door and moulding stock. Sold by piece or truck load. Virgin tidewater cypress mined from south Louisiana waterway, cut wet to spec. Or sold in log form.

Vermont

Trow & Holden Co.
45 So. Main St.
Barre, VT 05641
Tel: (800) 451-4349
Fax: (802) 476-7025
Stone carving and splitting tools, mortar-removal tools.
E-mail: trowco@aol.com

Second Harvest Salvage & Demo
PO Box 194-E, RR1
Jeffersonville, VT 05464
Tel: (802) 644-8169
Specializing in hand hewn frames and antique flooring and lumbers.

North Woods Joinery
PO Box 1166
Burlington, VT 05402-1166
Tel: (802) 644-5667
Fax: (802) 644-2509
Traditional post and beam construction: homes, barns, steeples, bridges, towers.

Wisconsin

Abatron Inc.
5501-95th Ave.
Kenosha, WI 53144
Tel: (414) 653-2000
Fax: (414) 653-2019
Wood, concrete, metal restoration products; adhesives; moldmaking compounds.
E-mail: info@abatron.com
Web site: http://www.abatron.com

Standard Tar Products Co., Inc.
2456 West Cornell St.
Milwaukee, WI 53209-6294
Tel: (800) 825-7650
Fax: (414) 873-7737
"Organiclear" protective wood coatings & finishes for log homes & restoration.

Nova Scotia

Acorn Timber Frames, Ltd.
RR 1
Hantsport, Kings County, NS, Canada
B0P 1P0
Tel: (902) 684-9708
Fax: same
Traditional joinery: homes, churches, farm/garden/tourism/vacation structures, great rooms, restorations. Serving Canada and alluring locations with your requirements since 1978

Structural Insulated Panels

Georgia

Upper Loft Design, Inc.
Rt. 1 Box 2901
Lakemont, GA 30552
Tel: (706) 782-5246
Fax: (706) 782-6840
A timberframe design/build and turn-key housewright company.
Web site: http://www.upperloft@stc.net

Indiana

Angela's Unique Homes–Panel Pros
7096 NCR 490 W.
Bainbridge, IN 46105
Tel: (765) 739-1268
Specializing in panel installs for "Thermocore Panel" systems. General contracting–construction managers.

Maine

Maine Panel
PO Box 277
Rockland, ME 04841
Tel: (207) 236-2369
Fax: (207) 236-8568
Manufacturer of stress-skin panels for timber frame homes. Available with urethane or EPS. Priced to be competitive. Installation available.

Minnesota

AFM Corporation
PO Box 246, 24000 W. Hwy. 7, Ste. 201
Excelsior, MN 55331
Tel: (612) 474-0809
Fax: (612) 474-2074
Manufacturers of insulated structural building panels.
E-mail: afmcorp@worldnet.att.net
Web site: www.afmcorp-spsfoam.com

New York

Pine Grove Post & Beam Builders
4 Bates Road
Johnson City, NY 13790
Tel: (607) 754-0821
Fax: (607) 748-5946
Custom designed timber framed homes, barns, buildings, and additions.

Vermont

Vermont Stresskin Panels
RR 2 Box 2794
Cambridge, VT 05444
Tel: (802) 644-8885
Fax: (802) 644-8797
Stresskin panel enclosure systems for timber frame structures.

Foard Panel, Inc.
8 Marlboro Avenue
Brattleboro, VT 05301
Tel: (802) 254-3972 Fax: same
Manufacturers and professional installers of high-quality urethane and EPS panels.
E-mail: shippees@sover.net

Kentucky

Fischer Sips
1843 Northwestern Pkwy.
Louisville. KY 40203
Tel: (800) 792-7477
Structural insulated panels.

Solar

California

Alternative Energy Engineering, Inc.
PO Box 339
Redway, CA 95560
Tel: (800) 777-6609 Fax: (707) 923-3009
Energy from solar, wind or water power. Photovoltaics, lighting, solar fans, fridges and books. 112 page catalog for $3.

Integral Energy Systems
109 Argall Way
Nevada City, CA 95959
Tel: (800) 517-6527
Fax: (916) 265-6151
Solar water pumping, electric systems and hot water. Propane appliances. Full spectrum lighting.

Real Goods Renewables
555 Leslie St.
Ukiah, CA 95482
Tel: (800) 919-2400
Fax: (707) 462-4807
Photovoltaic and other renewable energy system consultation, design, and sales.

Sierra Solar Systems
109-MC Argall Way
Nevada City, CA 95959
(800) 517-6527
(916) 265-6151
Solar electric, pumping, hot water, wind, hydropower and energy efficient lighting. Catalog $5.
E-mail: solarjon@oro.net
Web site: http://www.sierrasolar.com

Idaho

Backwoods Solar Electric Systems
8530 Rapid Lightning Creek Road
Sandpoint, ID 83864
(208) 263-4290
All the equipment with lower than usual prices. Catalog $3.

Maine

Talmage Solar Engineering, Inc.
18 Stone Road
Kennebunkport, ME 04046
Tel: (207) 967-5945
Fax: (207) 967-5754
Design and sale of solar electric components for off-grid or utility interface.
E-mail: tse@talmagesolar.com
Web site: www.talmagesolar.com

Massachusetts

New England Solar Electric, Inc.
PO Box 435
Worthington, MA 01098
Tel: (413) 238-5974
$3 for 64 page catalog/design guide, solar electric kits, components, gas refrigerators, other appliances and information you need to live independently with solar electricity.

Montana

Sunelco
PO Box 1499
Hamilton, MT 59840
Tel: (406) 363-6924, (800) 338-6844
Complete source for solar modules, batteries, inverters, water pumps, energy effecient lights, and propane appliances. Catalog $4.95.

North Carolina

Enertia Building Systems, Inc.
13312 Garffe Sherron Road
Wake Forest, NC 27587
Tel: (919) 556-0177
Fax: (919) 556-1135
Design/prefabrication of solid wood solar/geothermal environmental homes.

Vermont

Vermont Sun Structures, Inc.
42 Walker Hill Road
Williston, VT 05495
Tel: (802) 879-6645
Glulam timber framed sunrooms & greenhouses, fully "weeped" & water tight!

Strawbale

Arizona

The Canelo Project
HCL Box 324
Elgin, AZ 85611
Tel: (520) 455-5548
Fax: (520) 455-9360
Straw bale building/earthen floors and plasters, workshops, resources, consulting.
E-mail: absteen@dakotacom.net
Web site: http://www.deatech.com/canelo

The Last Straw
PO Box 42000
Tucson, AZ 85733
Tel: (520) 882-3848
The Last Straw: the quarterly journal of straw-bale construction.
E-mail: thelaststraw@igc.apc.org
Web site: http://www.netchaos.com/+ls

Out On Bale By Mail
1039 E. Linden St.
Tucson, AZ 85719
Tel: (520) 624-1673
Fax: (520) 299-9099
Educational materials for straw bale building. Help for owner builders.
E-mail: outonbale@aol.com

Sustainable Systems Support
PO Box 318
Bisbee, AZ 85603
Tel: (520) 432-4292
Offers books and videos on plastered straw bale construction, including an excellent 90 min. "how-to" video with a 62 page manual. Wall raising workshops and consultations.

Colorado

Solar Energy International
PO Box 715
Carbondale, CO 81623
Tel: (970) 963-8855
Fax: (970) 963-8866
Hands-on workshops on renewable energy and environmental building technologies.
E-mail: sei@solarenergy.org
Web site: http://www.solarenergy.org

Massachusetts

Greenspace Collaborative
PO Box 107
Ashfield, MA 01330
Tel: (413) 369-4905
Buildings of straw bales and other natural materials detailed for the northeastern climate.

Maine

Wentworth Timberframes
PO Box 1116, 45 Mason Street
Bethel, ME 04217
Tel: (207) 824-4237
25 years experience. Hewn, rough-sawn, or hand-planed timbers. Mortise and tenon joinery. Owner friendly

Proclay
C/O Fox Maple
PO Box 249
Brownfield, ME 04010
Tel: (207) 935-3720
Fax: (207) 935-4575
Light-clay infill techniques, clay & lime plasters, clay building materials, workshops and consulting.
E-mail: foxmaple@nxi.com

Minnesota

Community Eco-Design Network
PO Box 6241, 3151-29th Ave. S, #103
Minneapolis, MN 55406
Tel: (612) 306-2326
Super-insulated construction planbook, design services, northern climate strawbale building system.
E-mail: erichart@mtn.org
Web site: http://www.umn.edu/n/home/m037/kurtdand/cen

New Hampshire

Straw Works
152 West Main St.
Conway, NH 03818
Tel: (603) 447-1701
Fax: (603) 447-6412
Design for those wishing to walk lightly upon the earth.
E-mail: Straw-Works@juno.com

Ohio

Natural Homesteads
13182 N. Boone Road
Columbia Station, OH 44028
Tel: (440) 236-3344
Natural building design / consultation; slide presentations; straw-bale and cob workshops.

Oregon

Sustainable Architecture
PO Box 696, 910 Glendale Ave.
Ashland, OR 97520
Tel: (541) 482-6332
Fax: (541) 488-8299
Architectural services integrating full spectrum of healthy, holistic building.

Aprovecho Research Center
80574 Hazelton Road
Cottage Grove, OR 97424
Tel: (541) 942-8198
Fax: (541) 942-0302
Demonstration research and education center for sustainable living.
E-mail: apro@efn.org/~apro
Web site: http://www.efn.org/~apro

Gringo Grip
4951 Netarts Hwy. W. #2041
Tillamook, OR 97141
Tel: (800) 734-8091
Fax: (800) 734-8071
A simple thru-the-bale anchor for fastening cabinets, interior wall sections, electrical boxes, fixtures, and pipe to straw-bale walls.

Vermont

Yestermorrow Design/Build School
RR 1 Box 97-5
Warren, VT 05674
Tel: (802) 496-5545
Fax: (802) 496-5540
Offers hands-on courses in residential design and "green" construction.
E-mail: ymschool@aol.com
Web site: www.yestermorrow.org

Organic Oat Straw
RR#1 Box 520
Orleans, VT 05860
Tel: (802) 754-2028
Straw bales for building.

Washington

Greenfire Institute
PO Box 1040
Winthrop, WA 98862
Tel: (509) 996-3593
Fax: same
Straw bale construction training, consultation and design.
E-mail: greenfire@igc.org
Web site: www.balewolf.com

Sustainable Building

Arizona

The Last Straw
PO Box 42000
Tucson, AZ 85733
Tel: (520) 882-3848
The Last Straw: the quarterly journal of straw-bale construction.
E-mail: thelaststraw@igc.apc.org
Web site: http://www.netchaos.com/+ls

California

Sierra Timberframers
PO Box 595
Nevada City, CA 95959
Tel: (916) 292-9449
Fax: (916) 292-9460
Timberframed structures. Recycled wood & salvaged trees. Solar & sustainable designs preferred. Classes available.

Eos Institute
580 Broadway, Suite 200
Laguna Beach, CA 92651
Tel: (714) 497-1896
Fax: (714) 497-7861
Educational nonprofit for the study of sustainable living. Resources, consulting, and programs on ecological community design. Library, lectures, workshops.

Colorado

Solar Energy International
PO Box 715
Carbondale, CO 81623
Tel: (970) 963-8855
Fax: (970) 963-8866
Hands-on workshops on renewable energy and environmental building technologies.
E-mail: sei@solarenergy.org
Web site: http://www.solarenergy.org

DC, Washington

Passive Solar Industries Council
1511 K Street, Suite 600
Washington, DC 20005
Tel: (202) 628-7400
Fax: (202) 393-5043
PSIC independent nonprofit advancing climate responsive buildings.
E-mail: PSICouncil@aol.com
Web site: http://www.psic.org

Sandra Leibowitz
Eco-Building Schools
3220 N Street NW #218
Washington, DC 20007
$7 ($6 + $1 postage) for Eco-Building Schools: A directory of alternative educational resources in environmentally sensitive design. Detailed info on 35 eco-building schools across the U.S.
Web site: http://www.ecodesign.org/edi/eden

Iowa

Lite-Form International
PO Box 774, 1210 Steuben St.
Sioux City, IA 51102
Tel: (712) 252-3704
Fax: (712) 252-3259
Insulating forms for cast in place foundations & walls.
E-mail: liteform@pionet.net
Web site: http://www.pionet.net/~liteform/index.html

Agriboard Industries
PO Box 645
Fairfield, IA 52556
Tel: (515) 472-0363
Complete, OSB laminated, compressed wheat straw panel building systems.
E-mail: agriboard@lisco.com

Massachusetts

The Heartwood School
Johnson Hill Road
Washington, MA 01235
Tel: (413) 623-6677
Fax: (413) 623-0277
Workshops in homebuilding, timber framing, woodworking, and more.
E-mail: info@heartwoodschool.com
Web site: www.heartwoodschool.com

Greenspace Collaborative
PO Box 107
Ashfield, MA 01330
Tel: (413) 369-4905
Buildings of straw bales and other natural materials detailed for the northeastern climate.

Jack A. Sobon: Architect/Builder
PO Box 201, 613 Shaw Road
Windsor, MA 01270-0201
Tel: (413) 684-3223
Fax: same
Specializing in design and construction of sustainable wooden architecture.

Maine

Talmage Solar Engineering, Inc.
18 Stone Road
Kennebunkport, ME 04046
Tel: (207) 967-5945
Fax: (207) 967-5754
Design and sale of solar electric components for off-grid or utility interface.
E-mail: tse@talmagesolar.com
Web site: www.talmagesolar.com

Wentworth Timberframes
PO Box 1116, 45 Mason Street
Bethel, ME 04217
Tel: (207) 824-4237
25 years experience. Hewn, rough-sawn, or hand-planed timbers. Mortise and tenon joinery. Owner friendly.

Proclay
C/O Fox Maple
PO Box 249
Brownfield, ME 04010
Tel: (207) 935-3720
Fax: (207) 935-4575
Light-clay infill techniques, clay & lime plasters, clay building materials, workshops and consulting.
E-mail: foxmaple@nxi.com

Michigan

Renaissance Developments
10704 Oviatt Road
Honor, MI 49640
Tel: (616) 326-4009
Sustainable building, healthy creative dreamspaces, bau-biologie, owner-builder involvement welcome.

Montana

Center For Resourceful Building Technology
PO Box 100, 516 S. Orange
Missoula, MT 59806
Tel: (406) 549-7678
Fax: (406) 549-4100
Non-profit educating the public on environmentally responsible construction practices.

North Carolina

Enertia Building Systems, Inc.
13312 Garffe Sherron Road
Wake Forest, NC 27587
Tel: (919) 556-0177
Fax: (919) 556-1135
Design/prefabrication of solid wood solar/geothermal environmental homes.

New Mexico

Natural House Building Center
2300 West Alameda, A5
Santa Fe, NM 87501
Tel: (505) 471-5314
Fax: (505) 471-3714
Hands-on workshop: timber framing, straw-clay construction, earth floors & plastering.

New Hampshire

Springpoint Design
2210 Pratt Road
Alstead, NH 03602
Tel: (603) 835-2433
Fax: (603) 835-7825
Architectural design / consulting: health, sustainability, efficiency—timber frames, alternative enclosures.

Oregon

Cob Cottage Co.
PO Box 123
Cottage Grove, OR 97424
Tel: (541) 942-2005
Fax: (541) 942-3021
Information and workshops on building with cob (sand, clay, straw).
Web site: http://www.deatech.com/cobcottage

Sustainable Architecture
PO Box 696, 910 Glendale Ave.
Ashland, OR 97520
Tel: (541) 482-6332
Fax: (541) 488-8299
Architectural services integrating full spectrum of healthy, holistic building.

Terry F. Johnson Building Design
1013 NW Taylor Ave.
Corvallis, OR 97330
Tel: (541) 757-8535
Fax: (541) 753-4916
Custom plans for timber framed homes, barns and outbuildings.
E-mail: sarah@peak.org

Aprovecho Research Center
80574 Hazelton Road
Cottage Grove, OR 97424
Tel: (541) 942-8198
Fax: (541) 942-0302
Demonstration research and education center for sustainable living.
E-mail: apro@efn.org/~apro
Web site: http://www.efn.org/~apro

Groundworks
PO Box 381
Murphy, OR 97533
Tel: (541) 471-3470
Workshops and handbook available on cob (hand-sculpted earth) construction.
Web site: http://www.cpros.com/~sequoia

Pennsylvania

Hugh Lofting Timber Framing, Inc.
339 Lamborntown Road
West Grove, PA 19390
Tel: (610) 444-5382
Fax: (610) 869-3589
Company dedicated to practicing green architecture with sustainable materials.
E-mail: hlofting@aolcom

Tennessee

ORNL Buildings Technology Center
PO Box 2008, 1 Bethel Valley Road
Oak Ridge, TN 37831
Tel: (423) 574-4345
Fax: (423) 574-9338
Whole wall & roof R-value
measurements.
E-mail: jef@ornl.gov
web site: www.ornl.gov/roofs+walls

Virginia

Masonry Heater Association Of North
America
11490 Commerce Pk. Dr., Suite 300
Reston, VA 20191
Tel: (703) 620-3171
Fax: (703) 620-3928
Association of builders, designers &
researchers of masonry heaters.
Web site: http://mha-net.org/

Vermont

Yestermorrow Design/Build School
RR 1 Box 97-5
Warren, VT 05674
Tel: (802) 496-5545
Fax: (802) 496-5540
Offers hands-on courses in residential
design and "green" construction.
E-mail: ymschool@aol.com
Web site: www.yestermorrow.org

Environmental Building News
RR 1, Box 161
Brattleboro, VT 05301
Tel: (802) 257-7300
Fax: (802) 257-7304
The leading publication on
environmentally responsible design and
construction.
E-mail: ebn@ebuild.com
Web site: http://www.ebuild.com

Washington

Bear Creek Lumber
PO Box 669, 495 Eastside County
Road
Winthrop, WA 98862
Tel: (800) 571-7191
Fax: (509) 997-2040
Western cedar, fir, redwood. Traditional
patterns, decking, timbers and beams.
Delivery available nationwide.

West Virginia

Wind Bell Hollow/C.J. Jammer
HC 40 Box 36
Lewisburg, WV 24901
Tel: (304) 645-6466
Design/drafting of timber framed homes
and other natural house designs.

Ontario

Bear Timber Frame Homes
PO Box 124
Ajax, Ont, Canada L1S 3C2
Tel: (905) 428-6505
Designers of timber frame and energy-
efficient (R2000) homes.

Sustainable Wood Supply

California

Crossroads Recycled Lumber
PO Box 184
O'Neals, CA 93645
Tel: (209) 868- 3646
Fax: same
Demolition salvage, portable sawmills,
dead & dying trees, timbers, flooring.

Natural buildings.

Michael Evenson Natural Resources
PO Box 157
Petrolia, CA 95558
Tel: (707) 629-3679 Fax: same
Recycled old growth redwood, Douglas-
fir, custom remilling.
E-mail: evenson@igc.apc.org

Jefferson Recycled Woodworks
PO Box 696, 1104 Firenze Ave.
McCloud, CA 96057
Tel: (916) 964-2740 Fax: (916) 964-2745
Reclaimed timbers, lumber and millwork.
Milled to your specifications.
E-mail: goodwood@telis.org
Web site: http://www.ecowood.com

Colorado

Greenleaf Forest Products, Inc.
102 Greenleaf Lane
Westcliffe, CO 81252
Tel: (719) 783-2487
Fax: (719) 783-0212
Logs, poles and rough-sawn from
sustainably-managed private forests.

Florida

Tropical American Tree Farms
C/O AAA Express Mail, 1641 NW 79th
Avenue
Miami, FL 33126
Tel: (800) 788-4918, 011 (506) 787-0020
Fax: 011 (506) 787-0051
Growing precious tropical hardwoods on
tree farms in Costa Rica.
E-mail: tattfsa.sol.racsa.co.cr

Massachusetts

Karp Woodworks
136 Fountain Street
Ashland, MA 01721
Tel: (508) 881-7000
Fax: (508) 881-7084
Sustainably harvested certified tropical
& domestic woods. "Furnature," an
organic, sustainable and chemical-free
line of upholstered furniture. "Certified
Serenity", a line of comfortable and
colorful sunroom/patio furniture from
certified sustainable sources.

Green River Lumber, Inc.
PO Box 329
Gt. Barrington, MA 01230
Tel: (413) 528-9000
Fax: (413) 528-2379
Manufacturer of certified and non-
certified plank hardwood flooring.

Bamboo Fencer
31 Germania St.
Jamaica Plain, MA 02130-2314
Tel: (617) 524-6137
Fax: (617) 524-6100
Manufactures and imports fences,
gates, and other products.
E-mail: Dave@bamboofencer.com
Web site: http://www.bamboofencer.com

Maryland

Craftwright-Timber Frame Company
100 Railroad Ave., #105
Westminster, MD 21157
Tel: (410) 876-0999
Custom hand-crafted timber frames,
antique frames and timbers available.

Maine

Natural Knees
281 Hartland Road
St. Albans, ME 04971
Tel: (207) 938-2380
Natural grown knees for timber frame
construction and boat building.
E-mail: kneeman@somtel.com

Michigan

Northern Land & Lumber Co.
7000 P Rd.
Gladstone, MI 49837
Tel: (906) 786-2994
Fax: (906) 786-2926
Primary manufacturer of log home kits &
components.
E-mail: nlandl@up.net
Web site: www.deltami.org/nlandl

Minnesota

The Woodworkers' Store
4365 Willow Dr.
Medina, MN 55340
Tel: (800) 279-4441
Fax: (612) 478-8395
Woodworking hardware, wood, tools and
know-how.
E-mail: rocklerl@pclink.com
web site: www.woodworkerstore.com

Midwest Hardwood Corp.
9540 83rd Ave. N
Maple Grove, MN 55369
Tel: (612) 425-8700
Fax: (612) 391-6740
Northern hardwood lumber
manufacturer.
E-mail: MWHWD@ix.netcom.com

New Mexico

Plaza Hardwood, Inc.
5 Enebro Court
Santa Fe, NM 87505
Tel: (800) 662-6306
Fax: (505) 466-0456
Distributor of wood flooring and lumber
from certified sustainable forest
resources.

Ohio

Hochstetler Milling
552 St. Rt. 95
Loudonville, OH 44842
(419) 281-3553, (419) 368-0004
Oak timber 4-sided planing. Pine log
home logs 10 profiles.

Pennsylvania

Conklin's Authentic Barnwood
RR 1, Box 70, Butterfield Road
Susquehanna, PA 18847
Tel: (717) 465-3832
Fax: same
Supplier antique barnwood, hand-hewn
beams, flooring and rustic materials.
E-mail: conklins@epix.net
Web site: conklinsbarnwood.com

Vermont

Tree Talk
PO Box 426, 431 Pine Street
Burlington, VT 05402
Tel: (802) 865-1111
Fax: (802) 863-4344
Multimedia CD-ROM on wood. 900
species. Database. Video. Pictures.
Maps.
E-mail: wow@together.net
Web site: www.woodweb.com/~treetalk/
home.html

Belgian Woodworks
1068 Ireland Road
Starksboro, VT 05487
Tel: (802) 453-4787
Custom mouldings, banisters and
newels in sustainably harvested
northern hardwoods.

Washington

Environmental Home Center
1724 4th Ave. South
Seattle, WA 98134
Tel: (800) 281-8275, (206) 682-8275
Retail / wholesale—environmentally
responsible building materials and
decorating supplies.
E-mail: info@enviresource.com
Web site: www.enviresource.com

British Columbia

Evergreen Specialties
1619 Evelyn
North Vancouver, BC, Canada V7K 1T9
Tel: (604) 988-8574
Fax: (604) 988-8576
Dry fir, cedar. Architectural beams,
poles, lumber, decking, masts &
planking.

Thatch

Fox Maple School Of Traditional
Building
PO Box 249
Brownfield, ME 04010
Tel: (207) 935-3720
Fax: (207) 935-4575
Workshops for introductory & advanced
timber framing. Other workshops
available in the areas of thatch, clay and
alternative building systems. Fox Maple
strives for quality craftsmanship, with a
view towards a sustainable future.
E-mail: foxmaple@nxi.com
Web site: http://www.nxi.com/WWW/
joinersquarterly

Custom Roof Thatching & Supplies
PO Box 62054
Cincinnati, OH 45262
Tel: (513) 772-4979
Fax: (513) 772-6313
Has thatched in U.S. since 1986. A
guide to roof thatching in the U.S. $6.00
web site: http://www.roofthatch.com

Liberty Cedar
535 Liberty Lane
W. Kingston, RI 02892
Tel: (800) 882-3327, (401) 789-6626
Fax: (401) 789-0320
Naturally decay-resistant exterior wood
products specializing in wood roofing.

South County Post & Beam
521 Liberty Lane
West Kingston, RI 02892
Tel: (401) 783-4415
Fax: (401) 783-4494
A full service timber frame company &
wide pine flooring supplier.

Timber Framers

California

Sierra Timberframers
PO Box 595
Nevada City, CA 95959
Tel: (916) 292-9449
Fax: (916) 292-9460
Timberframed structures. Recycled
wood & salvaged trees. Solar &
sustainable designs preferred. Classes
available.

Pacific Post & Beam
PO Box 13708
San Luis Obispo, CA 93406
Tel: (805) 543-7565
Fax: (805) 543-1287
Full service timber frame and truss
design and build.

Colorado

Leopard Creek Timberframe Co.
PO Box 51, 2980 Hwy.62
Placerville, CO 81430
Tel: (970) 728-3590
Fax: same
Hand-crafted timber frame homes,
located in southwest Colorado. Call for
information.

Connecticut

Post & Beam Homes, Inc.
4 Sexton Hill Road South
East Hampton, CT 06424
Tel: (860) 267-2060, (800) 821-8456
(Connecticut only)
Fax: (860) 267-9515
Pine, oak, Doug fir or recycled lumber.
Frames hand-crafted in our workshop.
Our expert timber framers will construct
anywhere.

C&C Home Builders, Inc.
3810 Old Mountain Road
West Suffield, CT 06093
Tel: (860) 668-0382
Building in the New England-New York
area using white oak and traditional
joinery.

Delaware

Timber Frame Systems, Inc.
PO Box 458, 28 Main St.
Frankford, DE 19945
Tel: (302) 732-9428 Fax: (302) 537-4971
Manufacturer of custom post & beam
frame kits.

Florida

R.G. White Construction
PO Box 14734, 5800 Firestone Road
Jacksonville, FL 32238
Tel: (904) 778-8352
Fax: same
Building fine quality cracker style and
craftsman style homes.

Georgia

Hearthstone Log & Timberframe Homes
120 Carriage Drive
Macon, GA 31210
Tel: (800) 537-7931 Fax: (912) 477-6535
21 years experience, CADD design,
professional erection and dry-in
services.
E-mail:
hearthstonehomes@mindspring.com
Web site: www.mindspring.com/
~hearthstonehomes

Upper Loft Design, Inc.
Rt. 1 Box 2901
Lakemont, GA 30552
Tel: (706) 782-5246 Fax: (706) 782-6840
A timberframe design/build and turn-key
housewright company.
Web site: http://www.upperloft@stc.net

Idaho

Jeff Pedersen—Logsmith
PO Box 788, Hwy. 93 North
Challis, ID 83226
Tel: (208) 879-4211
Fax: (208) 879-5574
Traditional broadax-hewn dovetail and
round log scribe-fit log homes. Broadax-
hewn and round log timber frames.
E-mail: jplogs@cyberhighway.net

Alternative Timber Structures
1054 Rammel Mt. Rd.
Tetonia, ID 83452
Tel: (208) 456-2711
Fax: same
Custom door manufacturer, custom
sizes, interior & exterior—Davis Frame
rep—

Illinois

Windlass Timber Framing, Inc.
137 N. Center St.
Naperville, IL 60540
Tel: (630) 355-1788
Fax: same
Timber frame barn removal, repair,
erection and sales.

The Edge Woodworks
Rt. 1 Box 179
Grafton, IL 62037
Tel: (618) 786-2442
Traditional hand-crafted joinery, portable
sawmill, owner-builder friendly.
E-mail: edgewrks@gtec.com

Indiana

Timbersmith, Inc.
4040 Farr Road
Bloomington, IN 47408
Tel: (812) 336-7424
Our frames exhibit traditional wooden
joinery and can be finely detailed to
produce one-of-a-kind creations.

Kentucky

The Raven River Co., Inc.
125 Twin Creek-Connorsville Road
Sadieville, KY 40370
Tel: (606) 235-0368
Fax: same
Artisans of fine timber frames and other
things.
E-mail: ravenriver@kitt.net

Massachusetts

New England Preservation Services
95 West Squantum Street, Suite 705
Quincy,MA 02171
Tel: (617) 472-8934
Fax: (617) 770-8934
Restoration of 18th & 19th century
homes and barns.
E-mail: 74131.1254@Compuserve.com

The Heartwood School
Johnson Hill Road
Washington, MA 01235
Tel: (413) 623-6677
Fax: (413) 623-0277
Workshops in homebuilding, timber
framing, woodworking, and more.
E-mail: info@heartwoodschool.com
Web site: www.heartwoodschool.com

Colonial Restorations
26 Main St.
Brookfield, MA 01506
Tel: (508) 867-4400
Structural restoration/repair of post &
beam homes or barns.

Jack A Sobon: Architect/Builder
PO Box 201, 613 Shaw Road
Windsor, MA 01270-0201
Tel: (413) 684-3223
Fax: same
Specializing in design and construction
of sustainable wooden architecture.

Ellison Timberframes
20 Six Penny Lane
Harwichport, MA 02646
Tel: (508) 430-0407
Award-winning design/build company.
No steel connections used.

Maryland

Craftwright-Timber Frame Company
100 Railroad Ave., #105
Westminster, MD 21157
Tel: (410) 876-0999
Custom hand-crafted timber frames,
antique frames and timbers available.

Maine

New Dimension Homes, Inc.
PO Box 95, RR1
Clinton, ME 04927
Tel: (207) 426-7450
Fax: (207) 426-8837
Affordable panelized western red cedar
post & beam homes & sunrooms.

Wentworth Timberframes
PO Box 1116, 45 Mason Street
Bethel, ME 04217
Tel: (207) 824-4237
25 years experience. Hewn, rough-
sawn, or hand-planed timbers. Mortise
and tenon joinery. Owner friendly

Connolly & Co. Timber Frame Homes &
Barns
10 Atlantic Highway
Edgecomb, ME 04556
Tel: (207) 882-4224
Fax: (207) 882-4247
Custom timber frame homes & barns
built to last. Traditional oak pegged
mortise and tenon joinery. Design
services. Project management. Frames
to complete projects. Visit our facility in
Maine and observe our commitment to
excellence.
E-mail: connolly@lincoln.midcoast.com

Authentic Timberframes
Route 302, RR 2 Box 698
Bridgton, ME 04009
Tel: (207) 647-5720
Timber frame homes, barns, cottages,
camps and signs. Traditional joinery,
hand-crafted frames.
E-mail: tenon@maine.com
Web site: http://timberframe.maine.com

Barnstormers
RR 1 Box 566, North Rochester Road
East Lebanon, ME 04027-9730
Tel: (207) 658-9000
The barn recycling specialists. Antique
barns resourced, restored, shipped &
reassembled nationwide. Authentic
timber framing. Vintage lumber.

TYhe Timber Frame Apprenticeshop
PO Box 249
Brownfield, ME 04010
Tel: (207) 935-3720
Fax: (207) 935-4575
Workshops for introductory & advanced
timber framing. Other workshops
available in the areas of thatch, clay and
alternative building systems. Fox Maple
strives for quality craftsmanship, with a
view towards a sustainable future.
E-mail: foxmaple@nxi.com
Web site: http://www.nxi.com/WWW/
joinersquarterly

Michigan

Millcreek Classic Homes
1009 Parchment Drive SE
Grand Rapids, MI 49546
Tel: (616) 949-3012
Fax: (616) 949-4477
Design and build Riverbend timber
frame custom homes.

Minnesota

Sandro's Woodshed
20018 486th Ave.
Hendricks, MN 56136
Tel: (605) 479-3875
Custom timber frames. Cabinetry and
furniture built with all natural materials—
no plywood or particle board—non-toxic
finishes available.

Nebraska

Great Northern Woodworks, Inc.
30694 Polk St. NE
Cambridge, MN 55008
Tel: (612) 444-6394
Fax: (612) 444-9552
Timber frame structures, including
design, cutting, raising and panel
enclosure.

Missouri

Timberland Design / Hearthstone
15444 Clayton Road, Ste. 325-6
St. Louis, MO 63011
Tel: (800) 680-8833, (314) 341-8833
Fax: (314) 341-8833
Architect, Hearthstone distributor,
specializing in timber frame/log designs
& packages.

North Carolina

Mountain Construction Enterprises
PO Box 1177, 353 Devonwood Drive
Boone, NC 28607
Tel: (704) 264-1231
Fax: (704) 264-4863
Custom traditionally mortised oak timber
frames with stress skin panels.
E-mail: Mtnconst@skybest.com
Web site: http://blowingrock.com/nc/
timberframe

Timberfab, Inc.
PO Box 399, 200 W. Hope Lodge St.
Tarboro, NC 27886
Tel: (800) 968-8322
Fax: (919) 641-4142
Log and timber frame structures,
components and supplies
E-mail: tfab@coastalnet.com
Web site: http://www4.coastalnet.com/
timberfab

Goshen Timber Frames, Inc.
104 Wykle Road
Franklin, NC 28734
Tel: (704) 524-8662
Fax: same
Ongoing workshops and
apprenticeships in timber framing and
design; design services; frame sales.
E-mail: goshen@dnet.net
Web site: http://
www.timberframemag.com

New Hampshire

Timberpeg
PO Box 5474
W. Lebanon, NH 03784
Tel: (603) 298-8820
Fax: (603) 298-5425
Custom designed timber frame homes
and commercial structures since 1974.
E-mail: info@timberpeg.com
Web site: www.timberpeg.com

Great Northern Barns
PO Box 912E, RFD2
Canaan, NH 03741
Tel: (603) 523-7134
Fax: (603) 523-7134 *51
Great Northern Barns dismantles and
erects antique barn frames.
E-mail: ejl@endor.com
Web site: www.greatnorthernbarns.com

Day Pond Woodworking
PO Box 299, Rt. 114
Bradford, NH 03221
Tel: (603) 938-2375
Over 17 years experience building
custom timber frame homes, etc.

Specialty Timberworks
PO Box 261, Brownfield Road
Eaton, NH 03832
Tel: (603) 447-5625
Fax: same
Designers & fabricators of new, and
reconstruction of antique timber frames.
3-D CADD services.

A.W. Corriveau Timber Frames
PO Box 421
Gilmanton, NH 03237
Tel: (603) 267-8427
Quality hand cut and erected timber
frames in oak, hemlock or pine.
Competitive prices due to low overhead.
Satisfaction guaranteed.

New Mexico

Natural House Building Center
2300 West Alameda, A5
Santa Fe, NM 87501
Tel: (505) 471-5314
Fax: (505) 471-3714
Hands-on workshops: timber framing,
straw-clay construction, earth floors &
plastering.

New York

Tea House Design, Inc.
PO Box 99, 11 Benedict Road
Waccabuc, NY 10597
Tel: (914) 763-3078
Fax: (914) 763-6165
27 years experience. 100 mile radius
NYC. Innovative and diligent.

New Energy Works Of Rochester, Inc.
1755 Pioneer Road
Shortsville, NY 14548
Tel: (716) 289-3220
Fax: (716) 289-3221
Timber frame production, reclaimed
wood milling; interior woodworks and
design.
E-mail: jononewt@aol.com

Timberbuilt
10821 Schaffstall Dr.
N. Collins, NY 14111
Tel: (716) 337-0012
Fax: (716) 337-0013
We design, cut, erect and enclose fine
timber frame structures.

Alternate Energy Systems
PO Box 344
Peru, NY 12972
Tel: (518) 643-0805
Fax: (518) 643-2012
Masonry heaters-timber frame and log
homes-a natural blend-call.

Pine Grove Post & Beam Builders
4 Bates Road
Johnson City, NY 13790
Tel: (607) 754-0821
Fax: (607) 748-5946
Custom designed timber framed homes,
barns, buildings, and additions.

Cepco Tool Co.
PO Box 153, 295 Van Etten Road
Spencer, NY 14883
Tel: (607) 589-4313
Fax: same
Board straightening/joining tools,
Bowrench deck tool, Quick-Jack
construction jack.

Legacy Timber Frames, Inc.
691 County Rd. 70
Stillwater, NY 12170
Tel: (518) 279-9108
Fax: (518) 581-9219
Custom designed, traditional timber
frame construction.

Rondout Woodworking, Inc.
29 Terra Road
Saugerties, NY 12477
Tel: (914) 246-5879
Fax: (914) 246-5845
Restoration specialist. Agricultural-
industrial, waterwheels, windmills, barns,
timber frames.

Ohio

Heartwood Timber Frames
6660 Heartwood Place
Swanton, OH 43558
Tel: (419) 875-5500
Fax: same
Crafting beautiful timber frames, panel
homes, and masonry heaters.

Hearthstone Log & Timberframe Homes
4974 Wortman Road
Zanesville, OH 43701
Tel: (614) 453-6542
Fax: same
Oak or pine timber frames, and square,
hand-hewn log homes.

Pennsylvania

Hessel Valley Timber Framing
2061 Jackson Run Road
Warren, PA 16365
Tel: (814) 489-3018
Unique combinations of Medieval
European and early American
timberframe carpentry.

Hugh Lofting Timber Framing, Inc.
339 Lamborntown Road
West Grove, PA 19390
Tel: (610) 444-5382
Fax: (610) 869-3589
Company dedicated to practicing green
architecture with sustainable materials.
E-mail: hlofting@aolcom

Pocono Mt. Timber Frames
PO Box 644, Rt. 115
Brodheadsville, PA 18322
Tel: (717) 992-7515
Fax: (717) 992-9064
Design, fabrication, and erection of
timber frame barns and houses.
E-mail: etreible@ptd.net
Web site: www.pmtf.com

Bruce Cowie Timber Frames
Rt. 34 Box 354
York, PA 17406
Tel: (717) 755-6678
Custom hand-crafted traditional timber
framing.
E-mail: bruce220@juno.com

Oregon

Confluence Design & Construction
PO Box 1258, 1013 NW Taylor
Corvallis, OR 97339
Tel: (514) 757-0511
Fax: (541) 753-4916
"Where thinking and doing are still one."
Design, frames, consultation

Rhode Island

South County Post & Beam
521 Liberty Lane
West Kingston, RI 02892
Tel: (401) 783-4415
Fax: (401) 783-4494
A full service timber frame company,
wide pine flooring supplier.

South Carolina

Southern Breeze Timberworks
PO Box 635
Travelers Rest, SC 29690
Tel: (864) 834-3706
Quality hand-wrought joinery.

South Dakota

Northern Lights Woodworks
24144 Pine Grove Road
Rapid City, SD 57701
Tel: (605) 399-9909
Design and construction of timber frame homes and other timbered projects.

Tennessee

Hearthstone, Inc.
1630 E. Hwy. 25-70
Dandridge, TN 37725
Tel: (800) 247-4442
Fax: (423) 397-9262
Traditionally joined timber frames and finely crafted dovetailed log homes.
E-mail: sales@hearthstonehomes.com
Web site: www.hearthstonehomes.com

Virginia

Blue Ridge Timberwrights
2030 Redwood Drive
Christiansburg, VA 24073
Tel: (540) 382-1102
Fax: (540) 382-8039
Designers and manufacturers of hand-crafted timber frame structures.

Dreaming Creek Timber Frame Homes, Inc.
2487 Judes Ferry Road
Powhatan, VA 23139
Tel: (804) 598-4328
Fax: (804) 598-3748
Oak, southern yellow pine. Lengths to 45 ft. Custom planing to 8" x 20". Fax tally for prices. Ship nationwide.

Vermont

Liberty Head Post & Beam
PO Box 68, Main Road
Huntington, VT 05462
Tel: (802) 434-2120
Fax: (802) 434-4929
Custom designed timber frames—authentically joined in the Vermont tradition.

North Woods Joinery
PO Box 1166
Burlington, VT 05402-1166
Tel: (802) 644-5667
Fax: (802) 644-2509
Traditional post and beam construction: homes, barns, steeples, bridges, towers.

Kondor Post & Beam
RR 2 Box 2794
Cambridge, VT 05444
Tel: (802) 644-5598
Fax: (802) 644-8735
Post & beam frames for residential & lite commercial buildings.
E-mail: kondor@sover.net
Web site: kondorinc.com

Vermont Frames
PO Box 100, Rte. 116 Varney Hill Road
Hinesburg, VT 05461
Tel: (802) 453-3727
Fax: (802) 453-2339
Traditional affordable timber frame homes. Building nationwide.
E-mail: foamlam@sover.net
Web site: http://www.sover.net/~foamlam

Washington

Timber Framers Guild of North America
PO Box 1075
Bellingham, WA 98227-1075
Tel: (360) 733-4001
Fax: (360) 733-4002

Ark II Inc.
HCR 73 Box 67
Twisp, WA 98856
Tel: (509) 997-2418
Fax: (509) 997-4434
Fine quality timber frame & log buildings.

The G.R. Plume Company
1373 West Smith Road, Suite A-1
Ferndale, WA 98248
Tel: (360) 384-2800
Fax: (360) 384-0335
Architectural timber millwork fabricated from reclaimed Douglas fir.

Richard Berg, Architect
727 Taylor St.
Port Townsend, WA 98368
Tel: (360) 379-8090
Fax: (360) 379-8324
Architectural practice specializing in comfortable, energy-efficient, quality timber framed homes.
E-mail: rberg@olympus.net

Timbercraft Homes, Inc.
85 Martin Road
Port Townsend, WA 98368
Tel: (360) 385-3051
Fax: (360) 385-7745
Since 1979, high quality timber frame structures, components, and architectural engineering.
E-mail: info@timbercraft.com
Web site: http://www.timbercraft.com

Old World Timber Frames
22130 SE Green Valley Road
Auburn, WA 98092
Tel: (253) 833-1760
Heirloom quality timber frame homes and buildings. Contact Ben Beers.

British Columbia

Gateway Timberframe Construction
8576 Ebor Terrace
Sidney, BC, Canada V8L 1L5
Tel: (250) 655-3476
Fax: (250) 656-7455
Full construction services. Quality timbers & workmanship. Panels.

Steward Management Ltd.
11110-284th Street
Maple Ridge, BC, Canada V2W 1T9
Tel: (604) 462-7712
Fax: (604) 462-8311
Recyclers of old growth timbers-will cut & plane to size.

Manitoba

Pride Builders Ltd.
Box 12, GRP. 4
Dufresne, Manitoba, Canada R0A 0Y0
Tel: (204) 878-3926
Fax: (204) 878-3927
Design services, frame cutting & raising, with either your general contractor or ours.

Nova Scotia

Acorn Timber Frames, Ltd.
RR 1
Hantsport, Kings County, NS, Canada B0P 1P0
Tel: (902) 684-9708
Fax: same
Traditional joinery: homes, churches, farm/garden/tourism/vacation structures, great rooms, restorations. Serving Canada and alluring locations with your requirements since 1978.

Ontario

Alderaan Stone/Timber Homes
PO Box 313, 6-14845 Yonge Street
Aurora, Ontario, Canada L4G 6H8
Tel: (905) 713-0001
Fax: (905) 713-0134
Traditional materials and craftsmanship. Comprehensive custom reproductions of early Canadian homes.
Web site: www.craftsman-book.com

The Timbersmith Log Construction, Limited
General Delivery
Hillsdale, Ontario, Canada L0L 1V0
Tel: (705) 725-2585
Fax: (705) 725-2590
Log and timber frame custom hand-crafted homes.

Northern Timberhouse, Ltd.
PO Box 71, Hwy. 35 South
Minden, Ontario, Canada K0M 2K0
Tel: (705) 286-3791
Fax: (705) 286-6168
Canadian timber frames and hand-crafted log homes since 1980.
E-mail: nortim@halhinet.on.ca

Bear Timber Frame Homes
PO Box 124
Ajax, Ont, Canada L1S 3C2
Tel: (905) 428-6505
Designers of timber frame and energy-efficient (R2000) homes.

Timbers

Arizona

Sirocco Trading Company
110 East Wing Drive
Sedona, AZ 86336
Tel: (520) 204-2516
Fax: (520) 282-3716
Recycled wood products, solid timbers, boards; Douglas fir, redwood, more.
E-mail: eeh3@sedona.net

California

Granberg International
PO Box 70425, 200 South Garraro Blvd.
Richmond, CA 94807-0425
Tel: (510) 237-2099
Fax: (510) 237-1667
Manufacturer of the Alaskan sawmill. Attachments and accessories for sharpening chainsaws.
E-mail: granberg@aol.com
Web site: www.granberg.com

Pacific Post & Beam
PO Box 13708
San Luis Obispo, CA 93406
Tel: (805) 543-7565
Fax: (805) 543-1287
Full service timber frame and truss design and build.

Maxwell Pacific
PO Box 4127
Malibu, CA 90264
Tel: (310) 457-4533
Douglas fir, redwood, pine, cedar, barnwood, used and new.

Michael Evenson Natural Resources
PO Box 157
Petrolia, CA 95558
Tel: (707) 629-3679
Fax: same
Recycled old growth redwood, Douglas-fir, custom remilling.
E-mail: evenson@igc.apc.org

Ontario

Recycled Lumberworks
596 Park Blvd.
Ukiah, CA 95482
Tel: (707) 462-2567
Fax: (707) 462-8607
Quality recycled old growth timber, clear heart redwood lumber from 100 year old vat staves and Douglas fir flooring is our specialty.

Colorado

Greenleaf Forest Products, Inc.
102 Greenleaf Lane
Westcliffe, CO 81252
Tel: (719) 783-2487
Fax: (719) 783-0212
Logs, poles and rough-sawn from sustainably-managed private forests.

Connecticut

Hull Forest Products
101 Hampton Road
Pomfret Center, CT 06259
Tel: (860) 974-2083
Fax: (860) 974-2963
Producers of quality oak timbers, band sawn, up to 26'6" long.
Web site: http://www.HullForest.com

Post & Beam Homes, Inc.
4 Sexton Hill Road South
East Hampton, CT 06424
Tel: (860) 267-2060, (800) 821-8456 (Connecticut only)
Fax: (860) 267-9515
Pine, oak, Doug fir or recycled lumber. Frames hand-crafted in our workshop. Our expert timber framers will construct anywhere.

Delaware

Timber Frame Systems, Inc.
PO Box 458, 28 Main St.
Frankford, DE 19945
Tel: (302) 732-9428
Fax: (302) 537-4971
Manufacturer of custom post & beam frame kits.

Florida

Tropical American Tree Farms
C/O AAA Express Mail, 1641 NW 79th Avenue
Miami, FL 33126
Tel: (800) 788-4918, 011 (506) 787-0020
Fax: 011 (506) 787-0051
Growing precious tropical hardwoods on tree farms in Costa Rica.
E-mail: tatfsa.sol.racsa.co.cr

R.G. White Construction
PO Box 14734, 5800 Firestone Road
Jacksonville, FL 32238
Tel: (904) 778-8352
Fax: same
Building fine quality cracker style and craftsman style homes.

Idaho

Stein & Collett
PO Box 4065, 201 South Mission Street
McCall, ID 83638
Tel: (208) 634-5374
Fax: (208) 634-8228
Beams, flooring, doors, stair systems. Both new and recycled woods custom architectural millwork. Unique and unusual species are our specialty.

Massachusetts

W.D. Cowls, Inc.
PO Box 9677, 134 Montague Road
North Amherst, MA 01059-9677
Tel: (413) 549-1403
Fax: (413) 549-0000
Timbers to 26', NELMA certified to grade boards, structural lumber and timbers.

Maryland

Vintage Lumber Co., Inc.
PO Box 104, 1 Council
Woodsboro, MD 21798
Tel: (800) 499-7859
Fax: (301) 845-6475
Reclaimed, remilled and remarkable tongue and groove antique wood flooring.
E-mail: woodfloors@vintagelumber.com
Web site: www.vintagelumber.com

Maine

Natural Knees
281 Hartland Road
St. Albans, ME 04971
Tel: (207) 938-2380
Natural grown knees for timber frame construction and boat building.
E-mail: kneeman@somtel.com

Michigan

Northern Land & Lumber Co.
7000 P Rd.
Gladstone, MI 49837
Tel: (906) 786-2994
Fax: (906) 786-2926
Primary manufacturer of log home kits & components.
E-mail: nlandl@up.net
web site: www.deltami.org/nlandl

Minnesota

Duluth Timber Company
PO Box 16717
Duluth, MN 55816
Tel: (218) 727-2145
Recycled timbers and planks from U.S. and Canada. Doug fir, redwood and pine. Resawn beams, flooring; "as is" wholesale timbers.

North Carolina

Harmony Exchange
Route 2, Box 843-A
Boone, NC 28607
Tel: (800) 968-9663
Antique, reclaimed & new growth. Flooring, timber trusses, decking, exposed beam systems, siding & more. Catalog.

New Hampshire

Great Northern Barns
PO Box 912E, RFD2
Canaan, NH 03741
Tel: (603) 523-7134
Fax: (603) 523-7134 *51
Great Northern Barns dismantles and erects antique barn frames.
E-mail: ejl@endor.com
Web site: www.greatnorthernbarns.com

New York

M. Fine Lumber Co., Inc.
175 Varick Ave.
Brooklyn, NY 11231
Tel: (718) 381-5200
Fax: (718) 366-8907
Buyer & seller of reusable lumber, timber & flooring available.
E-mail: MerritF@Fine-Lumber.com
Web site: www.Fine-Lumber.com/Lumber.html

Pioneer Millworks
1755 Pioneer Road
Shortsville, NY 14548
Tel: (716) 289-3220
Fax: (716) 289-3221
Reclaimed timbers from turn-of-the-century buildings, S4S or rough sawn. Hand-hewn barn timbers. Antique pine and fir flooring. Custom millwork.

Ohio

Hochstetler Milling
552 St. Rt. 95
Loudonville, OH 44842
Tel: (419) 281-3553, (419) 368-0004
Oak timber 4-sided planing. Pine log home logs 10 profiles.

Pennsylvania

Conklin's Authentic Barnwood
RR 1, Box 70, Butterfield Road
Susquehanna, PA 18847
Tel: (717) 465-3832
Fax: same
Supplier antique barnwood, hand-hewn beams, flooring and rustic materials.
E-mail: conklins@epix.net
Web site: conklins barnwood.com

Pocono Mt. Timber Frames
PO Box 644, Rt. 115
Brodheadsville, PA 18322
Tel: (717) 992-7515
Fax: (717) 992-9064
Design, fabrication, and erection of timber frame barns and houses.
E-mail: etreible@ptd.net
web site: www.pmtf.com

Rhode Island

Liberty Cedar
535 Liberty Lane
W. Kingston, RI 02892
Tel: (800) 882-3327, (401) 789-6626
Fax: (401) 789-0320
Naturally decay-resistant exterior wood products specializing in wood roofing.

Tennessee

Hearthstone, Inc.
1630 E. Hwy. 25-70
Dandridge, TN 37725
Tel: (800) 247-4442
Fax: (423) 397-9262
Traditionally joined timber frames and finely crafted dovetailed log homes.
E-mail: sales@hearthstonehomes.com
web site: www.hearthstonehomes.com

Texas

What Its Worth, Inc.
PO Box 162135
Austin, TX 78716
Tel: (512) 328-8837
Fax: same
Recycled heart pine. Timbers, planks, custom flooring, cabinet, door and moulding stock. Sold by piece or truck load. Virgin tidewater cypress mined from south Louisiana waterway, cut wet to spec. or sold in log form.

Precision Woodworks
507 E. Jackson St.
Burnet, TX 78611
Tel: (512) 756-6950
Fax: same
New products from antique longleaf pine and other used timbers.

Utah

Trestlewood (A Division Of Cannon Structures, Inc.)
PO Box 1728, 241 W 500 N, Suite A
Provo, UT 84603-1728
Tel: (801) 375-2779
Fax: (801) 375-2757
Wholesaler of recycled Douglas fir, redwood, SYD, etc. Timbers & products.
E-mail: bradnate@burgoyne.com

Virginia

Blue Ridge Timberwrights
2030 Redwood Drive
Christiansburg, VA 24073
Tel: (540) 382-1102
Fax: (540) 382-8039
Designers and manufacturers of hand-crafted timber frame structures.

Dreaming Creek Timber Frame Homes, Inc.
2487 Judes Ferry Road
Powhatan, VA 23139
Tel: (804) 598-4328
Fax: (804) 598-3748
Oak, southern yellow pine. Lengths to 45 ft. Custom planing to 8" x 20". Fax tally for prices. Ship nationwide.

Vermont

Second Harvest Salvage & Demo
PO Box 194-E, RR1
Jeffersonville, VT 05464
Tel: (802) 644-8169
Specializing in hand hewn frames and antique flooring and lumbers.

North Woods Joinery
PO Box 1166
Burlington, VT 05402-1166
Tel: (802) 644-5667
Fax: (802) 644-2509
Traditional post and beam construction: homes, barns, steeples, bridges, towers.

Washington

Bear Creek Lumber
PO Box 669, 495 Eastside County Road
Winthrop, WA 98862
Tel: (800) 571-7191
Fax: (509) 997-2040
Western cedar, fir, redwood. Traditional patterns, decking, timbers and beams. Delivery available nationwide.

R.W. Rhine, Inc.
1124 112th St. E
Tacoma, WA 98445
Tel: (253) 531-7223
Fax: (253) 531-9548
Salvage timbers, piling and wood products.

Resource Woodworks
627 E. 60th Street
Tacoma, WA 98404
Tel: (206) 474-3757
Fax: (206) 474-1139
Custom milling & planing of reclaimed Douglas fir timbers, also flooring & trim package available. We ship anywhere.

British Columbia

Evergreen Specialties
1619 Evelyn
North Vancouver, BC, Canada V7K 1T9
Tel: (604) 988-8574
Fax: (604) 988-8576
Dry fir, cedar. Architectural beams, poles, lumber, decking, masts & planking.

Steward Management Ltd.
11110-284th Street
Maple Ridge, BC, Canada V2W 1T9
Tel: (604) 462-7712
Fax: (604) 462-8311
Recyclers of old growth timbers--will cut & plane to size.

Tools

California

Abbey Tools
1132 N. Magnolia
Anaheim, CA 92801
Tel: (800) 225-6321

Bailey's
PO Box 550, 44650 Hwy. 101
Laytonville, CA 95454
Tel: (800) 322-4539
Fax: (707) 984-8115
Free catalog: world's largest mail order woodsman supplies company.
E-mail: baileys@bbaileyscom
Web site: http://www.bbaileys.com

Granberg International
PO Box 70425, 200 South Garraro Blvd.
Richmond, CA 94807-0425
Tel: (510) 237-2099
Fax: (510) 237-1667
Manufacturer of the Alaskan sawmill. Attachments and accessories for sharpening chainsaws.
E-mail: granberg@aol.com
Web site: www.granberg.com

Makita U.S.A., Inc.
14930 Northam St.
La Mirada, CA 90638
Tel: (714) 522-8088
Fax: (714) 522-8194
Corded and cordless portable electric power tools.

Connecticut

Constitution Saw Co.
310 Nutmeg Road South
South Windsor, CT 06074
(203) 289-7696

Florida

International Tool Corporation
2590 Davie Road
Davie, FL 33317
Tel: (800) 338-3384
Fax: (954) 792-3560
Woodworking & construction power tools at the guaranteed lowest prices.
Web site: http://www.internationaltool.com

Idaho

Woodhouse
PO Box 801
Ashton, ID 83420
Tel: (208) 652-3608
Fax: (208) 652-3628
Supplying all specialized tools and materials for log-timber construction. Providing owner and/or professional with largest selection of quality products available.

Barr Specialty Tools
PO Box 4335
McCall, ID 83638
Tel: (800) 235-4452
Fax: (208) 634-3541
Quality hand-forged framing chisels, slicks, adzes, draw knives, and gouges for the serious woodworker. Simply the best.

Illinois

Estwing Mfg. Co.
2647 8th St.
Rockford, IL 61109-1190
Tel: (815) 397-9558
Fax: (815) 397-8665
Manufacturer of world's first & finest all steel hammers.
E-mail: estwing@estwing.com
Web site: www.estwing.com

Frog Tool Co., Ltd.
2169 IL Rt. 26
Dixon, IL 61021
Tel: (800) 648-1270
Fax: (815) 288-3919
Timber framing and handling tools, hand woodworking tools, books. Catalog $5.

S. B. Power Tool Co.
4300 W. Peterson Ave.
Chicago, IL 60646
Tel: (800) 301-8255
Fax: (773) 794-6615
Skil and Bosch portable power tools and accessories.

Indiana

Wood-Mizer Products, Inc.
8180 W. 10th Street
Indianapolis, IN 46214
Tel: (317) 271-1542
Fax: (317) 273-1011
Transportable sawmills and accessories: lowers lumber costs and improves quality.
E-mail: adindy@woodmizer.com
Web site: http://www.woodmizer.com

Trusty-Cook, Inc.
10530 E. 59th St.
Indianapolis, IN 46236
Tel: (317) 823-6821
Fax: (317) 823-6822
Deadblow urethane hammers and sledges for maximum power, sustained impact.

Massachusetts

U.S. Cutting Chain Mfg. Co.
PO Box 437, 95 Spark Street
Brockton, MA 02403
Tel: (508) 588-0322
Fax: (508) 583-7808
Heavy duty chain mortisers, mortise chains, guide bars and sprockets.

Maine

Lie-Nielsen Toolworks, Inc.
PO Box 9
Warren, ME 04864
Tel: (800) 327-2520
Fax: (207) 273-2657
Makers of heirloom quality hand tools for woodworkers.
E-mail: toolwrks@lie-nielsen.com
Web site: http://ww.lie-nielsen.com

Barn Masters, Inc.
PO Box 258
Freeport, ME 04032
Tel: (207) 865-4169
Fax: (207) 865-6169
Makita tools for timber framing: chain mortisers, stationary routers, chisel mortisers, groove cutters, circular saws, 6" x 12" planers, tenon cutters. Free brochure.

Minnesota

Tools On Sale Div. Of Seven Corners Hdwr., Inc.
216 West 7th Street
St. Paul, MN 55102
Tel: (800) 328-0457
Fax: (612) 224-8263
496 page catalog of power tools and related accessories featuring the most respected brands in the business.

The Woodworkers' Store
4365 Willow Dr.
Medina, MN 55340
Tel: (800) 279-4441
Fax: (612) 478-8395
Woodworking hardware, wood, tools and know-how.
E-mail: rocklerl@pclink.com
Web site: www.woodworkerstore.com

Missouri

Woodmaster Tools
1431 N. Topping Ave.
Kansas City, MO 64120
Tel: (816) 483-7203
Make mirror-smooth custom molding with the Woodmaster planer/molder.

North Carolina

Country Workshops
90 Mill Creek Road
Marshall, NC 28753
Tel: (704) 656-2280
Tools, books and instruction in traditional woodworking with hand tools
E-mail: langsner@countryworkshops.org
Web site: countryworkshops.org

Klingspor's Sanding Catalogue
PO Box 3737
Hickory, NC 28603-3737

North Dakota

Tool Crib Of The North
PO Box 14040, 1603 12th Ave. N
Grand Forks, ND 58206-4040
Tel: (701) 780-2882
Fax: (701) 746-2869
96 color pages of woodworking tools and accessories, free!
E-mail: kcolman@corpcomm.net
Web site: www.toolcribofthenorth.com

New York

Cepco Tool Co.
PO Box 153, 295 Van Etten Road
Spencer, NY 14883
Tel: (607) 589-4313
Fax: same
Board straightening/joining tools, Bowrench deck tool, Quick-Jack construction jack.

Lee Valley Tools Ltd.
PO Box 178012 East River St.
Ogdensburg, NY 13669-0490
Tel: (800) 871-8158
Fax: (800) 513-7885
Our 236-page full-color catalog has the widest selection of woodworking hand tools on the market.
Web site: http://www.leevalley.com

Crosscut Saw Company
PO Box 7871
Seneca Falls, NY 13148
(315) 568-5755

Martin J. Donnelly Antique Tools
PO Box 281
Bath, NY 14810-0281
Tel: (607) 776-9322
Fax: (607) 776-6064
Antique tools.
E-mail: MJDtools@servtech.com

Company Listings by Subject _____

Ohio

Miller's Sharpening Service
11301 N. Webb
Alliance, OH 44601
Tel: (330) 821-6240

Pennsylvania

Wilke Machinery Co.
3230 Susquehanna Trail
York, PA 17402
Tel: (717) 764-5000
Fax: (717) 764-3778
Distributors of quality woodworking
machinery and home of Bridgewood
Brand machinery.
Web site: www.wilkemach.com

Virginia

Quick Gauge, Inc.
5237 Clifton Street
Alexandria, VA 22312
Tel: (800) 916-9646
Fax: (703) 941-7415
Quick Clamp installs on any square for
fast & accurate layout of stair stringers &
rafters. Long-lasting aluminum. Dealers
welcome.

Vermont

Trow & Holden Co.
45 So. Main St.
Barre, VT 05641
Tel: (800) 451-4349
Tel: (802) 476-7025
Stone carving and splitting tools, mortar-
removal tools.
E-mail: trowco@aol.com

Tools Of The Trade
PO Box 2001, West Main St.
Richmond, VT 05477
Tel: (800) 375-5981
Fax: (802) 434-4467
The only magazine devoted exclusively
to tools for construction professionals.
Web site: www.bginet.com

Bethel Mills, Inc.
PO Box 61, 1 North Main
Bethel, VT 05032
Tel: (800) 234-9951
Fax: (802) 234-5631
Retail lumber, building materials, and
tools for the serious contractor.
E-mail: bml@sover.net
Web site: bethelmills.com

Washington

Systimatic
12530 135th Ave. NE
Kirkland, WA 98034
Tel: (800) 426-0035
Fax: (425) 821-0801
Manufacturer of carbide tipped circular
saw blades.

West Virginia

Woodcraft Supply
PO Box 1686, 210 Wood County
Industrial Park
Parkersburg, WV 26102
Tel: (800) 225-1153
Fax: (304) 428-8271
Quality woodworking tools, books,
hardware, hardwoods; plus tool
sharpening service.
E-mail: custserv@woodcraft.com
Web site: www.woodcraft.com

Videos

Alaska Craftsman Home Program, Inc.
PO Box 241647
Anchorage, AK 99524-1647
Tel: (907) 258-2247 (ACHP)
Fax: (907) 258-5352
Education and research advanced cold
climate home building techniques.
E-mail: achp@alaska.net
Web site: http://www.alaska.net/~achp

Bailey's
PO Box 550, 44650 Hwy. 101
Laytonville, CA 95454
Tel: (800) 322-4539
Fax: (707) 984-8115
Free catalog: world's largest mail order
woodsman supplies company.
E-mail: baileys@bbaileyscom
Web site: http://www.bbaileys.com

Canterbury Shaker Village
288 Shaker Road
Canterbury, NH 03224
Tel: (603) 783-9511
Fax: (603) 783-9152
From tree to beam–hand-hewing with
Dan Dustin. 58 minutes.
E-mail: shakervillage@mv.mv.com

Cob Cottage Co.
PO Box 123
Cottage Grove, OR 97424
Tel: (541) 942-2005
Fax: (541) 942-3021
Information and workshops on building
with cob (sand, clay, straw).
Web site: http://www.deatech.com/
cobcottage

Earthwood Building School
366 Murtagh Hill Road
West Chazy, NY 12992
(518) 493-7744
Fax: same, phone first
Teaches cordwood masonry and
underground housing. Books, videos
and workshops.
Web site: http://www.interlog.com/
newood

Fine Homebuilding Magazine
PO Box 5506, 63 S. Main Street
Newtown, CT 06470-5506
Tel: (203) 426-8171
Fax: (203) 270-6751
Homebuilders share tips, techniques
and reviews of tools and materials.
E-mail: fh@taunton.com
Web site: http://www.taunton.com

Freedom Builders
1013 Naples Drive
Orlando, FL 32804
Tel: (407) 647-5849
Fax: (407) 645-5652
Internet informational & advertising
site—log & t.f. design—video
productions.
E-mail: freedom@magicnet.net
Web site: www.magicnet.net/freedom

Goldec International Equipment, Inc.
6760 65 Ave.
Red Deer, Alberta, Canada T4R 1G5
Tel: (403) 343-6607
Fax: (403) 340-0640
De-bark logs with our chainsaw
attachment. The amazing Log Wizard!
E-mail: goldec@telusplanet.net
Web site: goldec.com

Iris Communications, Inc.
PO Box 5920
Eugene, OR 97405
Tel: (541) 484-9353
Fax: (541) 484-1645
Carefully selected books, videos and
software for green construction.
E-mail: iris@oikos.com
Web site: www.oikos.com

Lofty Branch Bookstore
PO Box 512
Victor, NY 14564
Tel: (716) 742-2607
Fax: (716) 289-3221
Over 350 timber framing, construction,
design and woodworking books/videos.
E-mail: loftybooks@aol.com
Web site: http://
members.aol.com.loftybooks

Lok-N-Logs, Inc.
PO Box 677, Route 12
Sherburne, NY 13460
Tel: (800) 343-8928, (607) 674-4447
Fax: (607) 674-6433
Producer of top quality, pre-cut log home
packages–lifetime limited warranty!
E-mail: lnlinfo@loknlogs.com
Web site: http://www.loknlogs.com
Catalog: $12.95

Natural Building Resources
Star Rt. 2, Box 119
Kingston, NM 88042
Tel: (505) 895-5652
Fax: (505) 895-3326
Books and videos on natural building.
Host—Natural Building Colloquium.
E-mail: blackrange@zianet.com
Web site: www.zianet.com/blackrange

Out On Bale By Mail
1039 E. Linden St.
Tucson, AZ 85719
Tel: (520) 624-1673
Fax: (520) 299-9099
Educational materials for straw bale
building. Help for owner builders.
E-mail: outonbale@aol.com

Sustainable Systems Support
PO Box 318
Bisbee, AZ 85603
Tel: (520) 432-4292
Offers books and videos on plastered
straw bale construction, including an
excellent 90 min. "how-to" video with a
62 page manual. Wall raising workshops
and consultations.

The Canelo Project
HCL Box 324
Elgin, AZ 85611
Tel: (520) 455-5548
Fax: (520) 455-9360
Straw bale building/earthen floors and
plasters, workshops, resources,
consulting.
E-mail: absteen@dakotacom.net
Web site: http://www.deatech.com/
canelo

Notes & Numbers

Company Index

Notes & Numbers

Notes & Numbers

Also published by Fox Maple Press

Joiners' Quarterly
The Journal of Timber Framing & Traditional Building

A Timber Framer's Workshop
*The Workshop Manual of the
Timber Frame Apprenticeshop*

Advanced Timber Framing
Timber Joinery for Hip & Valley Roof Framing

Soon to be released…

A Timber Framers' Library
*A compilation of the best timber framing articles in the
first 14 issues of Joiners' Quarterly*

To receive newsletters and press releases about
future books and publications in the Corn Hill Book Series,
traditional building workshops, and events at
Fox Maple School of Traditional Building,
please write to us.

Fox Maple Press, Inc.
P.O. Box 249
Corn Hill Road
Brownfield, Maine 04010
207-935-3720 • Fax 207-935-4575